The Epistemic Dimensions of I

Ignorance is a neglected issue in philosophy. This is surprising, for, contrary to what one might expect, it is not clear what ignorance is. Some philosophers say or assume that it is lack of knowledge, whereas others claim or presuppose that it is absence of true belief. What is one ignorant of when one is ignorant? And what kinds of ignorance are there? This neglect is also remarkable because ignorance plays a crucial role in all sorts of controversial societal issues. Ignorance is often thought to be a moral and legal excuse, it is a core concept in medical ethics and debates about privacy, and it features in religious traditions and debates about belief in God. This book does not only study an epistemic phenomenon that is interesting in itself, but also provides important tools that can be fruitfully used in debates within and beyond philosophy.

Rik Peels is an Assistant Professor at the Vrije Universiteit Amsterdam, the Netherlands. His primary research interests are the ethics of belief, ignorance, scientism, and various issues in the philosophy of religion, such as whether God has a sense of humour. He is the author of *Responsible Belief: A Theory in Ethics and Epistemology* (New York: Oxford University Press, 2016), the editor of *Perspectives on Ignorance from Moral and Social Philosophy* (London: Routledge, 2016), and the co-editor of *Scientism: A Philosophical Exposition and Evaluation* (New York: Oxford University Press, 2017).

Martijn Blaauw is Secretary General of the Faculty of Technology, Policy and Management, Delft University of Technology, the Netherlands. He is interested in the area of research where epistemology meets the technological challenges of the 21st century. He has published widely in epistemology, including papers in such journals as *Analysis, The Australasian Journal of Philosophy, and Episteme*. He is the editor of *Contrastivism in Philosophy* (London: Routledge, 2012).

Cover photo "Spring's Landfall" by Tom Chambers. www.tomchambersphoto.com

The Epistemic Dimensions of Ignorance

Rik Peels

Vrije Universiteit Amsterdam

Martijn Blaauw

Delft University of Technology

CAMBRIDGE
UNIVERSITY PRESS

University Printing House, Cambridge CB2 8BS, United Kingdom

One Liberty Plaza, 20th Floor, New York, NY 10006, USA

477 Williamstown Road, Port Melbourne, VIC 3207, Australia

314-321, 3rd Floor, Plot 3, Splendor Forum, Jasola District Centre, New Delhi - 110025, India

79 Anson Road, #06-04/06, Singapore 079906

Cambridge University Press is part of the University of Cambridge.

It furthers the University's mission by disseminating knowledge in the pursuit of education, learning and research at the highest international levels of excellence.

www.cambridge.org
Information on this title: www.cambridge.org/9781316625811

© Rik Peels and Martijn Blaauw 2016

First published 2016
First paperback edition 2018

A catalogue record for this publication is available from the British Library

Library of Congress Cataloging in Publication data
Peels, Rik, 1983– editor.
The epistemic dimensions of ignorance / [edited by] Rik Peels, Vrije Universiteit Amsterdam, Martijn Blaauw, Delft University of Technology.
New York : Cambridge University Press, 2016.
LCCN 2016025916 | ISBN 9781107175600
LCSH: Ignorance (Theory of knowledge) | Knowledge, Theory of.
LCC BD221 .E65 2016 | DDC 121–dc23
LC record available at https://lccn.loc.gov/2016025916

ISBN 978-1-107-17560-0 Hardback
ISBN 978-1-316-62581-1 Paperback

Not ignorance, but ignorance of ignorance is the death of knowledge.

attributed to Alfred North Whitehead

Contents

Introduction

Rik Peels and Martijn Blaauw

1   Ignorance and Epistemology

Epistemology is traditionally understood as the theory of knowledge and the theory of what is necessary for knowledge, such as reliability or epistemic justification. Matthias Steup, for instance, in his Epistemology entry to the *Stanford Encyclopedia of Philosophy* gives two definitions of 'epistemology'.[1] On the narrower definition, it is the study of knowledge and justified belief, while on the broader definition, it is the study of issues having to do with the creation and dissemination of knowledge in particular areas of inquiry. Ignorance, at first glance, seems to be the *opposite* of knowledge or, at least, something quite close to its opposite.

It is not surprising, therefore, that epistemologists have hardly paid any attention to ignorance. None of the major epistemology handbooks, for instance, devotes a chapter to it.[2] And in the vast epistemological literature of the last twenty years or so, the topic of ignorance is virtually absent. The only area where ignorance enters the discussion is in debates on radical scepticism.[3] Interestingly, ignorance has received attention in areas of philosophy *other than* epistemology. This illustrates, if nothing else, at least that the concept is useful in philosophical discussion.

In ethics, for instance, it is quite common to distinguish between acting *in* ignorance and acting *from* ignorance, since there is a fierce debate on whether or not it is necessary to act from ignorance in order for one's ignorance to count as an excuse for one's action or whether acting in ignorance suffices for that.[4] However, this debate concerns the relation between one's mental state of ignorance and one's actions, and as such does not seem to count as belonging to an 'epistemology of ignorance'.

---

[1] See Steup (2005).   [2] See, for instance, Audi (2011); Moser (2005).
[3] See, for instance, Unger (1975).
[4] See Guerrero (2007, pp. 63–64); Houlgate (1968, pp. 112–113); Rivera-López (2006, p. 135); Zimmerman (1997, p. 424).

Also, in discussions about facts and norms, ignorance is an important topic. One can be ignorant about facts and about norms – and thus also about epistemic norms. *Factive* ignorance is ignorance of certain facts about one's or other people's circumstances, such as the room's temperature or a person's criminal track record. *Normative* ignorance is ignorance of certain standards, principles, or norms, such as *moral* standards and *epistemic* standards.[5] However, the fact that one can be ignorant about epistemic norms does not mean that this type of ignorance counts as belonging to an 'epistemology of ignorance'.

This leaves much of the territory unexplored, though. An obvious question is, of course, what ignorance *is*. The dominant, standard view that we find tacitly assumed in much of the literature and hardly ever defended in any detail is that ignorance is the lack or absence of knowledge.[6] Remarkably, we also find an alternative view in the literature, even though, again, it is not spelled out in detail. On this alternative view, ignorance is the lack or absence of true belief.[7] The difference between the two views is that on the standard view, a true belief that falls short of knowledge is also ignorance, whereas on the new view it is not. In fact, it seems that intermediate positions are possible as well, such as the thesis that ignorance is the lack of *reliably formed* true belief or the absence of *justified* true belief.[8]

Epistemic questions regarding ignorance are, however, not confined to the question of what the nature of ignorance is. Here are some other questions about ignorance that, it seems, epistemologists are especially suited to answer:

- What is the difference between ignorance as *absence* of knowledge and ignorance as *lack* of knowledge?[9]
- What kinds of ignorance are there? Is ignorance in the case of false belief, for instance, crucially different from ignorance in case one cannot even grasp the proposition in question?
- In what respect does ignorance as not knowing the answer to a question differ from ignorance as to whether something is true?

[5] E.g., Harman (2011).
[6] Driver (1989, pp. 373–376); Fields (1994, p. 403); Flanagan (1990, p. 422); Houlgate (1968, p. 109); Unger (1975, p. 93); Zimmerman (1988, p. 75; 2008, ix).
[7] Goldman (1986, p. 26); Goldman and Olsson (2009, pp. 19–21); Guerrero (2007, pp. 62–63); Rivera-López (2006, p. 135); Van Woudenberg (2009, p. 375).
[8] In a short exchange with Pierre Le Morvan, we have tried to put on the agenda the issue of what the nature of ignorance is. See Le Morvan (2011, 2012, 2013); Peels (2010, 2011a, 2012).
[9] For an answer to this question, see Haas and Vogt (2015, pp. 18–19).

- Are there such things as ignorance-how and ignorance-of in addition to ignorance-that (propositional ignorance)? If so, how do these relate to propositional ignorance?
- How is ignorance related to other propositional attitudes, such as suspension of judgement and doubt?
- To what extent is ignorance context-dependent?
- Does ignorance come in degrees?
- Does ignorance have any epistemic value?
- What is the relationship between ignorance and assertion?
- How does ignorance relate to epistemic justification?
- Is there such a thing as group ignorance? If so, how should it be understood?
- When is ignorance rational?[10] Do the rationality conditions for ignorance differ from those of belief?

One may object that, even though these questions are interesting and even though epistemologists are well suited to answer them, they do not belong to the domain of *epistemology* proper, since ignorance is as remote from knowledge as anything could possibly be. This objection, however, fails to acknowledge that the scope of epistemology has significantly broadened during the last few years. Epistemologists pay attention to all sorts of propositional attitudes, such as hope, trust, faith and doubt, to such phenomena as insight and understanding, to epistemic virtues, such as wisdom, intellectual thoroughness and open-mindedness, and to epistemic vices, such as dogmatism and gullibility. In some cases, there is a clear connection with knowledge, but in many others, there is not. (We see the same pattern in other philosophical disciplines. Metaphysics studies that which exists – but a very interesting question is *what does not exist* – if only because the answer to this question can illuminate what existence is.) There is no reason, then, to think that philosophical reflection about ignorance does not belong to the domain of epistemology.

2   Ignorance beyond Epistemology

We have shown that the discussion about ignorance deserves a proper place in epistemology. However, ignorance is also a crucial theme in other philosophical disciplines and even beyond philosophy. The various perspectives on the epistemic dimensions of ignorance offered in this book

---

[10] It is widely acknowledged that ignorance can be rational. For an overview, see Somin (2015).

can be helpful for debates in these other fields. In this section, we will give four examples to illustrate this claim.

First, in *A Theory of Justice*, John Rawls provides a social contract account of justice in which the concept of ignorance plays a crucial role.[11] The core idea is that in our reasoning about the fundamental principles of justice, we should imagine ourselves to be free and equal persons who should jointly come to agree upon and commit themselves to certain core principles of justice. In order to guarantee that everyone's reasoning is maximally impartial, everyone is supposed to be ignorant of their personal social and historical circumstances. They *do* know certain general facts, such as interests people generally have and facts about psychology, biology, physics, and so on. But, due to their so-called *veil of ignorance*, they do not know what their personal circumstances will be. According to Rawls, imagining ourselves to be in such a situation helps us establish the principles of justice that we all ought to embrace. A thorough analysis of the epistemic dimensions of ignorance can help us to get a firmer grip on exactly what kind of ignorance the veil of ignorance requires. If ignorance is lack of knowledge, for instance, then Gettierized true belief will count as ignorance but, it seems, this is *not* the kind of ignorance that Rawls has in mind. So, what kind of ignorance is it? And is a certain *degree* of ignorance required here?

Second, it is widely acknowledged in the philosophical literature that ignorance sometimes counts as a *moral excuse*.[12] Ethicists have paid significant attention to whether blameworthy ignorance can also excuse or whether only blameless ignorance excuses,[13] and whether one is excused only if one acts *from* ignorance or also if one acts *in* ignorance.[14] These are important questions, but there are further questions to be asked about ignorance as a moral excuse that have to do with the *epistemic* dimensions of ignorance.[15] Imagine, for instance, that I *falsely believe* that the chocolate cake in front of me contains no poison whatsoever and that I am blameless for holding that belief. It seems that in that case, my ignorance that the chocolate cake is poisoned excuses me for giving it to my friend.

[11] See Rawls (1971).
[12] See, for instance, Brandt (1969, p. 349); Fischer and Ravizza (1998, pp. 12–13); Goldman (1970, p. 208); Rosen (2003, pp. 61–62); Smith (1983, pp. 543–571); Zimmerman (2008, pp. 169–205).
[13] According to some philosophers, blameworthy ignorance provides a *full* excuse (e.g., Ross 1939, pp. 163–164). Others argue that it provides only a *partial* excuse (e.g., Beardsley 1979, p. 578). And still others claim that it provides *no* excuse at all (e.g., Kornblith 1983, pp. 35–36). Smith (1983, pp. 548–551), distinguishes between these three views.
[14] The former is claimed or suggested by, for instance, Donagan (1977, pp. 128–130) and Zimmerman (1997, p. 424). The latter view is advocated by, among others, Houlgate (1968) and Rosen (2008, 598n).
[15] For an exploration of two of these questions, see Peels (2014).

Compare this situation to one in which I *suspend judgment* on the proposition that the chocolate cake is poisoned. In this situation as well the cake is poisoned, so, again, I am ignorant that it is. It seems that in this scenario, my ignorance does *not* excuse me, at least not fully. Whether or to what extent ignorance provides a moral excuse, then, seems to depend on what kind of ignorance is involved. Hence, a thorough exploration of the epistemic dimensions of ignorance will shed light on the conditions under which ignorance excuses.

Third, in several traditions that are partly philosophical, partly religious, ignorance plays a crucial role. One of these is the so-called *apophatic* tradition.[16] One of the core ideas in this tradition is that we are necessarily ignorant of the transcendent or God in particular. We find ideas along these lines with certain Neo-Platonists, such as Plotinus, Porphyry, Proclus, and Iamblichus. We find it in the writings of Jewish and Christian Medieval philosophers, such as Pseudo-Dionysius the Areopagite, John Scotus Eriugena, Maimonides, and Meister Eckhart, but also in the works of Islamic Medieval philosophers, such as Ibn al Arabi and Jalal al-Din Rumi. Nicholas of Cusa even wrote an entire book in which he defends the idea that there is such a thing as 'learned ignorance' about God: *De docta ignorantia* (1440 CE). Recently, the apophatic tradition has gained popularity and has been defended by employing the modern tools of analytic philosophy.[17]

Fourth, we see that in our current digital society, with its focus on big data and data mining, what can be known (and what can be known *about persons*) expands explosively. All our personal data are readily available to be 'mined' through the various online traces we leave in the digital world. Posts on Facebook, Twitter, or Instagram can be collected to construct a view on a persons' identity. In this way, people are being known by others even though they have not intentionally tried to achieve this. It is a by-product of our digital lives. The interesting consequence is that ignorance becomes a very important concept. For we do not want to be known by others in ways that we cannot control. We want to protect our privacy, and privacy can be defined in terms of ignorance.[18]

These are just a few cases that illustrate the relevance of ignorance in the broader context of philosophy. It would not be difficult to add examples: some kind of ignorance is required for employing certain *methods in scientific inquiry*, such as Randomized Controlled Trials in medicine studies, according to some philosophers science itself is *driven*

---

[16] For an exposition of the relation between the apophatic tradition and ignorance, see Franke (2015).
[17] See, for instance, Jacobs (2015).   [18] See, for instance, Blaauw (2013).

by ignorance,[19] ignorance can count as a *legal excuse*, ignorance plays a crucial role in *risk management*, and so on.[20] In fact, there is a field, called *agnotology*, that investigates culturally induced ignorance or doubt, in particular the kind of ignorance induced by the publication of misleading or inaccurate scientific data, such as those regarding the tobacco industry.[21] Such ignorance may be the result of governmental suppression, media neglect, or yet something else. Agnotology focuses on how these cultural influences induce ignorance, but it does *not* study what ignorance is, in what varieties it comes, and other epistemic dimensions of ignorance.

In another volume, entitled *Perspectives on Ignorance from Moral and Social Philosophy* (Rik Peels, ed., 2016), several moral, social, cultural, and legal issues regarding ignorance are explored.[22] In this volume, we confine ourselves mostly to the conceptual groundwork by exploring the epistemic dimensions of ignorance. Indeed, it is our aim in this volume to put the notion of ignorance on the epistemological agenda, by showing that there are a lot of non-trivial and interesting relations between ignorance and knowledge that warrant a thorough epistemological investigation of this concept.

3   Outline

Finally, let us introduce the essays in this volume. The first four essays map a terrain that has not received much attention in the philosophical literature, namely the nature of ignorance, the varieties of ignorance, degrees of ignorance, and the relation between ignorance and the closely related propositional attitude of doubt.

The opening essay by Pierre Le Morvan and Rik Peels explores the nature of ignorance, that is, it explores what it is to be ignorant. More specifically, it discusses two rival accounts of what are individually necessary and jointly sufficient conditions for being ignorant. These two accounts can be found in the literature and have recently received further articulation and defence. On the first view, called the Standard View, ignorance is the lack or absence of knowledge, whereas on the second view, called the New View, ignorance is the lack or absence of true belief. Rather than defending a particular account of ignorance, the essay spells out each of these two views in more detail and provides an overview of the main arguments for each of them. The reader will notice that the

---

[19] See Firestein (2012).   [20] For further examples, see Gross and McGoey (2015).
[21] For a recent introduction to agnotology, see Proctor and Schiebinger (2008).
[22] See Peels (2016).

controversy on the nature of ignorance will return in most of the other contributions to this volume.

In the second paper, Nikolaj Nottelmann discusses varieties of ignorance divided according to kind (what the subject is ignorant of), degree (the degree to which the subject is ignorant), and order (such as whether or not one is ignorant of one's ignorance). It provides analyses of notions such as factual ignorance, erotetic ignorance (ignorance of answers to questions), and practical ignorance (involving absence of know-how). After that, it discusses the interrelations between those kinds, arguing against so-called intellectualists that at least some instances of practical ignorance seem dissimilar in important respects to instances of the former kinds. Nottelmann also argues that we do not have strong reasons for regarding practical ignorance as a graded phenomenon, even if practical knowledge is. Finally, it is brought out that even if so-called Socratic ignorance, that is, first-order ignorance without second-order ignorance, is an important concept, still ignorance absolved only above the second order is of marginal significance.

In the third chapter, Berit Brogaard criticizes the Standard View, on which ignorance is lack of knowledge-that. She argues that this view is incorrect since lack of sufficient justification for one's true belief or lack of belief does not necessarily amount to ignorance. Her argument rests on linguistic considerations of common uses of 'ignorant' and its cognates. The phrase 'is ignorant of', she argues, functions differently grammatically and semantically from the phrase 'does not know', when the latter is used propositionally. 'Is ignorant of' does not have a genuine propositional use but is best understood as equivalent to 'is not knowledgeable of'. She further argues that 'knowledgeable' and 'ignorant' are relative gradable expressions. Relative gradables typically are associated with an implicit or explicit standard of comparison, give rise to borderline cases, and trigger the Sorites Paradox in their unmarked form. From these linguistic considerations, it follows that being ignorant admits of degree, and that one can fail to be ignorant despite lacking true beliefs concerning the propositions constituting a particular subject matter. The proposed treatment of knowledgeability and ignorance of facts and subject matters lends itself to an alternative reply to the problem of scepticism, which Brogaard calls the 'simple response'. Finally, she argues that ignorance can also reflect incompetence with respect to a particular activity. She defends the view that the latter is a case of lacking a particular kind of ability-involving knowledge-how, viz. practical knowledge of how to perform the activity in question.

In the fourth contribution to this book, Erik Olsson and Carlo Proietti discuss how ignorance relates to doubt. Both notions have received little attention from epistemologists, let alone the relation between the two. They start out by identifying what they consider to be the main conceptual ingredients of these two propositional attitudes. They then propose a semiformal account within the possible worlds framework of epistemic and doxastic logic. The upshot is that while ignorance can be construed as the absence of knowledge of any of the alternatives under scrutiny, doubt is a very special kind of ignorance. They develop two specific proposals for how to capture special features of doubt in their framework. One centres on the notion that doubt, as opposed to ignorance, requires maximum plausibility of opposing alternatives. The other is based on the assumption that, for an agent to doubt a proposition, she must entertain the question whether that proposition is true on her research agenda.

The next three essays discuss ignorance in relation to contemporary debates in epistemology: ignorance and contextualism, ignorance and arguments against anti-intellectualism, and the epistemic value that ignorance could have.

Michael Blome-Tillmann defends contextualism against the sceptic's claim that our ignorance about the external world is universal and ubiquitous. *Prima facie* convincing arguments have been produced in support of scepticism and a lively philosophical debate has emerged ever since Descartes introduced such an argument in his *Meditations*. In this chapter, Blome-Tillmann considers one such argument for our ignorance about the external world and outlines how *Epistemic Contextualism*—a contemporary view about the semantics of 'knowledge'-attributions—aims to resolve the threat posed by the argument. After discussing the contextualist's take on our alleged ignorance about the external world, he considers contemporary objections to contextualism that have proven influential in the recent literature. Along the way the paper discusses the issue of whether ascriptions of 'ignorance' are context-sensitive and develops a problem for absence-of-true-belief accounts of ignorance that have been popular in the recent literature.

On anti-intellectualism, whether a subject knows that p depends not only on traditional truth-conducive factors, but also on the stakes for her. Now, two of our most important sources of knowledge are testimony and memory. Thus, it would be problematic for any view of knowledge if it were in tension with the idea that these sources yield knowledge. For, it would leave us much more ignorant than we ordinarily take ourselves to be. In her chapter, Jessica Brown defends anti-intellectualism against the claim that it interrupts the transmission of knowledge by memory and testimony, and makes a demand of stakes-sensitivity on our practices that we do not meet. She argues that, when properly formulated, anti-intellectualism is not incompatible with plausible principles concerning the transmission of knowledge by memory and testimony. Further, she argues that there is a plausible reading of the stakes-sensitivity requirement which is compatible with anti-intellectualism and imposes no more work on us than would likely be imposed by the rival intellectualist view. She, thus, provides a defence against the objection that anti-intellectualism implies that we are significantly more ignorant than we normally think.

A third issue that has been hotly debated in the recent epistemology literature is the topic of epistemic value. The aim of Duncan Pritchard's paper is to relate some of the key themes in this literature to the specific topic of ignorance. In particular, he explores an important ambiguity in the very notion of epistemic value, and also examines how best to understand a distinctively epistemic kind of value. While there is often a straightforward epistemic disvalue to ignorance, he delineates some interesting cases in which ignorance is valuable, and valuable moreover in a manner that, he argues, is specifically epistemic.

The final three essays discuss the epistemic dimensions of ignorance in relation to issues that go beyond the purely cognitive, namely religious epistemology, hermeneutical injustice, and racial insensitivity. We have included these essays, even though they are not confined to the epistemic dimensions of ignorance. This is because religious epistemology is typically part of epistemology, the epistemology of race has interesting things to say on collective ignorance in its relation to individual ignorance, and group belief and group knowledge have recently become big issues in epistemology.[23]

In his essay, Justin McBrayer provides a broad taxonomy of the various roles that ignorance plays in the religious life. He assumes the Standard View on ignorance, which says that ignorance is lack of knowledge. This means that many people will be religiously ignorant in all sorts of ways. The religious life, McBrayer argues, is shaped as much by ignorance as by knowledge, both when it comes to religious theory and religious practice. Moreover, ignorance can be marshalled as evidence both for and against specific theoretical conceptions of the divine, but it is not decisive in either case. He also argues that certain kinds of ignorance are compatible with a life of religious virtue and religious faith. He concludes that religious ignorance need not paralyze us in the sense that one can live, hope, and worship as a theist, despite, or maybe even partly because of, our ignorance regarding the supernatural realm.

Miranda Fricker's contribution to this volume focuses on the relation between ignorance and injustice, especially hermeneutical injustice.

---

[23] See, for instance, De Ridder (2013); Mathiesen (2006).

Hermeneutical injustice is a specific kind of injustice, namely the kind that occurs when hermeneutical marginalization results in someone being unable to understand her own experience and/or render it intelligible to some significant social other. According to Fricker, the focus on ignorance as opposed to knowledge, just like the focus on injustice as opposed to justice, inverts the normal perspective taken in Anglo-American philosophy. She welcomes the inversion, because she takes it to bring to light some of the ways in which our epistemic practices can go wrong without the subject realizing it. In her paper, Fricker revisits both testimonial and hermeneutical injustice from the point of view of ignorance. However, her focus is mostly on discussions of *motivated ignorance* as a means of exploring one of the pressures that can perpetuate ignorance created by hermeneutical injustice. She does so principally in relation to the idea of 'white ignorance' as first put forward by Charles Mills. In the broad, 'white ignorance' is a label for a kind of motivated ignorance on the part of white people considered as a privileged racial class vis-à-vis the experiences and perspectives of black people. Fricker defends a certain view of how white ignorance relates to 'wilful' or motivated forms of hermeneutical injustice.

In the final essay of this volume, José Medina explores the relation between ignorance and racial insensitivity. In his paper, he offers an analysis of racial ignorance as a kind of insensitivity or numbness that reflects on the affective and cognitive aspects of people's inability to respond to racial injustices. His analysis highlights three key features of racial insensitivity: as an *active* (self-protecting) kind of ignorance, as a form of *meta*-ignorance, and as a form of *self*-ignorance. On the basis of this analysis, he argues for a robust notion of *shared* epistemic responsibility that can successfully handle issues of complicity and bystander responsibility. On Medina's view, until the epistemic responsibilities breached in racial ignorance are repaired, complicity with racial injustices cannot be uprooted. He argues that taking responsibility for epistemic injustices must begin with the *acknowledgment* of one's epistemic positions and relations, and with the *acknowledgment* of the epistemic privileges and epistemic limitations one has. He analyses several real-life examples as illustrations of epistemic failures and epistemic successes in racial relations, developing a critical discussion of the epistemic dimension of racial micro-aggressions and of what he calls micro-resistance. The paper concludes with a proposal for an ethics and pedagogy of discomfort, which exploits experiences of epistemic discomfort for the facilitation of ethical growth and the expansion of epistemic sensibilities.

We think that the contributions to this volume present a very nice overview of the relevance of ignorance to epistemological investigation and of the consequences of studying this concept for a variety of other epistemological questions. Therefore, we hope that this volume is only a first step towards the development of a full-blown 'epistemology of ignorance'.[24]

[24] We thank Irma Verlaan for her astute assistance in editing the final version of this book. A heartfelt thank you to our executive editor, Hilary Gaskin, our production editor, Rosemary Crawley, and our copy editor, Brian Black, for their hard work to make the publication of this volume possible. For helpful advice on the cover image, we would like to thank Maarten Buijs, Naomi Kloosterboer, Jojanneke van der Veen, and Irma Verlaan. Publication of this book was made possible through the support of a grant from Templeton World Charity Foundation. The opinions expressed in this publication are those of the authors and do not necessarily reflect the views of Templeton World Charity Foundation.

1   The Nature of Ignorance: Two Views

Pierre Le Morvan and Rik Peels

Introduction

Our purpose in this chapter is to explore the nature of ignorance. When we ask about its nature, we ask what it *is* to be ignorant. We address this question by considering two rival accounts that can be found in the literature, each of which specifies a distinct set of conditions taken to be individually necessary and jointly sufficient for ignorance.

The two rival accounts have recently been developed in more detail and defended on the basis of various arguments. In this chapter, we spell out these two different views and provide an overview of the main arguments for them. On the first view, called the Standard View, ignorance is lack or absence of *knowledge*, whereas on the second view, called the New View, ignorance is lack or absence of *true belief*. Among the adherents of the Standard View are Lloyd Fields, Susan Haack, Pierre Le Morvan, and Michael Zimmerman.[1] The New View is embraced, among others, by Alvin Goldman, Alexander Guerrero, Rik Peels, and René van Woudenberg.[2]

The chapter is structured as follows. First, we make a few preliminary comments by distinguishing various kinds of knowledge and explicating in more detail what the difference between the Standard and New Views amounts to (§ 2). Then, we provide a case for the Standard View (§ 3). We spell out three arguments that one might provide in favor of this conception: an argument from common usage (§ 3.1), an argument from unifying theorizing about knowledge and ignorance (§ 3.2), and an argument from ignorance of falsehoods (§ 3.3). Next, we provide a case for the New View (§ 4) by laying out three arguments in favor of it: an

---

[1] See Fields (1994, p. 403), Haack (2001, p. 25), Le Morvan (2011, 2012, 2013); Zimmerman (1988, p. 75; 2008, ix).

[2] See Goldman (1986, p. 26), Goldman and Olsson (2009, pp. 19–21), Guerrero (2007, pp. 62–63), Peels (2010, 2011a, 2012, 2014), Van Woudenberg (2009, p. 375).

argument from intuitions about cases of true belief that fall short of knowledge (§ 4.1), an argument from ignorance as an excuse (§ 4.2), and an argument from ignorance by acquaintance and procedural ignorance (§ 4.3). The purpose of Sections 3 and 4 is *not* to convince the reader of a particular view on ignorance, but merely to present arguments that adherents of these two views might advance in favor of them. We leave it up to the reader to decide which of the two views she or he finds more convincing. We conclude with a couple of retrospective and prospective remarks (§ 5).

2   Ignorance: Preliminaries

In this section we make two preliminary comments that will play an important role in the two following sections.

First, since on the Standard View, ignorance is the lack or absence of knowledge, it is important to note that it is widely thought that there are three different kinds of knowledge.[3] First, there is what is often called *factual or factive* knowledge, that is, knowledge that some specific proposition is true. Knowing that one's wife is at her office, that Abuja is the capital of Nigeria, and that 83 is a prime number belong to this class of knowledge. Second, there is *objectual* knowledge: knowing a certain object, where that object can but need not be a person. One can know one's friend, the taste of pineapples, one can know cities such as Berlin, and one can know what it is to be fired or to be in love. Third, there is *procedural knowledge*: knowledge of how to do something, how to perform some task.[4] Here are a few examples: knowing how to ride a bicycle, knowing how to open a wine bottle, knowing how the play the oboe, and knowing how to forgive someone who wronged one. We return to this threefold distinction below.[5]

---

[3] Many epistemologists have accepted the distinction between these three kinds of knowledge. There are a few exceptions, though. Some philosophers contend that both objectual and procedural knowledge are reducible to factual knowledge, or that they are a subspecies of factual knowledge. For some tentative arguments in favor of this thesis, see Snowdon (2004) and for an elaborate, mainly linguistic defense of it, see Stanley and Williamson (2001). We find this view unconvincing, but cannot elaborate on this issue here; for a good linguistic note on Stanley's and Williamson's article, see Rumfitt (2003).

[4] We prefer to talk about *procedural knowledge* rather than *knowledge-how*, for, as Paul Snowdon has convincingly argued, there are instances of knowledge-how that are not instances of procedural knowledge. See Snowdon (2004, p. 7).

[5] For an overview of these kinds of knowledge by one of those epistemologists, see Lehrer (2000, p. 5). For an influential account of the distinction between factive and procedural knowledge, see Ryle (1945, pp. 4–16; 1973, pp. 28–32, 40–41).

The second preliminary remark concerns only factual knowledge. As we said, on the Standard View, ignorance is lack or absence of knowledge. We should note, though, that there are five different ways in which one can lack knowledge that some proposition p is true – whether or not these five ways of lacking knowledge can be further divided into various ways in which one can lack knowledge:

(i) p is false;
(ii) S disbelieves the true proposition p;
(iii) S suspends belief on the true proposition p;
(iv) p is true and S neither believes that p, nor disbelieves that p, nor suspends belief on p;
(v) S believes the true proposition p, but S's belief that p lacks warrant, where warrant is that which turns true belief into knowledge.

The Standard and New Views agree that if one of the conditions (i) to (iv) is met, then we have a case of factive ignorance. Let us explain. For ease of exposition, we will start with (ii), (iii), and (iv), and then turn to, respectively, (i) and (v).

As to (ii) and (iii), if someone disbelieves or suspends judgment on, say, the true proposition that Napoleon lost the Battle of Waterloo in 1815, she is *ignorant* that he did, because it is true that he did. As to (iv), if someone neither believes that Napoleon lost the Battle of Waterloo in 1815, nor disbelieves that he did, nor suspends judgment on whether he did, for instance, because she has never even heard of Napoleon, then, surely, she is ignorant that he did.

Things are more complicated when it comes to (i). It seems clear that if someone, say, falsely believes that Napoleon lost the battle of Waterloo in 1799, then that person lacks knowledge that this was the case. But one might think that such a person is *not* ignorant that Napoleon lost the battle of Waterloo in 1799, since he did not. As we shall see below, the Standard and New Views differ on whether one can *only* be ignorant of truth. We address this issue below.[6]

Whether or not instances of (v) also count as cases of ignorance is a matter on which the Standard and New Views clearly disagree. In other words, they disagree on whether one is ignorant that p if one truly believes that p, but fails to know that p. On the Standard View, one is ignorant in such cases, whereas on the New View, one is not. In the following two sections, we will consider some arguments that might be advanced in support of each of these two views.

---

[6] As we later see, an intuition motivating the New View is that one can only be ignorant that p if p is true; accordingly, one cannot be ignorant that Napoleon lost the battle of Waterloo in 1799, because Napoleon lost that battle in 1815 rather than in 1799.

3   Ignorance as the Lack of Knowledge

On the Standard View, ignorance is the absence or lack of knowledge, with "ignorance" being an antonym of "knowledge." On the *prima facie* plausible assumption that the lack or absence of something *x* is the complement or contradictory of *x*, ignorance is simply the complement or contradictory of knowledge.[7] Michael Zimmerman takes a position that is at least close to the Standard View on ignorance when he says:

> Ignorance ... is a failure to know what is true. To know what is true, one must believe it (something that involves having a certain level or degree of confidence in it) and do so with adequate justification. Thus ignorance can come about in one of two ways: either by way of failure to believe the truth or by way of believing it without adequate justification.[8]

In this section, we attend to three arguments in favor of the Standard View.

3.1   *First Argument: Common Usage*

As a reflection of how ignorance is ordinarily understood, the idea that ignorance is lack of knowledge has considerable support from common usage of the term "ignorance." Of course, philosophical questions of the nature of something *x* are rarely, if ever, conclusively settled merely by considering common usage of a term for *x*. However, insofar as we seek to understand what is ordinarily meant by a term, considering such common usage has value, and philosophical critiques as to whether we really ought to conceive of *x* as ordinarily understood requires of course understanding how *x* is ordinarily understood in common usage.

In connection with such usage, consider the *Oxford English Dictionary*'s definition *1a* of the word "ignorance": "The fact or condition of being ignorant; want of knowledge (general or special)."[9] The current meaning of "ignorance" as an antonym of "knowledge" squares with its etymology as the English term "ignorance" comes from the Middle English "ignorance" or "ygnoraunce," from the Old French "ignorance," from the Latin "*ignōrāntia*," from the Latin "ignosco" derived from "in" (meaning: the opposite of) and "gnosco" (meaning: know).

English is not unique in this regard, as definitions of cognates of "ignorance" as antonyms of cognates of "knowledge" prove widespread. In fact, in numerous languages, spanning several distinct linguistic families, a cognate of "ignorance" is constructed as an antonym of

---

[7] Thus also Le Morvan (2011, 2012, 2013).   [8] See Zimmerman (2008, ix).
[9] "Ignorance" is also defined in terms of the lack of knowledge in the *Longman Dictionary of Contemporary English*, the *Merriam-Webster Dictionary*, the *Collins Dictionary*, and others.

a cognate of "knowledge."[10] We find this phenomenon in *many* languages. Here are just a few examples:[11]

	"Knowledge" Cognate	*"Ignorance" Cognate*
Burmese:	aasipanyar	aasipanyar kainnmaehkyinn
Chinese:	zhīshì	wúzhī
Danish:	viden	uvidenhed
Finnish:	tieto	tietämättömyys
Hebrew:	yediah	i yediah
Hindi:	jñāna	ajñāna
Malagasy	fahalalana	tsy fahalalana
Russian:	znaniya	neznaniye
Turkish:	bilgi	bilgisizlik[12]

The common usage of "ignorance" thus provides considerable evidence that it functions as an antonym of "knowledge" in English, and likewise for cognates in numerous other languages. This in turn suggests that taking ignorance to be the complement or contradictory of knowledge reflects how we ordinarily conceive of the nature of ignorance and its relationship to knowledge. Insofar as we maintain a presumption in favor of our ordinary way of conceiving of something – such that we presume it to be correct unless shown otherwise – we have a *presumptive* case in favor of the Standard View, and a presumptive case against the New View insofar as it denies the complementarity of knowledge and ignorance.[13]

3.2   *Second Argument: Unifying Theorizing About Knowledge and Ignorance*

Taking ignorance to be the complement of knowledge unifies theorizing about ignorance with theorizing about knowledge in that it seems that insights into the nature of knowledge automatically yield corresponding

---

[10] These linguistic families include the Austronesian, Dravidian, Finno-Ugric, Indo-European, Japonic, Semitic, Sino-Tibetan, Tai-Kadai, and Uralo-Altaic.

[11] Other examples of such languages are Azerbaijani, Basque, Bosnian, Bengali, Croatian, Czech, Dutch, Esperanto, Estonian, German, Greek, Gujarati, Hungarian, Irish, Japanese, Kannada, Korean, Latin, Latvian, Lao, Lithuanian, Macedonian, Malayalam, Marathi, Serbian, Slovak, Tajik, Tamil, Telegu, Thai, Uzbek, Welsh, and Yoruba.

[12] We are grateful to Pierre Le Morvan's colleague, the linguist David Stillman, for help in constructing this table. As Stillman has noted in correspondence, in the Germanic languages and the European Slavic languages, a term for "ignorance" is typically a calque (loan translation) of the Latin "ignosco." In the Romance languages, the Latin "ignorantia" has become "ignorància" in Catalan, "ignorance" in French, "ignoranza" in Italian, "ignorância" in Portuguese, "ignoranță" in Romanian, and "ignorancia" in Spanish.

[13] The Standard View is maintained by linguists such as Stephen Levinson (2000, p. 208), who notes that "not ignorant logically implies knows (because ignorance and knowledge are contradictories)."

putative insights into the nature of ignorance. This provides a conception of ignorance on which each kind of ignorance corresponds to one of the three kinds of knowledge that we discussed in the previous section: factive knowledge, objectual knowledge, and procedural knowledge. Accordingly, insights into the nature of knowledge automatically yield corresponding putative insights into the nature of ignorance. This is because, on the Standard View, ignorance has no substantive and positive nature of its own. Being purely privative and negational, its nature is completely determined by its contrast with the nature of knowledge. So conceived, the relationship between ignorance and knowledge proves analogous to the relationship between darkness and light inasmuch as darkness is the absence or want of light. It also proves analogous to evil understood in Augustinian terms as having no substantive or positive nature of its own inasmuch as it is nothing more than the privation or absence of good.[14] If ignorance thus has nothing more than a privative or negational nature relative to knowledge, then this nature can only be properly understood in contrast with the latter. Thus, every theory or conception of knowledge automatically yields by negation a theory or conception of its complement ignorance, and theorizing about both is thereby unified. To the extent that one finds such unification attractive, it counts in favor of the Standard View and against the New View.

Assuming for the sake of argument that the Standard View is correct, we exemplify below how insight into the nature of ignorance and its kinds can be gained by considering them in contrast with the nature of knowledge in its three varieties. We consider in turn factive, objectual, and procedural knowledge. First, the complement of factive knowledge is *factive ignorance* understood as the absence or lack of factive knowledge. Sam's being ignorant that Caesar crossed the Rubicon or Pam's being ignorant that monotremes are egg-laying mammals provide examples of such ignorance. Second, *objectual ignorance* is the absence or lack of objectual knowledge. Sam's being ignorant of this man's character or Pam's being ignorant of the taste of mango, for instance, provide examples of such ignorance. Third, *procedural ignorance* is the absence or lack of procedural knowledge. Sam's being ignorant of how to operate a forklift or Pam's being ignorant of how to calm a crying baby provide cases in point.

Factive knowledge has received the most attention in contemporary epistemology. Therefore, we will focus primarily on it in addressing the complementarity of knowledge and ignorance. In the literature, the most extensively discussed basic conception of factive knowledge takes it to be

[14] Augustine (2009, p. 43).

analyzable in terms of true justified belief with a codicil for Gettier-type counterexamples.[15] Let us attend to this conception in terms of its implications for understanding ignorance.

On this conception of factive knowledge, someone S's knowledge that p requires the satisfaction of the following four necessary conditions:

(i) a *doxastic* condition: S believes that p;
(ii) an *alethic* condition: p is true;
(iii) a *justificatory* condition: S believes that p with justification;
(iv) a *Gettier-proofing* condition: S's justification for believing that p must withstand Gettier-type counterexamples.

If ignorance that p[16] is the complement of knowledge that p, then someone S's failure to satisfy any of these putative necessary conditions for such knowledge suffices for S's being in the state of ignorance that p.[17] Corresponding to each of these sufficient conditions is a kind of factive ignorance that we may delineate as follows:

Ad (i): *doxastic ignorance* that p occurs when p is not believed. This can happen in four principal ways. One way is for someone to lack the capacity to form beliefs concerning p. Suppose, for instance, that Alex lacks the learning and/or conceptual repertoire to grasp the following proposition:

(1) Platypuses are monotremes.

If so, then Alex fails to believe (1). Suppose, by contrast, that Barbara has the capacity to believe (1), but withholds belief on it because she is doubtful of its truth. Barbara in this case also fails to believe (1), but does so by not exercising her capacity to believe it. Consider now Cindy who believes the contradictory of (1), namely that it is false that platypuses are monotremes. Assuming Cindy does not hold contradictory beliefs, Cindy does not believe that (1) either. Take also Dan who, while having the capacity to believe that (1), fails to believe this because it has never occurred to him.

Doxastic ignorance can thus arise from failing to believe a proposition because (a) one is incapable of believing it, (b) one withholds belief even

---

[15] We will later consider some other conceptions of factive knowledge in terms of their implications for understanding the nature of factive ignorance.

[16] René van Woudenberg has questioned whether it is proper English to say "S is ignorant that p." Here is why we think it is. According to the *Oxford English Dictionary*'s definition 2c of "ignorant," it can be used in sentences with a subordinate clause. The OED gives the following example: "I am ignorant that till now, I ever made you this offer." The construction has also been used by numerous philosophers. Here are two representative examples: (1) Ginet (1975, p. 16) writes: "it is conceivable that S should have been in doubt or ignorant that p"; (2) Hyman (2006, p. 900) writes: "For a verb-phrase of the form 'is ignorant that p' consists of a psychological verb followed by a 'that' clause."

[17] By contrast, on the New View, only if p is true does someone S's failure to satisfy condition (i) suffice for S's being in the state of ignorance that p.

though capable of believing it, (c) one believes its contradictory without inconsistency, or (d) one fails to believe it because it has never occurred to one to believe it.

Ad (ii): *alethic ignorance* occurs when a proposition is not true. Take the following false proposition:

(2) Platypuses are native to Tanzania.

Since (2) is false, no one can know that (2) is true. Since, on the Standard View, ignorance is the complement of knowledge, it follows that everyone is alethically ignorant that (2) is true. As we shall see below, adherents of the New View reject the possibility of alethic ignorance insofar as they maintain that one can be ignorant that p only if p is true.

Ad (iii): *justificational ignorance* occurs when a proposition is believed without justification. Suppose for instance that Alex believes (1) without justification, that is, without any reason or ground. Lacking justification for believing (1), Alex's belief does not satisfy a necessary condition for knowing that (1) is true, and thus satisfies a sufficient condition for justificatory ignorance that Alex is ignorant that platypuses are monotremes.[18]

Ad (iv): *Gettier-type ignorance* occurs when a proposition is true and believed with justification, but is subject to Gettier-type counterexamples.[19] Imagine for example that Sam sees w, w is a genuine Cartier watch, and Sam believes it to be a genuine Cartier watch because it looks to him to be so. Suppose then that Sam's belief is true and justified. Suppose as well, however, that w is ensconced in a display of a hundred counterfeit Cartier watches, and Sam is not able to distinguish w from the counterfeits, and w is only in the display by accident. Many are inclined to conclude that Sam does not know that w is a genuine Cartier watch even if he has a justified true belief that it is. If this conclusion is correct and on the Standard View's supposition that failure to meet a necessary condition for knowledge that p is a sufficient condition for ignorance that p, it follows that Sam is in a state of Gettier-type ignorance.

---

[18] Interestingly, different accounts of the nature of justification have a bearing on how to conceive of the nature of justificatory ignorance. For instance, Foundationalism results in a different account of justification than does Coherentism, and Externalism results in a different account than Internalism. Thus, various accounts of Foundationalism, Coherentism, Externalism, and Internalism will yield varying accounts of justificatory ignorance. Space constraints preclude discussing here the various ways in which such accounts can be developed.

[19] Here, we understand Gettier-type counterexamples in a broader sense than the original Gettier examples that involved inferences from false beliefs to justified true beliefs. A Gettier-type counterexample in this broad sense is any counterexample to knowledge understood as true justified belief.

In sum, if ignorance that p is the complement of knowledge that p as it is on the Standard View, and if knowledge that p is true belief that p with Gettier-proof justification, then ignorance that p occurs if (i) p is not believed, and/or (ii) p is not true, and/or (iii) p is believed without justification, and/or (iv) the justified belief that p is subject to Gettier-type counterexamples. Ignorance that p is *doxastic* in case of (i), *alethic* in case of (ii), *justificational* in case of (iii), and *Gettier-type* in case of (iv).

We have so far considered factive ignorance as the complement of factive knowledge where the latter is conceived of as true belief with Gettier-proof justification. Worth noting however is that alternative conceptions of factive knowledge lead to different complementary conceptions of factive ignorance. These alternative conceptions include taking factive knowledge to be (i) analyzable as true belief alone, (ii) analyzable as true belief with something other than justification, (iii) analyzable not as a species of belief but rather as an ability, and (iv) unanalyzable. Let us briefly consider each in terms of their implications for factive ignorance as the complement of factive knowledge.

Suppose that factive knowledge is nothing more than mere true belief as maintained for instance by Sartwell.[20] If so, then factive ignorance as its complement is nothing more than the absence or lack of true belief, and someone S is factively ignorant that p if p is not true and/or S does not believe that p. Thus, factive ignorance has only alethic and doxastic kinds.

Suppose that factive knowledge is true belief together with something other than justification. Let us call this something other than justification "O." Alternative accounts of O include:

- the *Nozickian truth-tracking* condition: if p were not true, S would not believe that p, and if p were true, S would believe that p;[21]
- the *Plantingan warrant* condition: S's belief that p results from the proper functioning of S's cognitive equipment, i.e., functioning as it was designed to function;[22]
- the *Safety* condition: S could not easily have believed that p is false.[23]

---

[20] See Sartwell (1991, 1992). For critical discussion, see Le Morvan (2002). Others, such as Goldman (2002a, 2002c) and Goldman and Olsson (2009), have argued that there is a weak sense of knowledge according to which it is nothing more than true belief. For critical discussion, see Le Morvan (2005, 2010).

[21] See Nozick (1981). For critical discussion see DeRose (1995).

[22] See Plantinga (1993a, 1993b). More fully stated: The Plantingan Warrant Condition specifies that a belief B is warranted only if B is produced by a properly functioning cognitive faculty in an environment fitting for that kind of cognitive faculty and is governed by a designed plan aimed at the production of true beliefs and that there is a high statistical probability that beliefs so produced will be true. For critical discussion, see the essays in Kvanvig. (1996).

[23] See Sosa (1999). For critical discussion, see Comesaña (2005).

Accepting any of these alternative accounts of factive knowledge leads to alternative complementary accounts of factive ignorance: in addition to its alethic and doxastic kinds, factive ignorance could result from a failure of truth-tracking, from a failure of proper functioning of cognitive equipment, or from a failure to safely believe that p.

Suppose that factive knowledge that p is not a species of true belief but rather an ability to "manifest various accurate representations of p" concerning the "epistemic diaspora" of p such as being able to answer questions accurately concerning p, to reason accurately concerning p, and to correctly use concepts related to p.[24] Accepting such an account of factive knowledge leads to a complementary account of factive ignorance according to which such ignorance arises from the failure to manifest various accurate representations of p concerning its epistemic diaspora.

Suppose that knowledge-first epistemology is correct and factive knowledge that p is, therefore, not analyzable at all but rather the most basic factive propositional attitude.[25] If so, then the complementary account of factive ignorance is simply that to be ignorant that p is to not know that p where such knowledge is the most basic factive propositional attitude.

In light of the considerations above, we have seen how the Standard View yields a unified account of knowledge and ignorance; insofar as such unification proves attractive, it counts in favor of the Standard View.

Worth noting in this context as well is that, by unifying theorizing about knowledge and ignorance, the Standard View avoids what may strike many as an implausible consequence of the New View, namely that merely having a true belief that p suffices for not being factively ignorant that p. Suppose for example that Sam in 2016 believes that an odd perfect number exists (that is, an odd number that is half the sum of all of its positive divisors including itself), and does so quite irrationally, or very unjustifiably, or as a result of a highly unreliable doxastic process. At this juncture in mathematical history, whether an odd perfect number exists remains an unsolved problem in number theory; suppose though that it is proven in 3016 that such a number exists. The New View entails that Sam *in 2016* is not factively ignorant that there is an odd perfect number, a consequence liable to strike many as quite implausible.[26] The Standard

---

[24] See Heatherington (2011). For critical discussion, see Madison (2012).
[25] See Williamson (2000). For critical discussion, see the essays in Greenough and Pritchard (2009).
[26] Of course, Sam in 2015 was not ignorant *of the proposition (proven true in 3016) that there is an odd perfect number*, but as discussed in the next section, knowledge *of* a true proposition is distinct from knowledge *that* it is true.

View (provided that knowledge that p is more than mere true belief that p) carries no such entailment.

3.3   *Third Argument: Ignorance of Falsehoods*

Can there be ignorance of falsehoods? We consider in this section a case for maintaining that there can be. The Standard View is fully compatible with such ignorance, and insofar as the New View is not, this provides further support for the Standard over the New View.

Propositions have truth-conditions. These truth-conditions can be distinguished from their satisfaction.[27] A proposition is true when its truth-conditions are satisfied, and, assuming bivalence, false when not. Consider the following three propositions:

(3) Damascus is north of Jerusalem.

(4) Mars is larger than Jupiter.

(5) An odd perfect number exists.

The first of these propositions is true. The second is false. The third is presumably true or false, but, as noted in the previous section, at this juncture in mathematical history we are not in a position to ascertain its truth-value.

In order to be in a position to know that, believe that, desire that, or doubt that a proposition is true (that is, that its truth-conditions are satisfied), one cannot be ignorant of the proposition itself and its con-comitant truth-conditions. Take, for instance, King Herod I (73 BCE–4 BCE), and consider the following two propositions:

(6) The most popular paid iOS app of 2014 was *Heads Up!*

(7) The most popular paid iOS app of 2014 was NOAA Hi-Def Radar.

It turns out that (6) is true while (7) is false.[28] In any event, being ignorant of these propositions, King Herod, since he lived more than 2000 years ago, was in no position to have any propositional attitude toward them. As such, he was ignorant *not* just that (6)'s truth-conditions are satisfied and that (7)'s truth-conditions are not, but in the even deeper sense of

---

[27] Whatever else they may be, it is widely agreed that propositions have truth-conditions. Whether they are nothing but their truth-conditions is more controversial, and not an issue that can be addressed here. For discussion on the ontology of propositions in relation to knowledge and ignorance of them, see Le Morvan (2015).

[28] www.apptrigger.com/2014/12/28/best-2014-popular-paid-ios-apps/

being ignorant of (6) and (7) themselves. King Herod I could not even grasp these propositions.

This example involving Herod, the adherent of the Standard View might suggest, illustrates how ignorance of propositions is not restricted to those that are true, and exemplifies how one can be ignorant of false ones too. In Herod's case, he lacked the conceptual repertoire to grasp not only true proposition (6) but also false proposition (7). Notice also that, even if one has the conceptual repertoire for having an attitude toward a proposition, one can still be ignorant of that proposition if one has not deployed this repertoire. Suppose, for instance, that President Obama has the conceptual repertoire to grasp (6) and (7), but has never deployed this repertoire. If so, one might think in a certain sense he is ignorant of these propositions.[29]

Turning now to knowledge of propositions as the complement of ignorance of them, the following points merit attention. First, adherents of the Standard View can argue that, although one can have knowledge of true propositions – e.g., Pierre Le Morvan has knowledge of (1) – one can also have knowledge of false ones – e.g., Pierre Le Morvan has knowledge of (2). Second, one can have knowledge of propositions one does not believe. For instance, Pierre Le Morvan has knowledge of (3), but does not believe it. Thus, one might think that knowledge of a proposition p does not share the putative necessary conditions of knowledge that p in terms of believing that p, p's being true, and having warrant for believing that p.[30]

In light of the reasoning above and the standard three-fold distinction that we made in Section 2 between factive, objectual, and procedural knowledge, we can conclude that the complement of ignorance *of* a proposition is not factive knowledge (knowledge that p). This leaves us with objectual and procedural knowledge. It is far from clear how this complement could be a form of procedural knowledge.[31] So we are left with objectual knowledge: the complement of ignorance *of* a proposition is an acquaintance with or knowledge of an entity, where the entity in

---

[29] Ignorance of a proposition can come in pre-conceptual and post-conceptual forms: if one lacks the conceptual repertoire requisite for having an attitude regarding a proposition, one is pre-conceptually ignorant of it, whereas one is post-conceptually ignorant of a proposition if, though having this conceptual repertoire, one has not deployed it so as to have such an attitude.

[30] "Warrant" is meant in the neutral sense for whatever it is that turns true belief into knowledge, and not in the particular sense of the specific account of warrant found in Plantinga (1993a, 1993b).

[31] A general point that extends beyond the question of the knowledge of propositions is that procedural and objectual knowledge seem to be different kinds of knowledge, and it is not evident that objectual knowledge is reducible to procedural knowledge.

question is a proposition. Such knowledge is not equivalent to knowledge *that p*, for although the latter entails knowledge *of p* since knowledge *of p* is a necessary condition for knowledge *that p*,[32] knowledge *of p* does not entail knowledge *that p* since knowledge *of p* is not a sufficient condition for knowledge *that p*.[33] Thus, knowledge *that p* should not be equated with knowledge *of p*.[34]

Accordingly, on the Standard View, the complement of ignorance *of* a proposition *p* is *not* knowledge *that p*. Its complement is rather knowledge *of p*—an acquaintance with or knowledge of an entity, where the entity in question is a proposition.[35] Such objectual knowledge may be occurrent (as when one is conscious of it) or dispositional (as when one retains it in memory), and occurs only if the knower has the concepts to grasp or comprehend the proposition. Knowledge of *p* is required to have – and is therefore entailed by, and a precondition of – knowledge that *p*, but also for having any propositional attitude concerning *p* such as believing that *p*, considering that *p*, doubting that *p*, hoping that *p*, or entertaining that *p*.

While the Standard View is fully compatible with the ignorance of falsehoods, insofar as the New View is supported by the idea we can *only* be ignorant of truths (and therefore not of falsehoods),[36] the above case for the ignorance of falsehoods supports the Standard over the New View.

Allowing for the ignorance of falsehoods also enables the Standard View to avoid a difficulty (at least an apparent one) the New View runs into. This difficulty arises when we consider that the New View defines factive ignorance *as the lack or absence of true belief*. Now a natural or intuitive understanding of a lack or absence of something *x* is that it is the complement of a presence of *x*; thus, if the presence of *S*'s true belief that *p* is <*S* believes that *p* and *p* is true>, then its absence is understood as ~<*S* believes that *p* and *p* is true> and this in turn is logically equivalent to <~*S* believes that *p* or ~*p*>. On this understanding of the absence of true belief then, ~*p* (namely, *p*'s being false) is a sufficient condition for the absence of true belief. Accordingly, if adherents of the New View were to accept this understanding of the absence of true belief, they would also

---

[32] Someone who is ignorant *of p* cannot know *that p*. See Le Morvan (2015).

[33] Just because someone *S* knows *of p*, it does not follow that *p* is true, or that *S* believes that *p*, or that *S*'s believing that *p* (if *S* does so) meets the anti-Gettier condition.

[34] This non-equivalence holds even if *p* is true, for even in such a case, knowledge *of p* is necessary but not sufficient for knowledge *that p*. Accordingly, knowledge *that* a proposition is true should not be equated with knowledge *of* a proposition that is true.

[35] See Le Morvan (2015) for a discussion of leading conceptions of the ontology of propositions and their epistemic implications.

[36] See Peels (2010, 2011a, 2012).

have to accept that p's being false is a sufficient condition for factive ignorance, and this contradicts the idea that we *cannot* be ignorant that p if p is false. To avoid this conclusion, adherents of the New View must provide an account of the absence of true belief on which the absence of true belief is *not* the complement of the presence of true belief, and this may strike many as an intuitively odd or unnatural way of construing this absence.[37] On the Standard View, by contrast, the absence of true belief is straightforwardly the complement of the presence of true belief, and so we can be, and in fact are, ignorant that p if p false.

One final related point concerning falsehood. An intuition invoked in support of the New View is that "ignorant that p" has the conversational implicature that p is true.[38] Thus, saying that S is ignorant that p conversationally implies that p is true. Does this show that we cannot be ignorant that p if p is false? Adherents of the Standard View can resist this conclusion by pointing out that conversational implicature is a matter of what is suggested or implied by an expression, not a matter of what it strictly speaking expresses. Moreover, "does not know that p" can also conversationally imply that p is true; for instance, to say "Pam doesn't know that platypuses are monotremes" can conversationally imply that platypuses are monotremes. But just because "does not know that p" can have this conversational implicature, it does not follow that the following widely held epistemological tenet is false: that p's being false is a sufficient condition for not knowing that p. *Mutatis mutandis* for "is ignorant that p."[39]

4   Ignorance as the Lack of True Belief

In the previous section, we considered ignorance as the absence or lack of knowledge. In this section, we consider an alternative conception of ignorance, namely ignorance as the absence or lack of true belief. If ignorance is the absence or lack of true belief, then none of the cases that are cases of true belief that fall short of knowledge are cases of

---

[37] Peels (2012, p. 743) has proposed that the absence of true belief can be understood instead as <S does not believe that p and p is true>. Note that this entails that the absence of true belief *cannot* be the complement of the presence of true belief, for <S does not believe that p and p is true> is not logically equivalent to ~<S believes that p and p is true>. Which of these ways of understanding the absence of true belief makes the most sense is a question we leave to our readers.

[38] See Peels (2010, 2011a, 2012).

[39] A critic of the Standard View might counter that "is ignorant that p" always has the conversational implicature that p is true, while "does not know that p" does not always have it. Whether this claim is true cannot be settled here and would be a good subject for linguistic inquiry and experimental philosophy.

ignorance – whether they are cases of Gettierized justified true belief, mere justified true belief, or even mere true belief. Since, according to adherents of the New View, one can be ignorant that *p* only if *p* is true, it follows that there are three kinds of ignorance:

(i) *Disbelieving ignorance*: one disbelieves that *p* while *p* is true.
(ii) *Suspending ignorance*: one suspends belief and disbelief on *p* while *p* is true.
(iii) *Deep ignorance*: one neither believes nor disbelieves nor suspends belief and disbelief on *p* while *p* is true.

A similar view is adopted by René van Woudenberg:

S is ignorant with respect to *p*, when (iiia) *S* neither believes nor disbelieves *p*, even though he has entertained *p* (rational ignorance). (iiib) *S* never so much as entertained *p* and accordingly neither believes nor disbelieves *p* (deep ignorance). (iv) *S* has the false belief that not-*p*. Each of these conditions is sufficient for ignorance. There is a way to connect and summarize the three sufficient conditions for ignorance by saying, as Alvin Goldman has done, that ignorance is "the absence of true belief"; after all, each of these conditions entails the absence of true belief.[40]

We should note that a fully spelled-out version of the New View will have to add several caveats to a rough analysis of ignorance along these lines. For one thing, it seems possible that one disbelieve the *true* proposition *p*, but know that, epistemically speaking, one really ought to have the attitude of *belief* toward *p*, but that, quite irrationally, one is unable to do so for psychological reasons. It is not at all clear that such a case will count as a case of *ignorance that p*, even though that is what the rough and ready version of the New View as presented above implies. However, since the aim of this paper is to sketch some important arguments for the Standard and New Views, we will leave such details for another occasion.

4.1   First Argument: Intuitions About Cases of True Belief that Fall Short of Knowledge

In order to sketch the first argument for the New View, let us consider some of the ways in which one can believe truly that *p* and yet fail to know that *p* and then consider whether they count as being ignorant that *p*.

Let us start with cases that just fall short of knowledge, such as Gettier-cases. An adherent of the New View might suggest that they do *not* seem to be cases of *ignorance*. Here is an example that can be used to illustrate the point. Imagine that Sam enters his living room and that he looks at the

---

[40] Van Woudenberg (2009, p. 375).

clock. The clock tells him that it is 7 p.m., so Sam comes to believe that it is 7 p.m. He knows that the clock normally works perfectly fine. However, unbeknownst to him, the clock stopped working twenty-four hours ago. Is Sam ignorant that it is 7 p.m.? It seems, the adherent of the New View might suggest, that it is implausible that Sam is ignorant in such a case. Of course, there are *other* propositions of whose truth Sam is clearly ignorant, such as that the clock stopped working twenty-four hours ago and that the clock is unreliable on this particular occasion. Of the truth of the proposition that it is 7 p.m. *itself*, however, Sam does not seem, to adherents of the New View, to be ignorant.

Next, they might suggest that even cases of *mere* true belief do not seem cases of ignorance. Consider Alfred from Columbia, Missouri who believes contrary to all the evidence that he is going to be the next president of the United States. He thus comes to believe the proposition q that the next president of the United States currently lives in Columbia, Missouri. As it turns out, the next president is Ms. Howard, a female member of Congress living in Columbia, Missouri, whom Alfred has never even heard of. In this case Alfred believes truly, but does not know that q. Is he *ignorant* that q is true? It seems to adherents of the New View that he is *not*. Again, there are all sorts of truths in the neighborhood that he *is* ignorant of and it is hard mentally to isolate q from all those others truths, truths such as *Ms Howard is going to be the next president of the United States, Ms Howard lives in Columbia*, and *The next president is currently a member of Congress*. We may be inclined to think that Alfred is ignorant that q is true because we know that he is ignorant of all these other propositions. If we focus on q, however, it seems – so the argument goes – that Alfred is *not* ignorant of q.

Now, let us assume with most epistemologists that knowledge is true belief that satisfies some further conditions in order to provide an anti-Gettier codicil. If both cases of true belief that just fall short of knowledge, like Sam's case, and cases of mere true belief, such as Alfred's case, do not count as cases of ignorance, then in-between cases will probably not count as cases of ignorance either. Here is why. If, on the one hand, such cases *had* a property that would make them cases of ignorance, then it seems to adherents of the New View that knowledge would also have that property and, therefore, be a case of ignorance. If, on the other hand, such cases *lacked* a property that would make them cases of ignorance, then it seems mere true belief would also lack that property and, therefore, be a case of ignorance. Thus, if both cases of mere true belief and cases of true belief that just fall short of knowledge are *not* cases of ignorance, then we can safely assume that in-between cases are not cases of ignorance either.

Note that each of the three steps of this argument needs to be successful in order for this argument to provide a good reason to embrace the New View, but that *not* all of them have to be successful in order for it to provide a good reason to reject the Standard View. If, for instance, mere true belief *is* a case of ignorance, but true belief that just falls short of knowledge is *not*, then the Standard View is false: ignorance is *not* the lack of knowledge. This means, of course, that there is a variety of potential views regarding the nature of ignorance that one might be willing to defend even if one thinks the Standard and New Views are mistaken, such as the view that ignorance is lack of Gettierized true belief, that it is lack of reliably produced true belief, that it is lack of true belief based on sufficient evidence, and so forth. Or one might defend a particular version of contextualism, arguing that which of these things ignorance is depends on the context of the cognitive subject in question. For the sake of clarity, in this paper we confine ourselves to the Standard and New Views.

4.2   Second Argument: Ignorance Excuses

Ever since Aristotle, it has been widely acknowledged among philosophers that ignorance – at least as long as it is *blameless* and if it is ignorance of the right kind of proposition – provides an excuse for wrong actions or omissions for which one would otherwise be blameworthy.[41] Here is an example. Imagine that it is Claire's birthday and that Sam decides to bake a chocolate cake for her. When Claire is away from the kitchen for a second, a jealous cousin poisons the cake. After Sam returns, he finishes preparing the cake and offers it to Claire, entirely ignorant that the cake has been poisoned. It seems clear that in such a case – again, as long as his ignorance is blameless – Sam is excused for offering Claire the poisoned chocolate cake and that it is his *ignorance* of the fact that the cake is poisoned that excuses him.

In some cases, ignorance counts as a full excuse: it removes *all* blameworthiness. In other cases, it is merely a *partial* excuse: it reduces the degree of one's blameworthiness, but it does not block blameworthiness altogether.[42] If, for instance, Sam suspends judgment on whether the chocolate cake is poisoned and still gives it to Claire, he is less blameworthy than if he is aware (believes truly) that the cake is poisoned, but

---

[41] See Aristotle (2003, pp. 123–129; pp. 145–147; pp. 299–305) (*NE* III.i.13–27; v.7–12; V.viii.3–12). For more recent examples, see Brandt (1969, p. 349), Fischer and Ravizza (1998, pp. 12–13); Goldman (1970, p. 208), Rosen (2003, pp. 61–62); Smith (1983, pp. 543–571), Zimmerman (2008, pp. 169–205).

[42] For some examples, see Peels (2014).

Sam is still blameworthy: in this case, he should *not* have offered Claire the chocolate cake.

The point of the second argument in favor of the New View is this: any kind of true belief that falls short of knowledge does *not* excuse. It does not even provide a *partial* excuse. However, ignorance (as long as it is blameless) excuses. It follows, by a simple *modus tollens*, that ignorance cannot be the lack of knowledge. The thesis that ignorance is lack of true belief, so the argument goes, is more plausible than the view that ignorance is the lack of knowledge, since each way in which one can lack a true belief – disbelieving ignorance, suspending ignorance, and deep ignorance – again, as long as it is blameless, seems to provide at least a partial excuse.

Let us elaborate on the earlier example to illustrate the point. Sam is in a situation in which he has baked Claire a birthday chocolate cake and he can give it to her or not. It seems to adherents of the New View that Sam's *knowing* that it is poisoned or his merely *truly believing* that it is poisoned does not make any difference to the degree of his blameworthiness: in both cases he is blameworthy to an equally high degree and he is not at all excused. For whether he knows or rationally believes or merely believes that the cake is poisoned does *not* make an important difference to his phenomenology. In all these cases, he *sincerely thinks* that the cake is poisoned; that is how reality appears to him.[43]

If, as many epistemologists believe, there are degrees of belief and if degrees of belief are to be spelled out in terms of conviction, then maybe one is more blameworthy if one is *certain* that the cake is poisoned than if one is merely *fairly convinced* that the cake is poisoned. Notice, though, that such varieties in degree of belief are not necessarily correlated with whether one *knows, believes on strong evidence, believes on weak evidence*, or *believes without any evidence*. One could in principle, quite irrationally, be one hundred percent sure without having any reasons or evidence. Thus, even though the degree to which one believes that, say, the chocolate cake is poisoned may make a difference to the extent to which true belief excuses, whether one *knows* or *justifiedly* believes, and so on, whether it is poisoned does not make a difference to that.

Adherents of the New View would stress that the suggestion here is *not* that a true belief that the cake is poisoned renders one blameworthy *to the highest degree possible*. Maybe someone who believes truly that the chocolate cake is poisoned and gives it to one's friend in order to do wrong for wrong's sake is even more blameworthy than someone who does so

---

[43] Given this argument, adherents of the Standard View need to develop a case for holding that one's being excused is a function of more than one's phenomenology or degree of conviction relative to a belief (or, as we point out below, argue that not all ignorance excuses).

merely because she is scared of the poisoning cousin.[44] In such cases, however, it seems that one's evil intention *adds* something to the degree of one's blameworthiness. Whether one believes or knows that the chocolate cake is poisoned makes no difference to the degree of one's blameworthiness: in both cases, one is not excused at all, not even partially.

Since, as we said, ignorance is widely acknowledged to count as an excuse, whereas it seems that true belief that fails to be knowledge does not, ignorance, one might think, cannot be absence of knowledge. What the discussion of ignorance in this section suggests is rather that ignorance is the lack of true belief.

Of course, one could simply propose to revise the widespread view that blameless ignorance excuses and say that *most* varieties of blameless ignorance excuse, but that *some* varieties of ignorance, such as blameless mere true belief and blameless mere justified true belief, do not. The New View, though, provides a unifying account of ignorance as an excuse, for it implies that *all* blameless ignorance provides at least a partial excuse and this captures the intuitions about excusing ignorance that, it seems, are widespread among philosophers.

4.3   There Is No Ignorance by Acquaintance or Procedural Ignorance

A third and final consideration in favor of the New View – one that cuts against the idea that the Standard View provides a unified account of ignorance – is the following. On the main rival view, the Standard View, ignorance is lack of knowledge. Given that there is not only factive knowledge, but also objectual knowledge and procedural knowledge, and given that people lack objectual knowledge and procedural knowledge with regard to many things, it would follow that people have objectual ignorance and procedural ignorance with regard to countless (the vast majority of) things. But that, one might think, seems problematic. Imagine that the following sentence is true:

> (8) Xavier *knows* Paris very well, because he has lived there for more than twenty years.

This is obviously a case of *objectual* knowledge: Xavier is familiar with Paris, since he has lived there for such a long time. If he has objectual knowledge of Paris and if the Standard View of Ignorance is correct, though, it would follow that he lacks objectual ignorance of Paris. But it seems to adherents of the New View that it is *not* correct to say:

---

[44] Thus, for instance, Beardsley (1979, p. 577).

(8′) Xavier is not at all *ignorant* of Paris, because he has lived there for more than twenty years.

Something similar seems to apply to another kind of objectual knowledge, namely knowledge of *people*. It is perfectly fine to say:

(9) She knows Albert since she moved to Oxford.

But again it seems to adherents of the New View that we would *not* say:

(9′) She is not ignorant of Albert since she moved to Oxford.

When it comes to such things as cities or countries and persons, there seems to adherents of the New View to be the absence or presence of *objectual knowledge*, but no such thing as the absence or presence of *objectual ignorance*. This is not to deny that we *do* use the expression "ignorance of X" in at least *some* cases in which X is not a person, a city a country or some such thing. We say, for instance:

(10) Marcel is ignorant of quantum physics.

(11) I was ignorant of their plans for the summer.

Adherents of the New View might suggest, though, that these are *not* cases in which someone is claimed to suffer from objectual ignorance. What the person in question seems to be ignorant of, one might think, rather seems to be a set of propositions – those constitutive of quantum physics and those that constitute a particular group of persons' plans for the summer. One might claim that something similar applies to expressions like "ignorant as to how to φ" and "ignorant of how to φ," such as they occur in the following sentences:

(12) They are ignorant as to how to escape from that prison.

(13) Fred is ignorant of how change a car's tire.

Arguing that the knowledge referred to in (12) and (13) is reducible to factive knowledge, that the truth of these sentences does not require there to be uniquely *procedural* knowledge, and to argue that something similar applies to other cases would be needed to complete the argument, but is beyond the scope of this paper. Again, if certain cases of objectual knowledge do not have objectual ignorance as their contradictory or complement, the Standard View is in trouble, but it does *not* follow that the New View is correct; more work would be needed for that, namely that every case of seemingly *objectual* or *procedural* ignorance is in fact a case of *factive* ignorance.

5   Epilogue

In this chapter, we have explored the nature of ignorance. In doing so, we have discussed two main rival views of its nature, namely the Standard and New Views, and three main arguments adduced in support of each.

As we shall see in some of the ensuing chapters, which view one takes on the nature of ignorance can make a significant difference to how one thinks of other philosophical issues. As Michael Blome-Tillmann points out, the Standard View implies that if contextualism about knowledge is correct, then so is contextualism about ignorance, whereas the New View implies that even if contextualism about knowledge is correct, it does not follow that contextualism about ignorance is correct. Justin McBrayer argues in Chapter 8 that one's understanding of the nature of ignorance makes a significant difference to several issues in the philosophy of religion, such as whether or not a large number of people are ignorant of God's existence. Some of these chapters also provide considerations that bear on the controversy between the Standard and New Views. Berit Brogaard, for instance, argues in Chapter 3 that being ignorant of how to do something is a special case of being ignorant of a fact – something that an adherent of the New View might gladly embrace.

Since these are just a couple of examples, we conclude that more work needs to be done, both on considerations in favor and against the Standard and New Views, and on spelling out the ramifications of each of these views in other areas of philosophy.[45]

---

[45] We thank Nikolaj Nottelmann and René van Woudenberg for their helpful comments on earlier versions of this paper.

2   The Varieties of Ignorance

Nikolaj Nottelmann

1   Introduction

This chapter aims to provide a useful taxonomy of ignorance types. It discusses instances of ignorance according to the following criteria:

1. Kind: what the ignorant subject is ignorant of
2. Degree: the degree to which the subject is ignorant
3. Order: for example, when a subject is ignorant of her ignorance, she may be said to suffer from second-order ignorance

No further criteria shall be of fundamental concern in this chapter.[1] In Section 2 I discuss ignorance of facts (factual ignorance), ignorance of answers to questions (erotetic ignorance[2]), and practical ignorance[3] (ignorance constituted by a lack of know-how). In passing, I also discuss ignorance of various kinds of entities, such as ignorance of objects, of persons, of event, and of properties. Section 2.3 deals with important questions concerning reducibility. First, in Section 2.3.1, it is discussed whether – and in which sense – erotetic ignorance reduces to factual ignorance. Second, in Section 2.3.2, I treat the intricate question whether practical ignorance reduces to erotetic ignorance. I point out difficulties for this latter "intellectualist" reduction.

In Section 3 I discuss how we may understand ignorance as occurring in degrees, and whether it is fruitful to distinguish between varieties such

---

[1] For example, some authors have argued that certain types of ignorance are constituted by the absence of true belief rather than the absence of knowledge. Such claims typically have taken inspiration from Alvin Goldman's analysis of ignorance as simply 'the absence of true belief' (see. e.g. 1999, p. 5), even if in adjoining contexts Goldman also sanctions a 'weak' conception of knowledge as simply true belief. However, the view is outspoken in Van Woudenberg (2009), who also remedies Goldman's failure explicitly to respect the factivity of ignorance. See also Peels (2010, 2011a, 2012) for defence of this 'New View' of (factual) ignorance. See Le Morvan (2011, 2012) for criticism.

[2] Thus named by Nicholas Rescher. See Rescher (2009, p. 29). From ancient Greek ἐρωτητικός (*erōtētikós*) – pertaining to questions.

[3] Some have preferred to call this type of ignorance 'procedural ignorance'. See for example Le Morvan and Peels, this volume, Chapter 1.

as 'deep' and 'shallow' ignorance. Finally, Section 4 treats briefly on the general importance of higher-order ignorance and its absolution.

As shall soon become clear the topics mentioned above each touch on a number of highly controversial and contested issues in contemporary epistemology, philosophical semantics, and the philosophy of mind. Thus, at best the present chapter may hope to present in a fair light the most important debates, and guide the reader to a firmer understanding of the philosophical stakes involved.

2   Varieties of Ignorance Divided According to What the Subject Is Ignorant Of

2.1   *Refining the Standard View of Factual Ignorance*

The *Oxford English Dictionary* defines ignorance as simply 'the want of knowledge (specific or general)'.[4] This view has been known as 'The Standard View'.[5] We may quickly realize that this definition is too simple. Like knowledge, ignorance (at least in one variety) is a factive state. You do not know that Santa Claus exists, since he does not. But this does not point to any ignorance on your part. A related problem with the *OED* definition is that often knowledge is absent, simply because the attributee is of the wrong kind: my coffee cup clearly does not know that it is snowing outside my house, since my coffee cup is a mindless material object. But to say that, therefore, my coffee cup is ignorant seems to involve some kind of pretense. Some thing's failure to know something, then, does not constitute ignorance, unless that thing is in a meaningful sense an ignorant subject. Thus, a fair analysis of factual ignorance seems be the following:

For any proposition p and any S, S is ignorant of the fact that p if, and only if:

1. S is an epistemic subject.
2. It is a fact that p.
3. S does not know[6] the fact that p.

I propose that we call (1) 'the epistemic subjecthood condition'; (2) 'the factivity condition'; and (3) 'the absence-of-knowledge condition'. I shall refer to the structure of this analysis as 'the tri-partite structure'. By an

---

[4] See Oxford English Dictionary Online. Stable URL: www.oed.com/view/Entry/91232, retrieved January 29, 2015.
[5] Thus Le Morvan (2012) defends 'the Standard View of Ignorance according to which ignorance is the lack or absence of knowledge'. Charitably, though, Le Morvan should be taken to respect the restrictions of factivity and subjecthood discussed here.
[6] Fans of the 'New View' may simply substitute 'S does not believe that p' here.

epistemic subject, I propose that here we simply understand an entity capable of some sort of knowledge. The only entities not ignorant of anything by definition are entities not knowing anything under any circumstances. Attributions of ignorance to anything but individual live human subjects shall play no role in the further proceedings, and such, I presume, uncontroversially qualify as epistemic subjects.[7] For ease of presentation, I have also assumed that all facts of which a subject could be ignorant are specifiable by way of a proposition. In other words I presume that 'S is ignorant of the fact that p' is equivalent to the somewhat archaic expression 'S is ignorant of p'.[8] But whatever facts are, arguably they are not simply true propositions. The latter have properties, most notably the property of being true, which facts do not share: the fact that you are human is not true or false, even if the proposition that you are human is. Still, we may suppose that it is only by way of her propositional knowledge that a subject may hope to avoid satisfying the absence-of-knowledge condition with regard to a certain fact. If this holds, we need only add the following *caveat*: if there be any facts not corresponding to true propositions, necessarily we are all ignorant of them.[9]

We should notice that even if in some sense factual ignorance is the inverse of factual knowledge, it does not require the relevant facts to be *knowable*. For example, our knowledge of the universe we inhabit seems fundamentally restricted by the light-cone, i.e. the vast conical section of the universe (considered as Minkowski space-time), from which electromagnetic radiation travelling in vacuum could reach us. Certainly it seems plausible that there is a fact of the matter concerning the number of DNA molecules in the huge portion of the Universe outside the light-cone. Even if this fact is unknowable, certainly we are ignorant of it.[10]

---

[7] I do so because it hardly matters to the current project whether for example groups, animals of various sorts or machines are capable of knowledge. This is not to say that such questions have no implications with regard to the general nature of knowledge, and, hence, the nature of ignorance.

[8] For example, in the American Standard Version of the Bible, Romans 6:3 asks: 'Or are ye ignorant that all we who were baptized into Christ Jesus were baptized into his death?'

[9] Sorting out the exact metaphysical nature of facts and propositions and their interrelations clearly lies far outside the scope of the present chapter. But see for example Mulligan and Correia (2013).

[10] Such cases seem to put under some pressure the 'New View' of (factual) ignorance, according to which one escapes ignorance simply by forming a true belief. See e.g. van Woudenberg (2009), Peels (2010). Even if I should for some quirky reason form a true belief concerning the number of DNA molecules outside the light-cone, it still seems odd to say that I am not ignorant of the relevant fact. However, as mentioned earlier, an in-depth evaluation of the New View lies outside the bounds of the present chapter. See here Le Morvan and Peels, this volume, Chapter 1.

2.2   *Towards Understanding Other Varieties of Ignorance*

Not all ignorance concerns facts. Or at the very least, as we shall soon see this assumption would short-circuit important debates. Still the tri-partite structure may be employed en route to a wider understanding of ignorance. In general, ignorance seems to require epistemic subjecthood. And in general ignorance seems to require the absence of some variety of knowledge.[11] However, as we shall soon see, offering helpful generalized versions of the absence-of-knowledge and factivity conditions is no easy matter. We may understand a generalized factivity condition as that which, together with epistemic subjecthood and the absence of some form of knowledge, suffices for some form of ignorance. Obviously, a first suggestion is that this requirement amounts to there *being something*, of which the ignoramus is ignorant. But what does this 'something' amount to for kinds like erotetic – or practical – ignorance?

We may begin by setting aside the easier cases: for ignorance of various entities, the actuality of the entity is clearly required. For example, nobody is ignorant of the present king of France, since there is no such actual person. The same consideration applies to ignorance of objects (objectual ignorance) and ignorance of events. Ignorance of properties, if there is such a thing, is more difficult. Informally, the factivity requirement here comes to there being a property, which some epistemic subject fails to know. But what does this mean? Unfortunately one's answer will depend heavily on one's preferred property metaphysics. If one takes the 'Platonist' position that properties are actual abstract objects, of course ignorance of properties falls into place as a curious kind of objectual ignorance. But many philosophers have thought that if properties exist, they exist in a sense more complex than that. For instance, an extreme minimalist view would have it that properties only exist in the sense that they are actually instantiated: if no actual objects are red, redness does not exist for anyone to be ignorant of.[12] This is hardly the place to digress into the difficult topic of property metaphysics. Suffice it to say that depending on which metaphysical view of properties is correct, due to the factivity

---

[11] Again, the 'New View' will deny this in the case of factual ignorance.

[12] Of course, such a rigorous minimalism would be hard pressed to explain very much concerning the way we normally talk of properties. See Swoyer and Orilia (2014, section 5.1.1). But less radical proposals in a similar vein have been influential. For example, Armstrong (1978) famously defends the highly parsimonious view that properties must have been instantiated in order to exist and that only predicates belonging to the basic vocabulary of our best science should be seen as referring to properties. See e.g. Künne (2006) for an insightful treatment of the question of property existence and its various senses.

condition the extent to which one can be ignorant of properties may vary in a dramatic sense.

To sum up the results so far: if we allow 'entity' as a liberal appellation for objects, persons, events, and properties, ignorance of all such entities conform to the following schema:

(Ignorance of an entity[13]) S is ignorant of entity E if, and only if,

1. S is an epistemic subject.
2. E exists (i.e. there is such an entity as E).
3. S does not know[14] E.

Erotetic ignorance (i.e. ignorance of answers to questions) is a more complex phenomenon. Here arguably the factivity condition requires that the relevant question has at least one correct answer in the actual world[15]: nobody is ignorant of where the present king of France lives, since the embedded question has no correct answer. But the absence-of-knowledge condition here cannot merely require that there is one correct answer that the subject fails to know. Consider the question 'Who came to the party?' If John and Joan were in fact the only guests at the party, 'John and Joan came to the party and no one else came' seems like a complete correct answer[16] to that question. That is, if I know this answer, surely I am not ignorant of who came to the party. Yet still there could be many correct answers which I fail to know.

---

[13] It should be clear why I cannot simply call this 'objectual' ignorance. Many relevant entities are not objects, at least not in any straightforward sense.

[14] I consider the difficult condition of specifying the metaphysical nature of the knowledge relation across all types of entities as being outside the scope of the present chapter.

[15] Of course that correct answer need not have been determined yet. Otherwise, erotetic ignorance of the future would be excluded by definition, unless determinism is true. This seems like a highly unwelcome result. It may be objected here that the treatment is still too simple, since seemingly sometimes we (self-)ascribe erotetic ignorance, when – and partly because – we are unsure whether the embedded question will ever have a correct answer. For example, I may claim ignorance of whether I have an immortal soul, since I am unsure if the notion of an immortal soul makes any sense in the first place. But arguably here I am really uncertain whether I am erotetically ignorant, since I am uncertain whether there is even a genuine question, whose correct answer I do not know. For lack of space, I cannot pursue this difficult debate further in the present context.

[16] The notion of a complete correct answer, or 'true complete answer' harks back to the ground-breaking Groenendijk and Stokhof (1982) according to which questions denote functions from possible worlds to true complete answers. See for example Stanley (2011, pp. 48–60) for an insightful discussion of that question semantics. It should be noted that a complete true answer need not entail all true answers. For example, intuitively a complete answer to the party-question true in the actual world is one correctly specifying exactly for all entities within a relevant domain, whether they came or did not come to the party. Such a true complete answer need not specify everything true about those entities, e.g. whether they are married to one another, insofar as this is irrelevant to providing the former information.

Suppose Joan is your sister and John is her husband. But I do not know this. So 'Your sister and her husband came' is one correct answer to the party-question that I fail to know. Thus, failure to know a correct answer cannot be the right absence-of-knowledge condition for erotetic ignorance.[17]

In order to fill in the tri-partite structure, arguably we have to complicate matters and distinguish between complete erotetic ignorance and partial erotetic ignorance (for further thoughts on degrees of ignorance, see Section 3). Complete erotetic ignorance is not as complicated as partial erotetic ignorance. Here the absence-of-knowledge condition must amount to the subject not knowing *any* correct answer at all. For example, if Betty knows that John came to the party, Betty is not completely ignorant of who came to the party. Yet, she does not escape being to some degree ignorant of who came to the party, until she knows a complete correct answer.

As pointed out above, if a subject *S* knows a *complete* correct answer to the question *Q*, *S* is not *to any degree* ignorant of *Q*. Consequently, the absence-of-knowledge condition on *partial* erotetic ignorance amounts to *S* not knowing *any* complete correct answer to the relevant question. In terms of the party example, there could be multiple complete answers correctly specifying for everyone within the relevant domain who came, and who did not come, to the party. Just by knowing one of those answers, *S* entirely escapes ignorance of who came to the party. However, it should be noticed that often settling what counts as a complete answer to a question is difficult for more than one reason: first, some questions are ambiguous between so-called 'mention-all' and 'mention-some' readings. For example, the question 'Where can I buy an Italian newspaper in New York City?' could be interpreted in the mention-all way as requesting an exhaustive list of Italian newspaper vendors in New York City. Or it could be interpreted in the mention-some way as requiring only knowledge of a single such vendor.[18] Also the level of accuracy required of a complete answer may vary with context. For example, normally it would seem ridiculous even on the mention-some reading to ascribe any kind of ignorance of where to buy an Italian newspaper in New York to a subject who knows the exact New York address of a suitable vendor. But in certain contexts we may judge such a subject ignorant of where to buy the newspaper, unless she also knows precisely where on the relevant premises an Italian newspaper is sold.

---

[17] Could one argue that the proposition <your sister and her husband came to the party and no one else came to the party> is the same as <John and Joan came to the party and no one else came to the party>? No. Surely there are worlds where the second proposition is true and the first is not, for example worlds in which John and Joan recently divorced or never married.

[18] For a discussion of the 'mention some' vs 'mention all' problem, see for example Stanley (2011, pp. 115–122).

Despite such complexities, hopefully the basic notion of a complete correct answer is clear enough for the present purposes.

The analysis undertaken above yields, where Q is an embedded question:

(erotetic ignorance, complete) S is completely ignorant of Q if, and only if,

1. S is an epistemic subject.
2. Q has at least one correct answer in the actual world.
3. S does not know any correct answer to Q.

(erotetic ignorance, partial) S is partially ignorant of Q if, and only if, S is not completely ignorant of Q and

1. S is an epistemic subject.
2. Q has at least one correct answer in the actual world.
3. S does not know any complete correct answer to Q.

We shall now turn to practical ignorance, which is arguably the most difficult kind of ignorance for which to fill in the tri-partite structure. Here the key question concerning factivity is this: What is required for practical ignorance, apart from epistemic subjecthood and a lack of know-how? To answer this question, unfortunately we must lock horns with the controversial subject, which is the nature of know-how. First we should notice the peculiar feature of English that know-how does not simply refer to knowledge ascribed by way of the 'know how' locution, but rather the 'know how to' locution: for example, we would not say that a subject failing to know how Caesar died thereby lacks any know-how.[19]

As a start, what the subject does not know, when she ignorant of how to φ, is any way which would qualify as *a way to* φ. So seemingly the factivity condition on practical ignorance comes simply to there being *a way to* φ. But this observation does not take us far. Possibly, 'there being a way to φ' could come to very different things depending on the value of φ and the context of ascription. An important wide-ranging debate concerns whether knowing a way to φ is always constituted by knowing a suitable answer to the question of how to φ. This 'intellectualist'[20] position contrasts with

---

[19] As Ian Rumfitt wittily remarks, saying that knowing how Trotsky was killed is part of a competent historian's know-how is like saying that knowing why Trotsky was killed is part of her know-why (Rumfitt 2003, p. 166).

[20] The label 'intellectualism' harks back to Chapter 2 of Ryle (1949), which launches a forceful attack on the so-called 'Intellectualist Legend' concerning know-how. However, modern intellectualists do not have much in common with Ryle's target here. Ryle maintained that 'intelligent practice is not a step-child of theory' (1949, p. 26). However, modern intellectualists are not committed to erotetic knowledge being always or typically 'theoretical'. Rather, key modern proponents of intellectualism hold that often erotetic knowledge may be linked to distinctive 'practical ways of thinking'. See here not least Stanley (2011, pp. 122–130). Also it

'anti-intellectualism', according to which at least sometimes knowing a way to φ amounts to having an ability or skill, which does not reduce to knowing answers to the question of how to φ. For example, typically anti-intellectualists will insist that at least in some contexts ascribing knowledge of how to play a musical instrument does not merely amount to ascribing erotetic knowledge.

Before entering that minefield, it is important to sort out central matters neutral to the intellectualist question. No matter which side one takes, arguably one should concede that, for example, a lucky strike on my first try as a novice bowler does not demonstrate my knowing how to hit strikes.[21] If any ability is required for know-how, it is the ability (under relevant circumstances) to φ *skilfully*.[22] But taking an intellectualist approach to practical knowledge does not mean that one can forget about skills. I do not in any serious sense know a complete correct answer to the question of how to fly an airplane, if I only know that such-and-such actions be a way of taking it off the ground given a sufficient degree of dumb luck (pulling whatever cockpit handle appears relevant based on one's experiences in a crude flight simulator, say). Rather I need to know what constitutes a *skilful* way of flying the aircraft given that relevant external conditions are satisfied (the aircraft is functional, the weather is fit for flying, etc.). Thus, it should be neutral ground in the debate over intellectualism that the absence-of-knowledge condition for practical ignorance is more complex than meets the grammatical eye: it concerns absent knowledge of any way to φ skilfully, that is, of any way successfully manifesting φ-ing skills.

Now, if intellectualism is correct, given the treatment of erotetic ignorance previously discussed, all instances of practical ignorance should fall into place as instances of either complete or partial erotetic ignorance. But here we may take advantage of the observation that the relevant type of questions invariably command a 'mention-some' reading.[23] For example, 'John knows how to cook' says that John knows at least one way to cook, not that John knows *all* ways of cooking. So by knowing any correct

---

should be remarked that sometimes intellectualism is presented as the view that practical knowledge reduces to propositional knowledge. But the gist of intellectualism seems preserved even if erotetic knowledge does not straightforwardly reduce to propositional knowledge. Prominent defences include Stanley and Williamson (2001), Snowdon (2004), Stanley (2011).

[21] The example derives from Noë (2005, p. 280).

[22] The relation between skills and abilities is not entirely easy to specify. It seems tempting to employ Ernest Sosa's influential conception of competence as 'the disposition (ability) to succeed when one tries' (see e.g. Sosa 2015, p. 95) and then understand skill as the inner 'seat' of such a competence, that is, that in virtue of which the agent will succeed given favourable external conditions. See for example Sosa (2010, p. 465). I owe this point to Katalin Farkas in private correspondence.

[23] See Stanley (2011, p. 111).

answer to the question of how to cook, that is, knowing for some way that it is a way to cook, John knows all he needs to know, in order to entirely escape ignorance of how to cook. On the intellectualist understanding, then, practical ignorance must be a form of complete erotetic ignorance: if John does not know how to cook he does not know *any* correct answer to the question of how to cook (skilfully[24]).

Accordingly, on the intellectualist understanding, the factivity requirement for practical ignorance amounts to there being a correct answer to the question of how to φ skilfully. However, as we shall now see there are significant restrictions on the values φ can take here.

First, it seems pretty clear that the factivity condition cannot be satisfied if φ-ing is simply impossible. For example, it seems wrong to say that any epistemic subject is ignorant of how to write down the highest prime number, or ignorant of how to draw a triangle with an angular sum of 270 degrees, since clearly *nothing* could qualify as ways of doing those things. It seems equally odd to say that I am ignorant of how to travel faster than the speed of light, insofar as this would involve a violation of the laws of nature. So it seems that in the sense relevant to factivity there is no way of φ-ing, unless φ-ing is possible conditional on the actual laws of nature.[25]

Now, if the above considerations are agreeable to intellectualists, should they also satisfy anti-intellectualists concerning practical ignorance? Remember that they see such practical ignorance as not always constituted by erotetic ignorance: what the subject lacks when she fails to know how to φ is not knowledge of answers to a question. It is something different; a skill or an ability. Next, I shall briefly discuss the merits of anti-intellectualism.[26] Here I shall merely demonstrate that there is

---

[24] Here skilfulness seems tacitly implied. We would not say that someone cooks, unless she displays at least some cooking skills. The same point applies to many other action verbs. But obviously there are exceptions. For example, one can fall without falling skilfully (like a martial artist, say). This is why it seems strange to say that strictly speaking one knows how to fall, if that is not taken to imply that one knows how to fall skilfully.

[25] Could we plausibly impose an even narrower modal restriction on φ-ing? Perhaps we cannot, even if arguing for that point would take us too far off track in the present context.

[26] The exact dialectics of the debate over intellectualism is not often specified. It should be noticed that anti-intellectualists are not committed to rejecting that practical knowledge always involves erotetic knowledge, which would mean that complete erotetic ignorance suffices for complete practical ignorance. For example, an anti-intellectualist could (but need not) agree that an able cellist must know the answer to the question of how to play the cello, for example, because her very playing is in a sense a demonstration of a way to play the cello. Thus, intellectualism is not home free, even if it is established that all know-how involves question-answering propositional knowledge, cf. Stanley (2011, pp. 126–130). Rather, intellectualists must argue that practical knowledge is nothing over and above erotetic knowledge, that is, that for all instances of practical knowledge, there is some erotetic knowledge, which *suffices* for it. If relevant factivity and epistemic-subjecthood conditions are met, this yields by contraposition the intellectualist position that practical ignorance must always be constituted by erotetic ignorance.

no accommodating understanding of practical ignorance neutral on the intellectualist question, even if the factivity condition for practical ignorance suggested by the erotetic framework is also agreeable to anti-intellectualists. It seems that the knowledge-constituting skill set crucially important to the anti-intellectualist is precisely a skill set whose manifestation would count as a way of ϕ-ing skilfully, in so far as this is even possible – for example, the skill set characteristic of proficient cello playing, insofar as we ascribe ignorance of how to play the cello. So pointing to that set of skills and its manifestation conditions counts as a correct answer to the question of how to ϕ skilfully. Unless there is a correct answer here, it is hard to see that there is anything to be practically ignorant of, no matter how one stands in the intellectualist debate.

The absence-of-knowledge condition, however, must be a divisive issue. Here anti-intellectualists must maintain that even when the subjecthood and factivity conditions are satisfied, *pace* intellectualism the occurrence of practical ignorance does not entail that any erotetic knowledge is absent. This shows that there is no way to set up a neutral tri-partite analysis of practical ignorance, within which intellectualists and anti-intellectualists may work out their differences. The disagreement here strikes to a key necessary requirement for practical ignorance. So we shall have to line up two separate analyses:

For intellectualists all we need here is an instance of (erotetic ignorance, complete) with suitable explications:

(practical ignorance, intellectual) S is ignorant of how to ϕ, if and only if

1. S is an epistemic subject.
2. There is a correct answer to the question of how to ϕ skilfully (where ϕ-ing is compatible with the current laws of nature).
3. S does not know any correct answer to the question of how to ϕ skilfully.

Anti-intellectualists may concede that the above analysis holds for many ascriptions of practical ignorance. However, they characteristically must insist that there is another sense in which a subject can be practically ignorant, which is not captured above. Rather that sense is captured by:

(practical ignorance, anti-intellectual) S is ignorant of how to ϕ (in the anti-intellectualist sense), if and only if

1. S is an epistemic subject.
2. ϕ-ing skilfully is compatible with the current laws of nature.
3. S lacks appropriate ϕ-ing skills, for which erotetic knowledge would not suffice.

Above, I have examined various types of ignorance divided according to kind. Hopefully, I have covered some of the most interesting varieties.[27] I shall now turn to examining whether some of the kinds investigated are not basic, since they reduce to other kinds.

2.3   Questions of Reducibility

2.3.1   Does Erotetic Ignorance Reduce to Factual Ignorance?   Perhaps there are fewer basic varieties of ignorance than suggested earlier above? If erotetic ignorance reduces to factual ignorance, this would mean a dramatic simplification. Not only could we do away with an independent basic category of complete erotetic ignorance, we could also account for degrees of erotetic ignorance in terms of differences in factual ignorance. And if intellectualism is right, practical ignorance turns out to be a variety of factual ignorance as well.

First, however, we should get clear on the reductive relation investigated. We may begin by observing that we cannot hope for a crude global semantic reduction. For example, 'Betty is entirely ignorant of who came to the party' cannot simply mean for a specific range of facts that Betty is ignorant of them, since in different possible worlds very different facts are relevant to the truth of that ascription. For example, in some possible worlds the Pope came to the party. Hence in those worlds, if Betty is entirely ignorant of who came to the party, she is ignorant of the fact that the Pope came to the party. But it seems rather outlandish to claim that the Pope is somehow involved with the meaning of the first humble ascription.

Rather what matters is whether it is the case that:

For any instance of erotetic ignorance in a world w, there is a set of facts in w (past, present, future), such that the ignorant subject is ignorant of those facts, and this factual ignorance is necessary and sufficient for her erotetic ignorance.

---

[27] Any type of knowable could give rise to a kind of ignorance in so far as all not all tokens of that type are necessarily known by all subjects. Throughout the history of philosophy, necessarily known knowables of various sorts have been proposed. An immodest position here would be old-fashioned rationalist (Platonist or Cartesian) nativism. For a good account of Descartes' radically nativist epistemology see Newman (2005). In Newman's preferred phrasing, on this account some knowledge derives from 'the nature of the mind' (p.182). Thus, necessarily any epistemic subject possesses a great deal of knowledge, even if many subjects need to be reminded that they always possessed it. Following through on this epistemological subject would take us far off track in the present context. Suffice it to say that given we individuate kinds of ignorance as coarsely as we have so far done, nativists cannot object that we have cut out empty classes: Any remotely plausible nativism probably should concede that many subjects suffer from *some* ignorance of each kind treated above.

I shall now argue that in general erotetic ignorance seems to reduce to factual ignorance, in so far as erotetic knowledge reduces to factual knowledge. That is, if it holds that

For any instance of erotetic knowledge in a world w, there is a set of facts in w, such that S knows those facts, and this factual knowledge is necessary and sufficient for her erotetic knowledge.

The above reductive claim is not entirely uncontroversial, and some authors have explicitly opposed it. However, clearly the view has a great deal of plausibility.[28]

Consider now the case of complete erotetic ignorance. The absence-of-knowledge condition here demanded that S does not know any true answer to the embedded question. But if erotetic knowledge reduces to factual knowledge, if S were to know any true answer to the embedded question, necessarily she would have to know certain facts. So her lack of erotetic knowledge simply amounts to her lacking knowledge of those facts. Thus, the absence-of-knowledge condition on complete erotetic ignorance nicely translates into factual terms. The factivity condition for complete erotetic ignorance also reduces unproblematically: it demanded that the embedded question had at least one true answer in the actual world. But given a factual absence-of-knowledge condition, this true answer may now simply be stated in terms of one of the aforementioned facts, which S fails to know.

For partial erotetic ignorance the reduction works equivalently. Here the distinctive absence-of-knowledge condition demanded that S did not know any complete correct answer to the embedded question. Again, if

---

[28] Schaffer (2007) has aimed to replace the orthodox 'reductive' view of erotetic knowledge with a so-called 'question-including' conception. The basic idea is that in a non-reducible sense erotetic knowledge amounts to knowing an answer *as an answer to a particular question*. For example, according to Schaffer, knowledge that I am watching George Bush on TV cannot generally suffice for knowledge whether I am watching George Bush, since sometimes I may be said to know that Bush is on TV and also know whether he or Janet Jackson is on TV, even if I do not know whether he or the clever Bush impersonator Will Ferrell is on TV (p. 187). According to Schaffer here I know whether George Bush is on TV *as an answer to the former question*, but not as answer to the latter question. However, see for example Stanley (2011, p. 64) for the forceful rejoinder that Schaffer has only made explicit a general context-sensitivity of erotetic knowledge ascriptions without providing sufficient reason for thinking that this cannot be accounted for within a reductive framework. For example, insofar as a context dictates that I do not know whether Bush or Ferrell is in TV, it seems odd to say in that very same context that I still know that Bush is on TV. Stanley (2011, pp. 64–68) also discusses and rejects complex arguments against reductionism presented in recent work by Jonathan Ginzburg. Regrettably I have no space to discuss this debate here. Also I have no space to discuss the problems induced by the so-called Extended Mind Hypothesis, which some have taken to open a gap between standards for erotetic knowledge ascription as compared to propositional knowledge ascription. See here Farkas (2016).

erotetic knowledge reduces to factual knowledge, this absence of knowledge must amount to the absence of knowledge of certain facts. The factivity condition is taken care of like immediately above.

Hopefully, an example may help make those abstract points more accessible. Consider the ascriptions:

> Betty is entirely ignorant of who came to the party.
> Betty is fairly ignorant of who came to the party.

Here, the former ascription ascribes complete erotetic ignorance, whereas the latter ascribes partial erotetic ignorance. Suppose it is a fact that John and Joan were the only guests at the party. So it is also a fact that John came to the party. If erotetic knowledge reduces to factual knowledge, the only way Betty could fail to know any correct answer to the embedded question is by failing to know any fact amounting to such an answer. So she is entirely ignorant of who came to the party, because she is ignorant of any such fact. Also, the only way Betty could fail to know any complete answer to the embedded question is by failing to know relevant facts. So again Betty can only be partially ignorant of who came to the party in so far as she knows some facts whose associated propositions constitute true answers, even if she knows no facts appropriately associated with a *complete* true answer.

I shall now consider an important principled objection due to Torsten Wilholt against the reduction undertaken just above. If Wilholt is right, erotetic ignorance must be acknowledged as a basic form of ignorance, no matter if erotetic knowledge reduces to factual knowledge. His argument is worth quoting in full:

If I conceive of a particular piece of ignorance as an item of non-knowledge – that is, a true proposition that I do not yet know – then it seems that I would only be able to direct my epistemic efforts at such an item if I already knew it – and knew it to be a true proposition. What this shows is that our conscious ignorance in the present sense cannot be understood as a set of true propositions lying out there, waiting to be discovered. Instead our conscious ignorance is best understood as a set of questions.[29]

Wilholt here directs our attention to the fact that, for example, I cannot very well self-ascribe ignorance of the proposition that my bike is currently parked outside the lecture hall. For due to the factivity condition, this would require me to regard it as a fact that my bike is currently parked outside the hall. And this seems incompatible with my self-ascribing ignorance of that same fact.

---

[29] Wilholt (forthcoming, p. 5).

Wilholt's objection is closely related to the so-called 'Moore's Paradox'. In a 1944 lecture, G.E. Moore pointed out the oddness of the sentence-form '*p*, but I do not believe that *p*'.[30] Wilholt in effect points to a seemingly similar oddness afflicting '*p*, but I am ignorant of the fact that *p*'. I shall now argue that this oddness does not undermine reductionism.

What Wilholt has established at most amounts to the following: I must refer to any fact of which I claim ignorance by way of an *opaque* definite description. Erotetic expressions serve this purpose nicely. Perhaps I cannot sensibly claim ignorance of the fact that my bike is currently parked outside the hall. But I can sensibly claim ignorance of the correct answer to the question of whether this is so. This does not in any way conflict with the reductive claim that what is necessary and sufficient for my ignorance here is simply my ignorance of a proposition or a set of propositions, namely the proposition(s) denoted in the actual world by the expression 'the correct answer to the question whether my bike is currently parked outside the hall'.

Even if erotetic locutions often come very handy for making opaque reference to unknown facts, they are not our only means to that end. I could also sensibly say things like 'I am ignorant of all the facts you learned in yesterday's class'. Still, clearly erotetic expressions are often better suited for framing research agendas compared to other sensible ways of self-ascribing ignorance[31]: realizing that I do not know the correct answer to a question is often a good starting-point for getting to know its answer. Thus, Wilholt may indeed have pointed to a strong pragmatic reason for keeping the concept of erotetic ignorance in our repertoire. But this does not show for any instance of erotetic ignorance that it is not constituted by the subject's factual ignorance.

I conclude that insofar as erotetic knowledge reduces to factual (i.e. propositional) knowledge, erotetic ignorance is always constituted by factual ignorance. Even if Wilholt aptly points to the usefulness of the concept of erotetic ignorance for the ongoing framing of our epistemic goals, his argument does not undermine that conclusion.

---

[30] The term 'Moore's Paradox' derives from Wittgenstein (2009, p. 199, Part II, Section x, §87).

[31] Even if there are exceptions to this rule: if I have strong reasons to think that I am ignorant of certain important facts about the Universe known only to the Sage on the Mountain, but have no idea what those facts concern, only the mode of ignorance-ascription just employed seems to frame a fruitful research project: find that sage and get him to transmit his precious knowledge! Wilholt's excessive focus on erotetic self-ascriptions seems too biased against the role of testimony in the absolution of ignorance.

2.3.2   Does Practical Ignorance Reduce to Erotetic Ignorance? The question here concerns the fate of intellectualism, a position briefly touched upon earlier. According to intellectualism, practical ignorance is nothing but a special variety of erotetic ignorance; namely ignorance of answers to questions of the how-to-φ-skilfully type. If intellectualism is true, and erotetic ignorance reduces to factual ignorance, the result is a neat reduction of practical ignorance to factual ignorance.

As we saw above the epistemic subjecthood condition and the factivity condition did not give rise to divisive issues in the context of the intellectualist debate. So the crucial issue is really, whether the absence-of-knowledge condition for practical ignorance always only refers to the absence of erotetic knowledge, as would surely be the case if practical knowledge is never anything above erotetic knowledge. Thus, anti-intellectualism concerning practical ignorance would be vindicated indirectly, if it could be demonstrated that intellectualism gets our concept of practical knowledge wrong. Or it could be vindicated directly if we could point to a case where clearly a subject is practically ignorant, even if she has all the relevant erotetic knowledge we could ask for.

Both strategies raise many deep concerns which I cannot hope to treat adequately in this chapter, where I merely hope to establish two central points. First, I want to show how intellectualists may respond to paradigmatic purported counterexamples. Second, I want to argue that – contrary to what some intellectualists have thought – pointing to the context-sensitivity of practical knowledge ascriptions is not to intellectualism's advantage.

Several authors have noted that seemingly the 'know-how-to' expression in English does work divided between multiple expressions in other natural languages. For example, in French one may ascribe to a subject either *savoir-faire* or *savoir-comment-faire*, where the former type of knowledge seems more closely associated with an ability to engage in an activity; thus, 'Il sait nager' and 'Il sait comment nager' both could be translated into English as 'he knows how to swim', but arguably only the latter French expression clearly concerns erotetic knowledge.[32] In Russian very different verbs are used to attribute erotetic knowledge and know-how.[33] Thus it does not seem farfetched to claim that in English 'know-how-to' expressions are used to attribute two different kinds of knowledge, only one of which is essentially erotetic.

---

[32] See Rumfitt (2003, p. 165).
[33] Rumfitt (2003, p. 164). The Russian verb used for ascribing erotetic knowledge is *znat'*, for know-how *umet'* is used.

Consider now a conductor short of a cellist for her orchestra. The conductor may assign to her assistant the task of searching out a suitable candidate, sending her off with the words: 'Make sure you get me someone who really knows how to play the cello!' Here it seems strange to argue that the conductor merely asked for somebody with a wide stock of erotetic knowledge concerning cello playing. Rather, the conductor expressed a desire for a candidate with a suitable set of cello playing *skills*.[34] Whether and under which circumstances the candidate should also be able to manifest the required skills, seems a less determinate matter. For example, if the candidate is needed for a long-term contract, certainly it would not seem to run against the conductor's expressed desires, if the assistant returns with a world-renowned cello virtuoso, who is still recovering from a broken arm[35] or can only play given certain external conditions are met.[36]

Still, intellectualists are not without resources to accommodate such points. Thus Jason Stanley:

What happens when I acquire skill in the activity of catching fly balls? What happens is that I come to the realization that a certain way of catching a fly ball, which I think of practically, is a way that will give me counter-factual success in fly ball catching. That the acquisition of a skill is due to the learning of a fact, explains why certain acts constitute exercises of skill, rather than reflex. A particular action of catching a fly ball is a skilled action, rather than a reflex, because it is guided by knowledge, the knowledge of how to catch a fly ball.[37]

In terms of the cello example, Stanley would thus say that the conductor calls for an agent with a certain propositional or erotetic knowledge after all. Namely a practically rooted knowledge that (or whether) certain ways

[34] Of course it could be argued that the conductor's call for anything above an erotetic knower is a mere *conversational implicature*, hence does not concern the semantics of know-how ascriptions. This is because arguably the call is cancellable. For example, the conductor could add: 'But I only need an instructor here, so she need not be an able musician.' However, the anti-intellectualist could retort that this cancellation could equally be interpreted as the cancellation of a semantic ambiguity. See for example Carston (2002, pp. 138–139). I thank Esben Nedenskov Petersen for bringing this matter to my attention.

[35] Whether we should say of a *permanently* crippled cellist that she retains her knowledge of how to play, is a more difficult matter. Noë (2005, p. 283) argues that our answer should be determined by whether we see the cellist's injury as undermining her skills ('ability') or their manifestation ('enabling conditions not satisfied'). In many cases there may be no determinate answer here, not least as time passes and the cerebral basis of the relevant skill set decays.

[36] Several stellar musicians due to neurosis have been unable to perform given certain external conditions. For example, the legendary conductor Arturo Toscanini reputedly was highly superstitious, unable to conduct 13th performances, etc. Probably nobody would say that because of this Toscanini did not know how to conduct.

[37] Stanley (2011, p. 130).

of playing the cello are suitably modally robust[38] ways of achieving cello playing success.

Stanley's rejoinder to anti-intellectualism here is a strong one. It even purports to explain in an elegant way, what seemingly the anti-intellectualist cannot so easily explain; namely why we call the cellist's skill-set knowledge.[39] But obviously Stanley needs to account for the somewhat esoteric notion of a practical way of thinking. On behalf of anti-intellectualism, Alva Noë has argued that this notion is obscure, its introduction being simply an *ad hoc* attempt to rescue intellectualism.[40] Stanley in return has argued that the notion should be acceptable on any Fregean account of mental content, that is, an account according to which the same content may be presented to a subject in more than one cognitively significant way. Thus, allegedly, a musician could be surprised to learn that the chord progression she has considered theoretically is the very same chord progression that she has thought through practically without considering exactly which keys to press down or which fingering to use.[41]

This is not to the place to settle the current score on the intellectualist battlefield. However, I hope to strengthen at least slightly the anti-intellectualist side by making a few observations concerning the context-dependence of practical knowledge ascriptions. Stanley regards it as an established fact 'that ascriptions of knowing how, like all ascriptions of knowing-wh [i.e. erotetic knowledge], involve sensitivity to a domain'.[42] How this works is illustrated with an example due to Katherine Hawley:[43] in a British context it seems reasonable to infer from Sarah's knowing how to drive a car that she knows how to operate a manual transmission; in US contexts not so. This is nicely explained by the hypothesis that ways of driving with a manual transmission are not within the answer-domain relevant to the US context: here one need not know such a way in order to know a complete correct answer to the question of how to drive a car. As Stanley brings out, this type of context sensitivity is commonplace for

---

[38] Counterfactual success in Stanley's terminology amounts to 'success under some contextually determined range of circumstances', Stanley (2011, p. 127).

[39] Perhaps anti-intellectualists may simply insist that know-how locutions have been drawn in to fill a certain semantic role, for which English is otherwise ill equipped. If so, it does not seem like a very great surprise that the know-how locution was chosen for this job, given that typically practical knowledge does involve a great deal of erotetic knowledge of the type intellectualists invariably associate with it. Surely, for example, we would expect an able cellist to know the answers to a great deal of questions concerning cello playing.

[40] Noë (2005, p. 287).

[41] Stanley here appeals to Gareth Evans's Fregean 'intuitive criterion of difference' together with observations on musicianship due to Cristopher Peacocke. See Stanley (2011, pp. 123–124).

[42] Stanley (2011, p. 119).   [43] Hawley (2003).

erotetic knowledge ascriptions.[44] Let us grant that Stanley is right in all of this.

However, a closer inspection of the ways in which practical knowledge ascriptions are sensitive to context plays to the intellectualists' disadvantage. Or so at least I shall argue. First, we should remember that intellectualists must take practical knowledge as concerned with mention-some interpretations of the embedded question: in order to know how to ϕ, I need only know *one* way to ϕ skilfully. So the relevant comparison is with ascriptions like 'Betty knows where to buy an Italian newspaper in New York City' or 'John knows who to call in the case of an emergency'[45] under mention-some readings. Surely such ascriptions are context-sensitive. But, what is sensitive to context here is arguably the *level of accuracy* expected of the known answer. For example, in some contexts we may merely require Betty to know the address of a suitable vendor, whereas in other contexts we may require her to provide more detailed directions. In some contexts John is only required to know that it is appropriate to call a doctor. In other contexts, we may require a much more accurate answer, demanding John to make explicit which specific doctor to call for.

The kind of practical knowledge ascription typically harnessed by anti-intellectualists, however, does not seem to be context-sensitive with regard to any dimension easily parsed in terms of expected accuracy. For example, in the cello player example, perhaps the level of skill expected is a context-sensitive matter. If the conductor heads a professional symphonic orchestra, we may take her to demand a higher minimum skill level for practical knowledge than if she called for a cellist suitable for an amateur band. If so, this compares to Hawley's car driving example above. Yet it does not make much sense to say that this is simply a matter of an able British driver knowing more accurately how to drive as compared to the typical US driver. The US driver's skills are not less accurate, they are just different. Also surely there is a sense in which the virtuoso plays more accurately, that is, in terms of pitching and faithfulness to scores, but this seems beside the point. Arguably, what high-standard know-how ascription contexts call for is not always more accurate answers; sometimes it is simply better skills. The relevant scale here is not a scale of accuracy, but a scale of proficiency. Stanley's theory that ultimately skills are a special kind of propositions known under practical modes of presentation will hardly account for this: what the conductor wants in the high-level context as compared to the low-level context is not a cellist with more accurate

---

[44] Stanley (2011, pp. 118–119).   [45] Stanley (2011, p. 113).

thoughts about ways of manifesting her cello playing skills. It is simply a cellist with better skills.

The above argument does not show that intellectualism is false. But if successful, it points out that at least in some contexts practical knowledge ascriptions are context-sensitive in a manner very different from the typical way in which erotetic knowledge ascriptions are context-sensitive. So pace Stanley at least some observations on context-sensitivity play in the anti-intellectualists favour.

It seems clear that in many cases practical ignorance is simply complete ignorance of an answer to the question of how to φ, that is, erotetic ignorance, for example, ignorance of how to solve a chess puzzle. Still, in certain cases like the cello playing example above, practical ignorance seems to concern an inadequate level of relevant skill. We saw that Stanley made a forceful argument to the conclusion that such skills amount to propositional knowledge. If so, even here practical ignorance is a type of erotetic ignorance. But Stanley's framework seemed ill fit to accommodate the special way in which practical knowledge ascriptions are sometimes context-sensitive. Thus at the very least, the case for anti-intellectualism is very much alive: it is far from clear that all instances of practical ignorance reduce to erotetic ignorance.

3   Degrees of Ignorance

Some authors operate with a notion of so-called 'deep' ignorance. According to René van Woudenberg, in the context of 'being ignorant with respect to a [true] proposition p', an epistemic subject is 'deeply ignorant', in so far as she 'never so much as entertained p'.[46] On a quite different note, Torsten Wilholt reserves the label 'deep ignorance' for instances of erotetic ignorance beset with what, following Sylvain Bromberger, Wilholt calls a 'p-predicament': on the subject's view the relevant question admits of a correct answer, but she cannot see any answer to it not faced with decisive objections.[47]

It is not entirely clear why we should reserve the label 'deep ignorance' for the situation described by Van Woudenberg. In many cases, simply entertaining a true proposition, thus escaping 'deep ignorance' with respect to it, does not bring me any closer to escaping ignorance. For example, if there be indeed 123,456 intelligent races in our galaxy at the present moment, I may entertain that proposition as much as I like, yet

---

[46] Van Woudenberg (2009, p. 375). By 'never entertaining p' it seems natural to understand that the subject did never in any sense think about the issue whether p is the case.

[47] Wilholt (forthcoming, pp. 11–13), following Bromberger (1992).

I shall never be able to believe it or come closer to knowing it. In which interesting sense, then, has my ignorance with respect to that true proposition become any less deep?

Unlike Van Woudenberg, Wilholt seems to describe a condition typically associated with feelings of frustration. Not least if one considers answering the relevant question important. Yet again, it is not entirely clear why we should call this particular sort of erotetic ignorance 'deep' as compared to other varieties: if recklessly I neglect a decisive objection to my confident, but mistaken, answer, my ignorance is not 'deep' according to Wilholt. Yet certainly I may be further removed from knowledge, than were I 'deeply' ignorant, since my misguided confidence stands in the way of knowledge acquisition.

Thus, rather than starting from some conception of 'deep' ignorance, I find it more illuminating to discuss various senses in which an ignorance state could be more or less removed from a relevant kind of knowledge.

Factual knowledge does not admit of degrees. Either one knows a fact, or one does not. As already argued above, the same holds for complete erotetic ignorance, which is hardly surprising, if erotetic ignorance reduces to factual ignorance, as was suggested in Section 2.2 above.

Yet, as its appellation signifies, partial erotetic ignorance admits of degrees: here one knows some true answer to the relevant question, even if one does not know any complete correct answer. The 'depth' of such an ignorance state could be said to depend on the minimal distance between a true answer one knows and a complete correct answer, which one does not know. But, it should be clear that in general there is no precise way to measure depth in this fashion: suppose again that John and Joan were the only guests at a party. Anna knows only that John came to the party. Betty knows only that Jill did not come to the party. Clair knows that John and Jane came, and that Jill did not come, but she is unsure whether June also came. Nobody here knows a complete correct answer. But other things being equal it seems fair to say that Clair is the least ignorant, since she is closest to knowing a complete correct answer. Whether Anna or Betty is the most ignorant subject seems unclear.[48]

Also, at least sometimes ignorance of various entities like objects, persons, or events may be graded according to the ignorant subject's perceived remoteness from meeting the (perhaps contextually determined) standards for acquiring the relevant kind of knowledge. For

---

[48] We may speculate that our verdicts turn on the strength of the evidential relation between the answers known and a complete correct answer. Surely at least the complete correct answer here is more probable, conditional on the answer Clair knows as compared to the others. But arguably it would be foolhardy to build much on this observation.

example, we may judge that you are less ignorant of WWII as compared to me, in so far as you know far more historical details relevant to a full picture of that complex event. But arguably ranking various instances of ignorance here is even more hopeless than in the case of erotetic ignorance, where at least we had a decent conception of what counts as escaping ignorance altogether.

Now as to practical ignorance. On an anti-intellectualist reading, practical knowledge admits of a straightforward grading in terms of skill levels. For example, we may say that an expert cellist knows better than an amateur how to play the cello, since her skills are superior. Yet, even in a high-level context, it sounds cruelly hyperbolic to say of an able amateur that she is simply ignorant of how to play the cello. What we would naturally say is rather that the amateur does not play well enough. Perhaps when it comes to two unequally talented learners, we could get ourselves to say that the more accomplished of them is less ignorant than the other of how to play the cello, since her skills come closer to meeting the minimal standard for cello know-how. Still such graded ignorance ascriptions sound unnatural. Normally, we would just say that the talented learner is the more skilful cello student, or that she is closer to playing well. So it is not clear that the anti-intellectualist framework provides us with any strong reason for explicitly grading practical ignorance ascriptions.

Intellectualism here faces a different predicament. As we saw previously, the intellectualist is committed to seeing practical ignorance as a kind of complete erotetic ignorance. Of course answers to practical questions could be graded along various dimensions. Some answers may count as more impressive, more comprehensive, or more elegant than others. But if two ignorant agents each lack an answer to a practical question, there are no known answers to compare for quality. So this consideration cannot introduce degrees of practical ignorance. Also, intellectualists cannot plausibly appeal to contextually determined standards for the correctness of answers: as was argued in Section 2.3.2 above, in contexts like a high-level cello audition, it seems odd to say that – unlike the cello virtuoso – the amateur cellist cannot answer the question of how to play the cello to the contextually salient degree of accuracy. Rather, it seems natural to say that she knows the answer (or solution) to the question of how to play the cello like a decent amateur, even if she is ignorant of how to play like an expert cellist. But this makes her ignorant of the answer to a *different question* (how to play like an expert), not partially ignorant of an answer known by the expert.

This means that perhaps surprisingly neither intellectualism nor anti-intellectualism provides us with any strong reasons for understanding practical ignorance as a graded phenomenon: for any ϕ satisfying the relevant factivity condition, a subject is either simply ignorant of how to ϕ, or she knows how to ϕ. There are no clear theoretical reasons for postulating a middle ground.[49]

4   Higher-Order Ignorance

I am very much aware of my ignorance of how to fly a fighter jet. Still, very often a subject is ignorant of the fact that she is ignorant of something. For example, in an isolated society unacquainted with airplanes, everybody is ignorant of their ignorance of how to fly a fighter jet. Most likely, with regard to a vast number of facts and procedures such second-order ignorance characterizes every epistemic subject there has ever been or ever will be.

Thus, we may distinguish between cases, where a subject is also ignorant of her first-order ignorance, and cases where a subject is not thus ignorant. I propose that we call the second variety 'Socratic ignorance' in honour of Plato's teacher, who, according to popular legend, prided himself of this type of ignorance[50]. In short, Socratic ignorance is first-order ignorance without accompanying second-order ignorance. Its contrast we could call 'opaque ignorance'.[51]

Clearly an opaquely ignorant epistemic subject is at least highly likely also to suffer from ignorance of even higher orders: not only is she ignorant of the fact that she is ignorant of some fact. Most likely, she is also ignorant of the fact that she is ignorant of the fact that she is ignorant

---

[49] However, the 'New View' of factual ignorance may have resources to argue otherwise: If erotetic ignorance reduces to factual ignorance, and the absence-of-knowledge condition here should be replaced by an absence-of-belief condition, perhaps if belief comes in degrees, so does what I have here called 'complete erotetic ignorance'. The idea would probably be that a subject with a high degree of belief in a complete correct answer would count as less ignorant than a subject without anything but a low degree of belief in a complete correct answer. I thank Rik Peels for making that point.

[50] The most obvious quotation here occurs in Apology 21d where Socrates is attributed the lines: 'I am wiser than this man; it is likely that neither of us knows anything worthwhile, but he thinks he knows something, when he does not, whereas when I do not know, neither do I think I know; so I am likely to be wiser than he to this small extent, that I do not think I know what I do not know' (Plato 1997, p. 21). Strictly speaking, here and anywhere, Socrates does not explicitly claim knowledge of his ignorance, but this seems like a natural interpretation. However, Plato never attributed to Socrates the baffling claim to know only that he knows nothing. A likely source of this paradoxical gnomon and its attribution to Socrates is Diogenes Laertius II, 32. See also Vlastos (1985).

[51] I here follow Wilholt (forthcoming). Ravetz (1993) prefers the term 'ignorance squared'. Note that since some ignorance comes in degree, we may also talk, if we wish, of 'super-Socratic' ignorance. Here one is not even ignorant of the *degree* of one's first-order ignorance.

of that fact, and so on. But arguably, sometimes such an ignorance hierarchy may come to an end at a level above the second order, even if the epistemic circumstances will have to be rather exotic. By way of illustration, suppose I am a fiercely proud Abraham Lincoln biographer believing that I have unearthed every important fact there is to know about the 16th president of the United States. Now a rival biographer comes to me, conveying the following information: there is a single important fact concerning Lincoln, which you do not know, even if you think you know it. But since we are rivals, obviously I am not going to tell you which fact that is.

Suppose I know my rival to be a highly competent and almost pathologically honest source of information. I have every reason to think that she would not say this to me, unless she was right. Suppose also that unbeknownst to me the relevant fact concerns the current location of Lincoln's famous top hat. So I remain first-order ignorant, since I still do not know that fact. And I remain second-order ignorant too, since my rival was right that I still think I know the current location of Lincoln's top hat, even if I do not. Yet I may truthfully say that due to my rival's testimony I am no longer ignorant of my ignorance of my ignorance of the mysterious fact to which my rival just alluded.

Still, it is hard to see under which realistic circumstances ascriptions of ignorance above the second order would be of much concern. In contrast, we need only look to Socrates himself to appreciate why the intellectual ideal of replacing one's opaque ignorance with Socratic ignorance may hold an appeal, not least to the philosophically inclined.

5   Conclusions

This chapter has examined various types of ignorance divided according to kind, degree and order. Analyses were given of the notions of factual, objectual, erotetic and practical ignorance. It was argued that even if erotetic ignorance reduces to factual ignorance, it is at least questionable whether practical ignorance also reduces thus. It was suggested that we conceive of degrees of ignorance in terms of remoteness from knowledge. It was shown how this conception applies within the domain of partial erotetic ignorance. Also it was shown that we have no obvious reasons for conceiving of practical ignorance as a graded phenomenon, regardless of how we view its nature. Finally it was brought out that second-order ignorance commands a strong interest independently of first-order ignorance, but that ignorance absolved only above the second order seems like a peculiar phenomenon.

Much territory was covered above. For the sake of brevity many complex issues were left untouched or quickly set aside. Still, I hope that the investigations undertaken may prove useful to ongoing research concerning the general significance of ignorance within such fields as ethics, epistemology, semantics and the philosophies of mind and action.[52]

[52] I am grateful to Rik Peels, Martijn Blaauw and Jeroen de Ridder for very helpful comments on a previous version of this chapter. My work has benefited substantially from stimulating discussions with many people. I want to thank in particular Katalin Farkas, Esben Nedenskov Petersen, Torsten Wilholt and René van Woudenberg.

3   Ignorance and Incompetence: Linguistic Considerations

Berit Brogaard

1   Introduction

It's tempting to think that ignorance is just the opposite of knowledge. This view is usually referred to as "The Standard View" (see, e.g., Peels 2010, 2012; Le Morvan 2012, 2013). You are ignorant of something just when you do not know it. This temptation, I will argue, should be avoided. While we could introduce a new technical notion of ignorance and treat it as the complement of the notion of knowledge, our ordinary concept of ignorance is considerably more promiscuous in its application than our concept of knowledge.

We sometimes speak of people being ignorant simpliciter. However, like knowledge, ignorance is a matter of standing in a particular relation to either a proposition or a subject matter. If we say that John is ignorant, we normally mean that he is ignorant with respect to a fact or a subject matter that is salient in the given conversational context.

In this paragraph I argue on the basis of evidence from ordinary language use that there are three types of ignorance: ignorance of facts, ignorance of a subject matter, and ignorance of how to perform a particular activity. None of these uses is equivalent to our ordinary use of "do not know" or "fail to know," when "know" occurs propositionally. If you don't know that p, you do not know that p simpliciter. You cannot know that p a lot, a little or to some extent. Conversely, we can be a little bit ignorant of the fact that p, very ignorant of the fact that p, and ignorant of the fact that p to some extent. Ignorance to some extent of the fact that p entails having a partial belief (or other comparable attitude) that p is the case or having some but not all the evidence one could (fairly easily) have had that p is the case. While ignorance of a fact does amount to a failure to know the fact, a failure to know a fact does not entail complete ignorance. That is, one can fail to know a fact without being completely ignorant of that fact.

As we will see, when you are ignorant about a subject matter, this entails having little or no knowledge of the claims that constitute the subject matter. Since you can know a subject matter to some degree, you can also be ignorant about the subject matter to some degree.

Finally, you can be ignorant of how to perform a particular activity. To be ignorant of how to perform an activity is to fail to know how to perform the activity. You might have the ability to perform the activity but nonetheless fail to know how to do it and hence be ignorant of how to do it. In some cases in which you are ignorant of how to perform a particular activity, we say that you are incompetent with respect to that activity.[1] When you are incompetent, you fail to possess an executable ability to perform. For example, if you lack knowledge of how to write a term paper by failing to have an internalized ability to do so, you are incompetent in that area, viz. the area of writing term papers.

Being ignorant of how to do something, I argue, is a special case of being ignorant of a fact. You can be ignorant of how to perform a particular activity by failing to have internalized the procedure required to perform it. But this involves being ignorant of a fact, namely the fact that doing x, y, z, and so on, will make you perform the relevant activity.

The proposed treatment of ignorance of facts and subject matters lends itself to an alternative reply to the problem of skepticism, which I will call the "simple response." You are knowledgeable just when you fail to be ignorant. Knowledgeability and ignorance are both degree notions. It is possible to fail to have knowledge or justification, in a technical sense, about the external world, and yet be relatively knowledgeable about the facts in question.

2   "Ignorant" and "That" Clauses

Although it may seem that our ordinary concept of being ignorant of facts is equivalent to our ordinary concept of lack of knowledge, ordinary language use tells a different story. Most saliently perhaps, and as Peter Unger (1975, p. 175) has pointed out long ago, the verb phrase "to be ignorant" does not combine with a "that" clause. Consider:

(1)

(a) John did not know that Mary came.
(b) *John is ignorant that Mary came.

Unlike the "know" construction in 1(a), the "ignorant" construction in 1(b) is grammatically ill-formed. Googling the term "ignorant that" yields

---

[1] I say "in some cases," because there is also a purely intellectual sense of "knowledge-how" and "ignorance of how." Suppose I have been riding my bike for twenty years and I then lose both of my legs in an accident. After the accident, it seems that I still know how to ride a bike in the purely intellectual sense, even though I lack an executable ability to ride a bike.

some marginal uses of "ignorant that," as in "one can be miserable without knowing that he is miserable" – that is, happy only because he is ignorant that he is "really" miserable."[2] However, these uses are marginal. The string "he is ignorant that he is 'really' miserable" is not strictly grammatical in English.

"Ignorant" and its cognates do occur in sentences with "that" clauses but, as Unger (1975) notes, to get a grammatical sentence from 1(b) one must interpose additional words between the verb and the "that" clause, as in:

(2)

    (a) John was ignorant of the fact that Mary came.
    (b) John was ignorant as to whether Mary came.

"To be ignorant of" is thus not the complement of "to know" but rather of "to be knowledgeable," as in:

(3)

    (a) John was knowledgeable of the fact that Mary came.
    (b) John wasn't knowledgeable of the fact that Mary came.

Grammatically, the verb phrases "to be ignorant" and "to be knowledgeable" are on a par with constructions such as "to be un/aware," "to be cognizant," "to be proud" and "to be mindful," as illustrated in (4):

(4)

    (a) John was ignorant of the fact that Mary came.
    (b) John was knowledgeable of the fact that Mary came.
    (c) John was unaware of the fact that Mary came.
    (d) Lisa was cognizant of the fact that Mary came.
    (e) Amy was proud of the fact that Mary came.
    (f) Ellen was mindful of the fact that Mary came.

Like "to be un/aware," "to be cognizant," "to be proud" and "to be mindful," "to be knowledgeable of" and "to be ignorant of" combine with clauses of the form "the fact that p'. This difference between the occurrence of "knowledgeable" and "ignorant" versus "know" may seem a mere oddity of ordinary language. However, as we will see in the next section, it reflects a deeper difference. Unlike "to know" and "to fail to know," "to be knowledgeable of" and "to be ignorant of" are gradable expressions. In this respect, they are similar to gradable constructions, such as "to be proud of" and "to be mindful of."

---

[2] www.roangelo.net/logwitt/thrasymachus.html, retrieved on January 15, 2015.

3   Relative Gradable Adjectives

As I will now argue, "know" and "knowledgeable of" or "ignorant of" differ in terms of their gradability. To see this, let us begin with the standard case of gradable adjectives. Gradable adjectives denote relations between objects and degrees (Bierwisch 1989; Cresswell 1977; Heim 1985; Kennedy 1999; Von Stechow 1984). For example, "expensive" denotes a relation between objects x and degrees of cost d such that the cost of x is at least as great as d. The value of the degree argument is determined by degree morphology: comparative morphemes, degree modifiers, and so on.

The definitive mark of gradable adjectives is that they are acceptable in comparative constructions and with other degree morphology. Consider the following constructions containing the gradable adjectives "rich," "dry" and "flat":

(5)
  (a) Heavy cream is richer than milk.
  (b) This dough is not as flat as I would like it to be.
  (c) This air is too dry for my skin.

5(a) and 5(b) are comparative constructions, and 5(c) is a construction with a degree modifier. The felicity of these constructions strongly indicates that "rich," "dry" and "flat" are comparative adjectives.

Unlike gradable adjective, non-gradable adjectives are unacceptable in comparative constructions. Consider:

(6)
  (a) *Dinosaurs are more extinct than woolly mammoths.
  (b) *These two lines are less perpendicular than the other two we looked at.
  (c) *Elisa is not as pregnant as I would like her to be.

The infelicity of the sentences in (6) show that "extinct," "perpendicular" and "pregnant" are non-gradable. What goes for adjectives also goes for gradable versus non-gradable verb phrases. Consider:

(7)
  (a) Mary loves her mother more than her father.
  (b) Jane adores her boyfriend way too much.
  (c) *Aze unfriended Ted more on Facebook than Dan did.
  (d) *Sarah took the job too much on January 30.

The sentences in 7(a)–(b), in which "love" and "adore" occur in a comparative construction or with degree morphology, are felicitous, whereas the sentences in 7(d)–(e), in which "unfriend" and "take" occur in a comparative construction or with degree morphology, are not. This confirms that "love" and "adore" are gradable verbs, whereas "unfriend" and "take" are not.

Like "love" and "adore," "ignorant of" and the alternative construction "ignorant as to whether" are acceptable in comparative constructions and with degree morphology. Consider:

(8)

(a) John is more ignorant of the fact that Mary came than Dennis is.

(b) Eli is too ignorant of the fact that Nick is catching up to him.

(c) Chris is just as ignorant as to whether Mary came as Joan is.

The fact that "ignorant of" and "ignorant as to whether" can occur felicitously in these constructions strongly suggests that these constructions are gradable. Contrast that with "does not know":

(9)

(a) *John does not know the fact that Mary came as much as Dennis does.

(b) *Eli does not know enough the fact that Nick is catching up to him.

(c) *Chris does not know the fact that Mary came just as much as Joan doesn't.

"To not know," unlike "to be ignorant of" and "to be ignorant as to whether," is not a gradable expression.

There is, however, more than one type of gradable: absolute gradables and relative gradables (Kennedy, 2007). Let us focus again on the standard case of gradable *adjectives*. The positive form of a relative gradable adjective denotes a property of having a degree of a gradable concept expressed by the adjective that is as least as great as some implicit or explicit standard of comparison. For example, "tiny" denotes the property of having a degree of tininess that is at least as great as the standard of comparison of tininess.

It is well-known that the standard of comparison associated with the positive form of relative gradable adjectives can occur with a for-PP or other local constituents that make the standard of comparison explicit, as in "this apartment is tiny for an apartment in New York."

The fact that the standard of comparison can be made explicit with a for-PP suggests that when the standard of comparison is implicit, it is still present in the logical form as an implicit variable associated with the predicate. The wide range of possible interpretations of implicit standards of comparison further suggests that the value of the standard of comparison is determined on the basis of some discourse-salient property.

Now, there are three diagnostic tests for whether a gradable adjective is a relative gradable expression. The first mark of relative gradables is that sentences containing them vary contextually in truth-conditions depending on which comparison class is determined by context or is made explicit in the sentence structure. Consider, for instance:

(10)

(a) This apartment is tiny.
(b) This apartment is tiny for an apartment in New York.
(c) This apartment is tiny compared to the apartments I was looking at earlier this week.

When said about a 100 m^2 apartment in New York 10(a) would in most conversational contexts be judged false but it would be judged true if uttered by an apartment-hunting millionaire who has been touring $400+ \text{ m}^2$ apartments in New York that same week. 10(b) and 10(c) make the comparison class explicit. 10(b) is best interpreted as saying that this apartment has a significantly smaller size than the median size for an apartment in New York.

Note that making the comparison class explicit does not resolve the vagueness of the predicate. There is no contradiction in saying "This apartment's size is smaller than the median size for a New York apartment, but it is still not small for a New York apartment." So, "This apartment is small for an apartment in New York" does not mean that this apartment has a smaller than median size for an apartment in New York. Rather, it means that this apartment is somewhat smaller than the median size for an apartment in New York, where the value of "somewhat" is determined by a discourse-salient property.

As we will see below, this diagnostic for determining whether a gradable adjective or verb is relative or absolute is not super-reliable. In fact, there is a group of relative gradable adjectives and verbs that cannot occur with a standard of comparison in the absence of a modifier.

The second mark of relative gradable adjectives is that, owing to their inherent vagueness, they give rise to borderline cases. In the neutral sense of "borderline case," a borderline case is an individual that does not evidently fall under the predicate and that does not evidently not fall under the predicate. For example, a 20 m^2

apartment is clearly tiny even for New York standards, whereas an 800 m^2 apartment clearly is not tiny but it may be indeterminate either epistemically or semantically whether a 45 m^2 apartment is tiny for New York standards.

On one widely accepted group of approaches to vagueness known as "gap theories," the existence of borderline cases leads to truth-value indeterminacy (as opposed to an indeterminacy of our knowledge of which precisification is the semantic value of the predicate). On these approaches, "this 45 m^2 apartment is a tiny apartment" is neither definitely true nor definitely false. The indeterminacy is usually explained as follows. A subject-predicate sentence "a is F is true if the reference of a is a member of the extension of F." So, "this 45 m^2 apartment is a tiny apartment" is true if and only if the referent of "this 45 m^2 apartment" is a member of the extension of "tiny apartment." But it is not determinate what set is the extension of "tiny apartment." There is the set of all apartments less than 46 m^2, the set of all apartments less than 45 m^2, the set of all apartments less than 44 m^2, and so on. None of these sets determinately constitutes the extension of "tiny apartment." As the reference of "this 45 m^2 apartment" is a member of some but not all of the putative extensions of "tiny apartment," "this 45 m^2 apartment is a tiny apartment" is neither definitely true nor definitely false.

The third diagnostic of relative gradable adjectives is that owing to their inherent vagueness, they give rise to sorites paradoxes in their unmarked form, for instance:

1. An 800 m^2 apartment is huge for an apartment in New York.
2. If an apartment that is n m^2 is huge for an apartment in New York, then an apartment that is $n-1$ m^2 is huge for an apartment in New York.
3. An apartment that is 0 m^2 is huge for an apartment in New York.

The key feature of vague predicates which drives sorites paradoxes is the feature Crispin Wright (1975) calls "tolerance." A tolerant predicate P is one whose application is indifferent to small changes in the relevant respects. For example, "huge for an apartment in New York" is tolerant of sufficiently small changes in the relevant respect, viz. square meters. Tolerant predicates thus satisfy the following condition:

Tolerance
If a and b are observationally indistinguishable with respect to P, then P(a) ↔ P(b) is definitely true.

A standard approach thought to resolve sorites paradoxes is supervaluationism. Roughly, supervaluationism treats claims as definitely true if they are true on all precisifications, definitely false if they are false on all precisifications, and neither definitely true nor definitely false if they are true on some precisifications and false on others. One problem with supervaluationism, however, is that it entails that $V\{P(a_i) \ \& \ {\sim}P(a_i{+}1)/1 \leq i \leq n\}$ is definitely true. For example, regardless of how we precisify "huge for an apartment in New York" (e.g., larger than 100 m^2), it will always be the case that some pair $P(a_i) \ \& \ {\sim}P(a_i{+}1)$ is true (e.g., "an apartment that is 101 m^2 is huge, and it is not the case that an apartment that is 100 m^2 is huge"). Yet, when a_i and $a_i{+}1$ are observationally indistinguishable, this result is incompatible with the principle of tolerance. So, supervaluationism is incompatible with the semantic properties of tolerant predicates.

One way to resolve this conflict is to reject the standard version of tolerance and accept a contextual version that blocks transitivity. The non-contextual version of tolerance implies transitivity. If a is observationally indistinguishable from b, and b is observationally indistinguishable from c, and P applies to a, then P applies to c. However, this is not generally true. In a color spectrum, for example, even if a and b are perceptually indistinguishable, and b and c are perceptually indistinguishable, a and c may not be perceptually indistinguishable. If we dispose of transitivity, the second inductive premise in the sorites paradox is false.

Not all gradable adjectives are relative gradable expressions (Unger, 1975). Absolute adjectives are gradable but they are not associated with an implicit or explicit standard of comparison, they do not give rise to borderline cases, and they do not trigger sorites paradoxes in the unmarked form. There are two kinds of absolute adjectives: minimum standard absolute adjectives and maximum standard absolute adjectives (Kennedy 2007). Minimum standard absolute adjectives require their arguments to possess some minimal degree of the property they describe. Consider:

(11)

(a) This procedure is painful.
(b) The gold is impure.
(c) The door is open.

11(a) is true as long as the procedure hurts to some degree, 11(b) is true as long as the gold contains some amount of impurities, and 11(c) is true as long as there is some opening of the door.

Maximum standard absolute adjectives, on the other hand, require their arguments to possess some maximum degree of the property they describe. Some examples:

(12)

(a) This procedure is painless.
(b) The gold is pure.
(c) The door is closed.

12(a) is true only if the procedure doesn't hurt, 12(b) is true only if the gold contains no amount of impurities, 12(c) is true only if there is no opening of the door.

To see that absolute adjectives do not give rise to sorites paradoxes, consider the following sorites-like argument:

1. A door that is 10 inches open is open.
2. If a door is n inches open, then a door that is $n - 1$ inches open is open.
3. So, a door that is 0 inches open is open.

Despite having the same structure as standard sorites paradoxes, this argument is not a paradox. It is just plainly invalid. The reason that it is not a paradox is that we are not the least tempted to think that the inductive premise is true. Even if a door that is one inch open is open, it obviously doesn't follow that a door that is 0 inches open is open. In order for an adjective to give rise to a genuine sorites paradox, it must give rise to borderline cases. That the sorites-like argument above fails is not puzzling because absolute adjectives don't give rise to borderline cases.

As Chris Kennedy (2007) points out, there is a tendency to think that absolute adjectives sometimes give rise to borderline cases. Minimum standard absolute adjectives may seem to allow something more than a minimum standard, and maximum standard absolute adjectives may seem to allow something less than a maximum standard. This observation is not quite right, however. Such uses of absolute adjectives, though felicitous, are imprecise, just like common uses of "it's 3 o'clock," "this rod is 10 meters long" and "Boston is 90 miles from Amherst." There are various ways to account for imprecise uses of expressions pragmatically but none of them challenges the claim that absolute adjectives have truth conditions that make reference to fixed maximal or minimal standards of comparison.

4   Moderately, Relative Gradable Expressions

What we just said about relative and absolute gradable adjectives also applies to relative and absolute gradable verbs with some modifications. Not all relative gradable adjectives can occur with a standard of comparison in the absence of a degree modifier (e.g., "rather," "quite," "somewhat"). And the same goes for relative gradable verb phrases. Here are some examples of relative gradable adjectival and verb phrases that cannot occur with a standard of comparison, except in the presence of a degree modifier:

(13)

    (a) ?Amy sounds English for someone born in Sweden.
    (b) Amy sounds quite English for someone born in Sweden.
    (c) ?John is bald for someone who has had a hair transplant.
    (d) John is still rather bald for someone who has had a hair transplant.
    (e) *This shirt is red for a 2000-year-old shirt.
    (f) This shirt is really red for a 2000-year-old shirt.
    (g) *She loves him for someone who is unable to love.
    (h) She loves him a lot for someone who is unable to love.

The first sentence in each pair without a degree modifier is at best marginally acceptable, whereas the second sentence is perfectly fine. Like absolute adjectives but unlike standard relative gradable expressions, verb phrases and adjectival phrases like "sound English," "bald," "red" and "love" combine with proportional modifiers, as illustrated in (14):

(14)

    (a) The bottle is completely empty.
    (b) The door is partially closed.
    (c) *The house is completely expensive.
    (d) *The apartment is partially small.
    (e) Tina sounds completely English.
    (f) John is partially bald.

Though "sound English," "bald," "red" and "love" combine with proportional modifiers and cannot occur with a standard of comparison, they are nonetheless relative gradable expressions. Clear evidence that they are gradable comes from the fact that they are perfectly acceptable in comparatives and with other degree morphology, as shown by (15):

(15)

    (a) Chris sounds more English than Rose does.
    (b) John is too bald to be of use for this hair commercial.
    (c) He doesn't love me as much as I would like him to.

Moreover, the fact that they give rise to genuine sorites paradoxes shows they are not absolute gradable expressions. Here are two examples:

First argument

(1) A person who pronounces 3000 words in a 3000-word speech with a British accent sounds British.

(2) If a person who pronounces n words in a 3000-word speech with a British accent sounds British, a person who pronounces $n - 1$ words in a 3000-word speech with a British accent sounds British.

(3) So, a person who pronounces 0 words in a 3000-word speech with a British accent sounds British.

Second argument

(1) A person who thinks romantically about another person 1,000 minutes a day loves the other person romantically.

(2) If a person who thinks romantically about another person n minutes a day loves the other person romantically, a person who thinks romantically about another person $n - 1$ minutes a day loves the other person romantically.

(3) A person who thinks romantically about another person 0 minutes a day loves the other person romantically.

Both arguments are genuine sorites paradoxes. There is no obvious sharp cutoff between sounding British and not sounding British or between loving a person romantically and not loving her romantically. So, the second inductive premise is not simply obviously false. Moreover, we cannot explain the indeterminacy in terms of imprecision. When we say that it's 3:00 p.m. even though it is actually 2:59 p.m., or that the dishes are dry even though there are microscopic amounts of water on them, what we are saying is close enough to the truth to count as true for the purposes of the conversation. Someone who sounds almost like a native British speaker, on the other hand, really does sound British. We are not simply riding roughshod over precision, when we say they sound British. Let us call relative expressions of this type "moderately relative."

As moderately relative expressions differ from standard relative expressions, I propose to modify Kennedy's (2007) framework. Standard relative expressions, as discussed by Kennedy, quantify over degrees in the semantics even in the absence of a modifier or other degree morphology. For example, "this apartment is small" is to be read as saying that this apartment's size is somewhat smaller than some discourse-salient size. Sentences containing moderately, relative expressions behave differently. Except in the presence of degree or proportional modifiers or other degree morphology, these sentences do not quantify over degrees, they simply attribute an observational property to a subject. For example, "John is bald" expresses the proposition that John has the observational property of being bald. "John is quite bald," on the other hand, quantifies over degrees in the semantics. The sentence is to be read as saying that John has some degree of baldness that is greater than some discourse-salient degree of baldness. On this view, it is not because of reference to degrees that moderately relative adjectives give rise to borderline cases and trigger sorites paradoxes but because they express observational properties that trigger the initial appearance that they satisfy tolerance.

We can assign the following truth-conditions to sentences containing moderately relative adjectives: "John is bald" is just a standard subject-predicate sentence that is true if John has the observational property of being bald. "John is quite bald," on the other hand, is true iff there is a Q_1 and a Q_2 such that Q_2 is a discourse salient degree of baldness, and Q_1 is a degree of baldness which John has, and Q_1 is somewhat larger than Q_2.

A worry here arises. The view just outlined seems to counter the standard analysis of gradable adjectives as denoting relations between objects and degrees. One way to address this worry is to say that sentences with moderately relative adjectives quantify over degrees after all. For example, it may be suggested that "John is bald" is to be read as saying that John instantiates t degrees of baldness (where t is somehow implicitly assigned a value by the context). Note that if this suggestion is right, the context has to provide a precise value for the degree variable. The variable cannot simply be existentially bound. For suppose otherwise. Then "Lisa is as full as Amy is" should imply "Lisa is full" (as surely there is a degree to which Lisa is full"), but it does not (witness: "Lisa is as full as Amy but neither is very full at all").

The proposal just outlined is implausible for a number of reasons. For one, it provides the wrong results for typical secondary qualities. For example, "this tomato is red" cannot plausibly be read as saying that this tomato instantiates t degrees of redness; the sentence just says that this tomato has the quality red (Brogaard, 2010). For another, if moderately relative adjectives make implicit reference to degrees, then we cannot explain why they cannot occur with a standard of comparison in the absence of degree morphology.

I want to make a different suggestion, which is to say that in the case of moderately relative adjectives, reference to degrees is introduced by the degree morphology. On this view, moderately relative adjectives are partial functions from objects to truth-values (with a positive extension, a negative extension and an extension gap). Degrees are introduced by degree morphology like "quite" and "more than." For example, "quite interested in you" has the logical form "t interested in you $[C]$" (where C is a standard of comparison). "Dan is more interested in you than Jacob" has the logical form "more [than Jacob is t interested in you] [Dan is t interested in you]." This proposal can explain why moderately relative adjectives cannot occur with a standard of comparison: there is no implicitly specified degree to enter into the comparison. The proposal has the further advantage that it satisfies the intuitive principle that the meaning of "quite F" is a function of the meaning of "F." If this view is right, then standard relative adjectives and moderately relative adjectives differ in terms of whether the adjective makes reference to degrees in its positive form or whether the degrees are introduced by the morphology.

"To be knowledgeable of" and "to be ignorant of" are examples of moderately relative expressions. Below I will argue that they give rise to borderline cases and trigger sorites paradoxes. In the absence of a modifier they cannot occur with a standard of comparison, except marginally. Consider:

(16)

(a) *For someone who is not normally very reflective, John is knowledgeable of the fact that there is always a reason for actions taken.

(b) For someone who is not normally very reflective, John is quite knowledgeable of the fact that there is always a reason for actions taken.

(a) ?For someone who is normally very attentive, John is ignorant of the fact that Mary was there.

(b) For someone who is normally very attentive, John was quite ignorant of the fact that Mary was there.

"To be knowledgeable" and "to be ignorant of" are thus moderately relative gradable adjectives. In the absence of a modifier, "x is knowledgeable of the fact that p" and "x is ignorant of the fact that p" express the proposition that x has the property of being knowledgeable/ignorant of the fact that p. In the presence of a modifier, however, "x is quite knowledgeable of the fact that p" is to be read as saying that x has some degree of knowledgeability that is greater than some discourse-salient degree of knowledgeability. Likewise, "x is quite ignorant of the fact that p" is to be read as saying that x has some degree of ignorance that is greater than some discourse-salient degree of ignorance. So, the crucial difference between "x is knowledgeable/ignorant" and "x is quite knowledgeable/ignorant" is that only the latter quantifies over degrees in the semantics.

In the presence of a modifier, "to be knowledgeable" and "to be ignorant of" thus have interpretations that depend on a discourse-salient standard. They furthermore give rise to borderline cases both with and without a modifier. John can be neither definitely highly ignorant nor clearly not highly ignorant of the fact that his girlfriend is about to break up with him.

Turning to the third diagnostic for relative gradable adjectives, the fact that "is knowledgeable of," "is ignorant of" and related locutions trigger sorites paradoxes both in the presence and absence of a modifier yields further evidence that these locutions are relative gradable adjectives. Here is an example:[3]

1. Someone who notices 100 salient signs that his beloved is about to break up with him is not ignorant of this fact.
2. If someone who notices n salient signs that his beloved is about to break up with him is not ignorant of this fact, then someone who notices $n - 1$ salient signs that his beloved is about to break up with him is not ignorant of this fact.
3. So, someone who notices 0 salient signs that his beloved is about to break up with him is not ignorant of this fact.

The troublemaker here is the principle of tolerance: if a and b are observationally indistinguishable with respect to P, then $P(a) \leftrightarrow P(b)$ is definitely true. It is the apparent truth of the principle of tolerance that is responsible for the apparent truth of the inductive premise. Noticing one sign that p cannot obviously make a difference to whether "is ignorant of the fact that p" has application, but larger differences can, which suggests that while there is a way to proceed from ignorance to a lack of ignorance, there is no sharp cutoff between ignorance and a lack of ignorance.

"To be knowledgeable of," "to be ignorant of" and related locutions thus satisfy the characteristics for being relative gradable expressions: they are associated with an implicit or explicit standard of comparison, and they give rise to borderline cases and sorites paradoxes.

"To be ignorant of the fact that p" thus is not equivalent to "not to know the fact that p." While the latter may be context-sensitive (see e.g. Cohen 1987, 1997; DeRose 1995; Lewis 1996), it does not admit of degrees or borderline cases in a fixed context, whereas the former does.

Now, since we are interested in the ordinary-language concepts of knowledge and ignorance rather than specialized philosophical notions, linguistic considerations are our best guide to an adequate understanding of these concepts. So, the fact that "to be ignorant of the fact that p" is not equivalent to "not to know the fact that p" provides us with good reason to think that the thesis that ignorance is lack of knowledge is false.

5   Ignorance and Objectual Knowledge

Another way in which we express our thoughts about knowledgeability and ignorance is with the preposition "about," as in:[4]

---

[3] Let it be granted for argument's sake that the person in question does not still believe that all those signs are misleading and does not irrationally discard all those signs.
[4] Steven Beutler, "Chris Christie Is Ignorant About Ebola, But That Doesn't Mean He Was Wrong About Quarantines," *New Republic*, October 28, 2014. www.newrepublic.com/ar

(17)

(a) Chris Christie is knowledgeable about Ebola.

(b) Chris Christie is ignorant about Ebola.

In the constructions in (17), "to be knowledgeable" and "to be ignorant" function on a par with "to know" and "fail to know" when "know" is used objectually. One mark of the objectual "know" is that it does not translate into the same word as the non-objectual "know" in languages such as French, Italian, German and Danish. In German, for example, the objectual "know" translates as "kennen," whereas the non-objectual "know" translates as "wissen." Thus, "John knows Peter" translates in German as "John kennt Peter," whereas "John knows that Peter is the teacher" translates as "John weisst das Peter der Lehrer ist."

Some knowledge sentences are ambiguous between a "kennen" (or objectual) reading and a "wissen" (or non-objectual) reading. "Natalie knows the way to Key Biscayne" can be translated in German as either "Natalie kennt den Weg nach Key Biscayne" or "Natalie weisst den Weg nach Key Biscayne" (Brogaard 2005, 2008). The former requires that Natalie is familiar with the way to Key Biscayne, while the latter merely requires basic knowledge of the directions. Another case: "Stephanie knows the author of *Naming and Necessity*" can be read as saying that the author of *Naming and Necessity* is one of Stephanie's personal acquaintances but it also has a reading that requires for its truth that Stephanie know who the author of *Naming and Necessity* is, which she knows if she knows, say, that Saul Kripke is the author of *Naming and Necessity* or that the author of "Speaker's Reference and Semantic Reference" is the author of *Naming and Necessity*.

Constructions of the form "knows [subject matter]," by contrast, seem to be unambiguously objectual. They do not involve different lexical items in other languages. "Knows," as it occurs in "John knows quantum theory," for example, admits only of the objectual reading.

Objectual knowledge is not factive in the standard sense. One can, in a theoretically important sense of the terms, know Lewis' counterpart theory even if modal realism is false. To know a subject matter involves, among other things, an ability to provide answers to questions about the implications of the theory. But knowing a theory does not require the theory to be true. Another example: John can know Greek mythology without believing that any of the sentences in Greek mythology is true, witness the awkwardness of Eli's response in the following dialogue:

ticle/120013/chris-christies-Ebola-quarantine-new-jersey-wasnt-totally-wrong, accessed on December 23, 2014.

ELI: Zeus's hammer Mjollnir was made for him by the dwarfs Brok and Eitri.
NICK: You clearly don't know your Greek mythology. Mjollnir is Thor's hammer, and figures in Norse mythology. Zeus didn't use a hammer. When he was pissed he threw lightning bolts.
ELI: What are you talking about? Greek mythology is false. There is nothing there to know.

Eli, of course, is equivocating on the word "know." Even though Greek mythology is false, there is obviously something there to know, as long as "know" is construed objectually. Knowing Greek mythology, in the objectual sense, does not require the sentences in the story to be true. It only requires the known claims to be true according to Greek mythology. Thus, one cannot have real knowledge of a theory without the presence of true beliefs about which claims are essential to the theory in question, but one can have real knowledge without these claims being true. Objectual knowledge of a theory is thus in an important sense nonfactive. But there is also a sense in which it is factive. For it requires true beliefs about which claims are essential to the subject matter in question. It will, of course, be a vague matter how many claims one must know within a given subject matter to count as knowing the subject matter.

When "know" is used objectually, it is a moderately, relative gradable expression. First, in the presence of a modifier, sentences containing them vary contextually in truth-conditions depending on which comparison class is determined by context or is made explicit in the sentence structure. Consider:

(18)

(a) Elena knows quite a lot about Ebola.
(b) Elena knows quite a lot about Ebola for someone who has never been in school.
(c) Elena knows a lot more about Ebola than Alan does.

Second, when used objectually "know" gives rise to borderline cases in both the presence or absence of a modifier. For example, an Ebola expert at the medical school of University of Miami definitely knows a lot about Ebola, whereas a young child definitely does not know a lot about Ebola, but it may be indeterminate whether a person who has been attending to news posts about Ebola knows a lot about Ebola.

Third, when used objectually "know" gives rise to sorites paradoxes in both the presence or absence of modifiers. Consider, for instance:[5]

---

[5] Let it be granted for argument's sake that reading articles about Ebola is the only way to learn about it and that the person who reads these articles actually believes at least most of what they say.

1. Someone who has read 1,000 articles about Ebola knows a lot about Ebola.
2. If someone who has read n articles about Ebola knows a lot about Ebola, then someone who has read $n - 1$ articles about Ebola knows a lot about Ebola.
3. Someone who has read 0 articles about Ebola knows a lot about Ebola.

Ignorance about a subject matter is the inverse of knowledge and knowledgeability of a subject matter. If Chris is ignorant about Ebola, he fails to know the subject matter. Again, this does not require that the subject matter provides a true description of reality. You can be ignorant of Greek mythology by failing to know a significant number of the claims that constitute Greek mythology. Here, too, someone can be more or less ignorant about a subject matter. You may be somewhat but not completely ignorant about Greek mythology.

As "know [subject matter]" is semantically equivalent to "knowledgeable about [subject matter]," the latter is a moderately gradable expression. Hence, in the presence of a modifier sentences containing "knowledgeable about" and "ignorant about" vary contextually in truth-conditions depending on which comparison class is determined by context or made explicit in the sentence structure. Consider:

(19)

(a) Chris is quite ignorant about Ebola.
(b) Chris is quite ignorant about Ebola for a leading politician.
(c) Chris is more ignorant than Elan about Ebola.

"Knowledgeable about" and "ignorant about" furthermore give rise to border cases and sorites paradoxes both in the presence and the absence of a modifier. To illustrate:

1. Someone who has studied quantum mechanics for 60,000 minutes is very knowledgeable about quantum mechanics.
2. If someone who has studied quantum mechanics for n minutes is very knowledgeable about quantum mechanics, then someone who has studied quantum mechanics for $n - 1$ minutes is very knowledgeable about quantum mechanics.
3. Someone who has studied quantum mechanics for 0 minutes is very knowledgeable about quantum mechanics.

As in standard cases, it is the apparent truth of the principle of tolerance, if a and b are observationally indistinguishable with respect to P, then $P(a) \leftrightarrow P(b)$ is definitely true, that is responsible for the apparent truth of the inductive premise. Studying quantum mechanics for one minute cannot obviously make a difference to how knowledgeable one is about quantum mechanics, but larger differences can, say studying for 1,000 minutes, which suggests that while there is a way to proceed from being very knowledgeable to not being very knowledgeable, there is no sharp cutoff between being very knowledgeable and not being very knowledgeable.

6   A Simple Reply to the Skeptic

Our treatment of knowledgeability and ignorance of facts lends itself to an alternative reply to the problem of skepticism. Skepticism comes in many flavors: strong and weak, global and local (Fumerton 1995). Weak skepticism is the view that we cannot have *knowledge* of a certain subject-matter or of all subject-matters, whereas strong skepticism is the view that we cannot have *justified beliefs* about a certain subject-matter or about all subject-matters . Although weak skepticism is considered worrisome by some, one could argue that it is not too troublesome if we cannot have knowledge as long as we can have justified beliefs. Presumably, justified beliefs can play most, if not all, the functional roles that knowledge is thought to play. So, the really worrisome position is strong skepticism.

Elsewhere I provided a response to strong skepticism (Brogaard forthcoming). While this reply allows us to retain our entitlement to truly claim to be justified in our beliefs about the external world, there is a simpler reply to the skeptic, which may suffice for ordinary purposes. Both strong and weak skepticism, I will argue, can be refuted appealing to the distinction between knowledge of facts and knowledgeability of facts.

The standard skeptical argument proceeds by showing that the justification for some claim p is equally good justification for some alternative skeptical hypothesis q. For example, your perceptual evidence for thinking that the universe started billions of years ago is equally good evidence for the hypothesis that the universe started five minutes ago. If a deity had created the universe five minutes ago with its appearances of age and human beings rife with all their memories, things would phenomenally seem exactly as they actually do. Likewise, your perceptual evidence for thinking that there is an external world is equally good evidence for the hypothesis that we are all brains in vats. It is, of course, implausible to think that we somehow have direct conscious access to mind-independent physical objects in the non-veridical skeptical scenario. As we have the same justification in the actual world and the skeptical scenario, it is also implausible to think we have direct conscious access to mind-independent physical objects in the actual scenario, and hence it is unreasonable to think that we have non-inferential justification in the actual scenario. It follows that we don't have any non-inferentially justified beliefs about the external world. So, if we have justification for our beliefs about the external world, that justification is inferential. This is the first part of the standard skeptical argument. The next part consists in arguing against the possibility of inferentially justified beliefs about the external world. I am not going to repeat the details of that part of the argument here (but see Brogaard forthcoming).

Even if we grant that we cannot be justified in believing any empirical claims about the external world, however, it does not follow that we cannot be somewhat, or perhaps even highly, knowledgeable of the fact that the world is, roughly, as it appears to us. Recall that constructions of the form "x is quite knowledgeable of the fact that p" are to be read as saying that x has some degree of knowledgeability that is greater than some discourse-salient degree of knowledgeability. In most everyday conversational contexts, knowledgeability of the fact that p does not require that we are internally justified in believing that we are not subject to a hoax or that a global skeptical scenario does not obtain. All we need in order to be knowledgeable of facts about our environment is what our senses and reasoning abilities ordinarily provide us with.

This simple solution to the skeptical problem differs from the standard contextualist response to the problem of skepticism. Contextualists of a traditional bent model the semantics of "know" on the standard theory of indexicals (see e.g. Cohen 1987, 1997; Lewis 1996; DeRose 1995). On the standard theory, the content of an indexical depends on some parameter of the context of use. For instance, the content of "I" depends on a speaker parameter, and the content of "now" depends on a time parameter.

According to standard variety contextualism, the content of "know" depends on a speaker-dependent epistemic standard parameter that is supposed to be relative to what is salient to, or at stake for, the speaker. Whether someone is knowledgeable, on the other hand, will depend on a class of comparison. Just as a 450 m^2 apartment may be small in Miami but big in New York, so being knowledgeable of a fact to degree d may count as significant for one group of people but not for another. But degrees of knowledgeability are not influenced by which skeptical scenarios one happens to entertain at a given moment or which practical issues are at stake for one at the time in question.

Take Keith DeRose's (1992) bank case as an illustrative example. Keith and his wife are driving home on a Friday afternoon. They plan to stop at the bank on the way home to deposit their paychecks. But as they drive past the bank, they notice that the bank is crowded. Thinking that it is not very important that their paychecks are deposited right away, Keith says: "I know the bank will be open tomorrow, since I was there just two weeks ago on Saturday morning. We can deposit them Monday morning." But Keith's wife then reminds him of an important check that will bounce if they do not deposit their paychecks before Monday morning. She says: "Banks do change their hours. Are you certain that is not what is going to happen tomorrow?" Keith concedes, uttering: "Well, I suppose I do not really know that the bank will be open tomorrow after all."

These sorts of cases were originally used to argue in favor of a contextual account of "know" and have played a major part in the most influential defenses of contextualism (e.g., Cohen 1987, 1997; DeRose 1992). Whether these defenses are successful or not need not concern us here. What matters here is that while these types of cases may affect whether people know, they do not affect whether people are knowledgeable or how knowledgeable people are. Even when Keith concedes, uttering "I suppose I do not really know that the bank will be open tomorrow after all," he is no less knowledgeable of the fact that the bank will be open the next day. Of course, one might argue that Keith is less knowledgeable of the fact that the bank is open tomorrow once he becomes aware of the practical issue of the paychecks. One would be hard pressed to actually make a good case for this point, however. Nothing has changed in terms of his informational state. Since "know" is a success term, Keith may not know that the bank is open on Saturdays but if indeed it is open Keith is quite knowledgeable of that fact. After all, he was there two weeks ago and perhaps he has even looked up the hours on his iPhone. Whether he is knowledgeable or not does not depend on salient skeptical possibilities or what is at stake for the knowledge attributers or subjects but rather on how much information he has about the hours of the bank. Keith is less knowledgeable than the bank manager but more knowledgeable than his neighbor who never went to the bank on a Saturday and never bothered looking up the hours of the bank.

This particular solution to the problem of skepticism remains neutral on the question of whether one can possess knowledge or justification despite the skeptical challenge. It is thus providing us with an alternative epistemic value term that is relatively unaffected by changes in the salience of skeptical scenarios or the stakes of speakers or subjects. Unlike "know" and "justified," "knowledgeability" is a degree notion, which is not as easily undermined by stakes or salience of skeptical scenarios. So, the simple solution is not a solution to the skeptic's argument against justification and knowledge of empirical facts but is instead offering a new way to take the sting off of the skeptical argument by treating subjects who in principle neither know nor are justified in believing that p as potentially knowledgeable of the fact that p, when indeed p is true.

7   Ignorance-How and Incompetence

In addition to "knowledgeable or ignorant of the fact that p" and "knowledgeable or ignorant about S," we also speak of knowledgeability or ignorance of how to do A. Ignorance about how to perform an activity is also known as incompetence with respect to A-activities. For example, if you are ignorant of how to write a term paper, you are incompetent with respect to that activity: writing term papers. As we will see, however, you can fail to be ignorant of how to perform a particular activity in one sense, and yet be incompetent with respect to the particular activity.

To be knowledgeable of how to perform a particular activity is a variant on knowing how to perform the activity, and to be ignorant of how to perform the activity is to fail to know how to perform the activity.

There are two competing views of knowledge-how: intellectualism and anti-intellectualism. According to the reductionist varieties of intellectualism defended by Jason Stanley and Timothy Williamson (2001) and Berit Brogaard (2007, 2008, 2009), knowledge-how simply reduces to knowledge-that. To a first approximation, s knows how to A if there is a w such that s knows that w is a way to A. For example, John knows how to ride a bicycle if and only if there is a way w such that John knows that w is a way to ride a bicycle. John Bengson and Marc Moffett (2007) defend an anti-reductionist version of intellectualism which takes knowledge-how to require, in addition, that s understand the concepts involved in her belief.

According to the anti-intellectualist accounts originally defended by Gilbert Ryle (1946) and many others after him, knowledge-how requires the possession of a practical ability and so knowing that w (for some w) is a way to A does not suffice for knowing-how. For example, John knows how to ride a bicycle only if John has the ability to ride it; if John merely knows that w (for some w) is a way to ride a bicycle, John does not know how to ride a bicycle.

Elsewhere I have argued for a conciliatory position that is compatible with the reductionist variety of intellectualism: knowledge-how is reducible to knowledge-that. But there are knowledge states which are not justification-entailing and knowledge states which are not belief-entailing (Brogaard 2011).

Consider the following case of knowledge-how, in which the subject fails to have a justified belief that w (for some w) is a way to fix the faucet. The faucet in Jason's apartment leaks. Jason finds a faucet manual in the kitchen drawer and fixes it. However, unbeknownst to him, the manual was created by the previous owner's parrot who liked to step dance on the keyboard of the owner's old typewriter. Over the 50 years of step dancing the parrot had created a lot of nonsense but there was this one time where the parrot happened to hit the right keys and created something that made sense: The Faucet Manual. The owner never looked at it but had left it in the kitchen drawer where Jason found it. Under these circumstances, there is a way w such that Jason believes truly that w is a way to fix the faucet but the belief is acquired via a faulty method. So Jason cannot claim to have the knowledge that the method is a way to fix the faucet. Even so, it seems alright to say that Jason knows how to fix the faucet.

It is widely acknowledged that one can possess knowledge in virtue of possessing the right sort of cognitive capacities and exercising them in the right sort of way in the right sort of environment. Beliefs formed in this way are safe. They could not easily have been false. Further, a belief is reliably formed if, and only if, beliefs formed via the same method in the same sort of environment tend to give rise to safe beliefs. So, beliefs acquired through the exercise of an intellectual virtue are reliable. But, as I have argued on previous occasions, beliefs accompanied by the right sort of practical abilities also satisfy safety and reliability (Brogaard 2011). Abilities are stable traits. If you have the ability to A by doing P in S, then doing P in S is a way for you to A in worlds in which you are sufficiently physically similar to the way you actually are.[6] So, if you believe that doing P in S is a way for you to A, and you have the ability to A by doing P in S, then your belief is safe. In the closest worlds in which you believe that doing P in S is a way for you to A, doing P in S is a way for you to A.[7] So, in those worlds your belief is true. Moreover, your belief is reliably formed. Beliefs with the same sort of ground as your actual belief tend to be safe. Beliefs can thus be safe and reliably formed without being cognitively grounded.

We can thus distinguish two ways in which a knowledge state may be grounded: practically and cognitively. A cognitive ground, as envisaged here, is whatever makes the difference between mere true belief that p and cognitive knowledge that p, for instance, the fact that the belief was formed via a reliable and virtuous belief-forming method in the right sort of environment. A practical ground is whatever makes the difference between mere true belief that doing P in S is a way for one to A and knowing how to A, for instance, having the ability to A. Let us refer to both kinds of grounds as "justificatory grounds."

---

[6] I do not succeed in swimming by making swim-like movements if I am not submerged in enough water. So, I don't have the ability to swim by making swim-like movements. But I have the ability to swim by making swim-like movements while sufficiently submerged in water.

[7] At least assuming that the closest worlds in which you believe that doing P in S is a way for you to A are worlds in which you are sufficiently similar physically to the way you actually are.

Given this notion of a justificatory ground, let us now return to our case in which a subject appears to lack justification for his belief that there is a w (for some w) such that w is a way to perform A, yet knows how to perform A. Jason knows how to fix the faucet because there is a way w such that Jason knows that w is a way for him to fix the faucet in the right sort of environment. But what grounds his belief that doing P in the right sort of environment is a way for him to fix the faucet is not the fact that his belief was acquired via a faulty method but rather the fact that he has an ability which he acquired by reading the manual: the ability to fix the faucet by doing P in S. One cannot acquire propositional knowledge by using methods which yield the right result only accidentally. However, one can acquire a practical ability by using such a method. Thus, one can acquire the ability to A by relying on a method which yields the right result accidentally, and once one has the ability, it can then serve as a justificatory ground for one's true belief that doing P in S is a way for one to A. By reading the fake manual Jason acquires the true belief that doing P in S is a way for him to fix the faucet, and he acquires the ability to fix the faucet by doing P in S. The ability then serves as a justificatory ground for his true belief that doing P in S is a way for him to fix the faucet.

The position outlined here is not committed to the view that abilities to perform an activity are necessary or sufficient for knowing how to perform that activity. Having an ability is not necessary for knowing how to perform an activity, as I can know how to get to New York, even if I don't have the means to get there. Nor is having an ability sufficient for knowing how to perform an activity. Consider Paul Snowdon's well-known counterexample to the view that to know how to A just is to have the ability to A:

A man is in a room, which, because he has not explored it in the least, he does, as yet, not know how to get out of. In fact, there is an obvious exit which he can easily open. He is perfectly able to get out, he can get out, but does not know how to (as yet). (Snowdon 2004, p. 11)

It seems perfectly alright to say that the man has the ability to get out of the room (he just has to look around) and yet it seems highly plausible that he doesn't know how to get out. He does not know how to get out because there presently is no way w such that he knows that w is a way to get out.

The counterexample trades on an ambiguity in the word "ability." In one sense of the word, s has the ability to A just in case S is in an ability state with a content that represents a certain procedure for how to A, and S has the bodily capacities for carrying out the procedure. In another sense, S has the ability to A just in case S has certain bodily capacities which, if combined with the right sort of procedural information, will put S in a position to A. The man in Snowdon's example is not in a state with a content that represents a procedure for getting out. There is a procedure (namely looking around) which, when internalized by the man, will put him in a position to get out. Only the first kind of ability is essentially mind-involving and hence is of the sort that suffices for knowledge-how.

Returning now to ignorance, one can be ignorant of how to perform an activity by lacking a sufficiently internalized ability to perform the activity. For example, you can be ignorant of how to exit the room in Snowdon's case because you haven't internalized the ability you have to get out.

As with knowledge-how, incompetence and hence ignorance of how to perform a given activity come in two different flavors. You can know what exactly to do to perform a yoga backbend and yet be unable to perform it, because you aren't flexible enough. There is a sense in which you are not ignorant about how to perform a yoga backbend, as you could easily teach others who are flexible enough how to do it. But since you actually cannot perform the backbend yourself, you are ignorant of how to perform it in a different sense. In this case, you are incompetent with respect to the particular activity: performing a yoga backbend, although you are not incompetent with respect to related activities, such as teaching others how to perform the backbend.

8   Conclusion

I have argued the phrase "is ignorant" functions differently grammatically and semantically from the phrase "does not know," when the latter is used propositionally. "Is ignorant" does not have a genuine propositional use but is best understood as the converse of "is not knowledgeable." I have further argued that "being knowledgeable" and "being ignorant" are particular kinds of relative gradable expressions. Relative gradables typically are associated with an implicit or explicit standard of comparison, give rise to borderline cases and trigger sorites paradoxes in their unmarked form. From these linguistic considerations, I argued, it follows that being ignorant admits of degree and that one can fail to be ignorant despite lacking true beliefs concerning the propositions constituting a particular subject matter. The proposed treatment of knowledgeability and ignorance of facts and subject matters lends itself to an alternative, "simple" solution to the skeptical problem. I have furthermore argued that ignorance can also reflect incompetence with respect to a particular activity. The latter is a case of lacking a particular kind of ability-involving knowledge-how, viz. practical knowledge of how to perform the activity in question.[8]

---

[8] Thanks to Rik Peels for helpful comments on a previous version of this paper.

4   Explicating Ignorance and Doubt: A Possible Worlds Approach

Erik J. Olsson and Carlo Proietti

> I will suppose that the sky, the air, the earth, colors, figures, sounds, and all external things, are nothing better than the illusions of dreams, by means of which this being has laid snares for my credulity; I will consider myself as without hands, eyes, flesh, blood, or any of the senses, and as falsely believing that I am possessed of these.
>
> Descartes, *Meditations on First Philosophy (I)*

1   Introduction

The concepts of doubt and ignorance are notions that we could not easily do without, in ordinary life or in science. We express doubt in someone's report if we consider the proposition expressed improbable or find the reporter lacking in credibility. If asked about some matter of fact, we express ignorance to signify that we don't know that answer, implying that the inquirer needs to consult another source of information. A reference to our ignorance may make our otherwise blameworthy action morally excusable.[1]

In inquiry, doubt is probably the driving force, philosophical inquiry being no exception. Famously, Descartes (1647) made methodological doubt the cornerstone of his rationalism. Empiricists such as Locke (1690) or Hume (1739–40) relied on a notion of comparative doubtfulness, seeing less reason to doubt the verdict of the senses than, say, that of imagination. (Neo-)Kantians and Wittgensteinians agree that the possibilities for doubt are more restricted than traditionally assumed, arguing that for something to be in doubt other things must be taken for granted (Wittgenstein 1969). Pragmatists like Peirce (1958) highlighted the distinction between paper and living doubt, maintaining that the latter is what motivates inquiry. For fallibilists, including Popper, doubt in empirical propositions is recognized as a fact of life that can never be

---

[1] For the legal role of ignorance see Faust (2000a, 2000b).

completely relieved. Concerning ignorance, it is obviously the end point of many skeptical inquiries (e.g., Unger 1975).

In spite of their fundamental conceptual roles, doubt and ignorance have been accorded relatively little interest by formal epistemologists.[2] Thus, in comparison with the effort devoted to knowledge and belief since Hintikka (1962), the former concepts have received only sporadic attention in epistemic and doxastic logic.[3] Similarly, mainstream epistemologists have invested comparatively little energy in clarifying the nature of, and relation between, doubt and ignorance. They focused primarily on analyzing knowledge, justified belief and related concepts.

In general, the logical relations between, on the one hand, doubt and ignorance and, on the other, belief and knowledge are unclear. One might think that doubt and ignorance are simply the negations of belief and knowledge, respectively. But this is too simplistic: one may clearly fail to believe that roses are blue without thereby doubting this, namely, if one believes that roses have a color other than blue. In general, one may fail to believe that X because one believes not-X, without thereby being in doubt as to whether X. By the same token, one may fail to know that X simply by knowing that not-X, without being ignorant as to X. According to Van der Hoek and Lomuscio (2004) being ignorant as to X is more adequately defined as "not knowing that X and not knowing that not-X," excluding cases like the former.[4] Is this definition adequate? Can doubt be characterized in an analogous way? What is the difference between doubting that X and being ignorant as to X?

To answer these questions and pave the way for a precise analysis of these notions we will identify, in Section 2, some fundamental features of doubt and ignorance taking into account insights from different scholars and traditions, without any ambition to give a comprehensive historical overview or a complete panorama of different positions. In Section 3, we introduce the framework of possible worlds. Section 4 contains our proposals for how to explicate the concepts of doubt and ignorance. Our discussion throughout is exploratory rather than final, the focus being on suggesting new ways of thinking about the concepts in question in a more rigorous manner. Thus, the account we arrive at is "semi-formal" leaving a number of formal issues unresolved for future work.

---

[2] We adhere to the distinction between "formal" and "mainstream" epistemology made by Hendricks (2006). The former includes epistemic logics, Bayesian approaches and all other methods that make a fundamental use of mathematical modeling to analyze epistemological notions such as knowledge, belief, uncertainty. By contrast, "mainstream" or informal epistemology is marked by its major reliance on conceptual analysis.

[3] Hoek and Lomuscio (2004) is a notable exception.

[4] This use should be distinguished from the use in "John is ignorant (of the fact) that X," implying that X is true.

2   Ignorance and Doubt: Similarities and Differences

Doubt and ignorance can be viewed, alongside belief and knowledge, as attitudes of an agent toward a proposition. Belief and knowledge are normally thought of as *cognitive* states of an agent with respect to a specific propositional content. The first point to clarify is whether the same can be said of doubt and ignorance. Thus our first question will be:

1. Are doubt and ignorance (cognitive) states or are they (cognitive) processes?

While ignorance is clearly a state, doubt is a more difficult case. Indeed, compared to other attitudes doubt seems to be of a more "dynamic" nature. According to Russell doubt is indeed a process: "a vacillation, an alternative between belief and disbelief" (Russell 1984, p. 142).[5] Linguistic practice may provide some guidance on this point. While we can say that John is (actively) doubting something, we cannot say that John is (actively) knowing or (actively) ignoring something (in the relevant sense of "ignoring"). The strength of this evidence is, however, difficult to assess. For one thing, one can say that John is (actively) believing something, although belief is usually taken to be a state, not a process. In the absence of strong evidence to the contrary, it is reasonable when engaging in conceptual analysis to stick to the approach taken by Hintikka (1962) and others, that is, to first characterize attitudes as states "in a specious present" and then, in a second step, investigate the dynamics of those attitudes. However, there is something relevant in Russell's insight, for doubt is, compared to plain ignorance, a more active attitude toward its object. Indeed, when we doubt something we are weighing pros and cons with the ultimate aim of resolving our doubts so as to settle on a firm belief. Doubt can, at least from the idealized perspective of the logician, be seen as a kind of ignorance. However, the implication does not go in the other direction: there may be ignorance where there is no doubt. I may be ignorant as to whether it is raining in Oklahoma City but this does not imply that I am in doubt as to whether this proposition is true, for the simple reason that I may be indifferent to its truth. A person cannot be in doubt vis-à-vis a proposition about which he or she does not care in the first place.[6] We will return to this issue below.

A second important issue concerns the question whether doubt and ignorance are "purely theoretical" attitudes. Thus we may ask:

---

[5] Quoted from Thagard (2004, p. 392).
[6] Relativity to a context and a question are two salient features of doubt according to the views of both Wittgenstein and Austin, for example, Rasmussen (1974).

2. Are doubt and ignorance emotional and/or voluntary attitudes?

Again, in the case of ignorance this question seems to have an easy (negative) answer: to be ignorant as to X does not force one to have any specific feeling or volitional attitude toward X. On the contrary, very often we are not even aware of the things of which we are ignorant, which, given our vast ignorance and limited attentional span, is probably for the better.

Things change when we proceed to examine doubt. According to Thagard (2004) doubt is the prototype of a "hot" cognitive state, that is, one loaded with emotion. Thagard's analysis has a predecessor in C.S. Peirce, according to whom doubt is "an irritation that causes inquiry, which is a struggle to attain a state of belief" (1958). Thagard underpins his analysis by listing a number of conditions that he thinks are typically satisfied in cases of doubt:

1. Someone makes a claim about some proposition X.
2. Others notice that X is incoherent with their beliefs.
3. They care about the proposition because it is relevant to their goals.
4. They entertain emotions related to the proposition.
5. The emotions are caused by a combination of the claim, the incoherence and the relevance of the proposition.

The fact that doubting, according to the Peirce-Thagard analysis, involves a fundamental emotional component may seem like a major obstacle to any attempt to provide a logical analysis or formal description. But appearances deceive. Consider the concept of belief. Surely, belief is also accompanied, in most cases, by emotions and goals and yet this has not prevented logicians or formal epistemologists from making use of it or even analyzing it (i.e., in terms of probability). In fact, to the best of our knowledge no logical or probabilistic description of belief appeals to emotional aspects.

This is not to deny the relevance of the Thagard-Peirce analysis, but to stress that the goal of a formal account of the kind we are looking for is slightly different from that of a descriptive or psychological one. A formal characterization of a given propositional attitude typically aims at (and is limited to) listing the properties of the concept in question (e.g., knowledge and belief) with respect to its content and to its interaction with other concepts (e.g., Boolean operators such as "and," "or," "not"). This holds for both qualitative (e.g., Hintikka 1962) and quantitative characterizations of belief (e.g., Ramsey 1926).

Even if a formal characterization of belief and doubt need not refer to emotional phenomena, it should arguably explain why these concepts, in contrast to knowledge and ignorance, are emotionally loaded, or at least not make the emotional factor entirely inexplicable. As for doubt, the important point stressed by the Peirce-Thagard analysis from this perspective is that, when doubting, one is contrasting possible alternatives corresponding to live possibilities actually entertained as such. These possibilities are often enough not on a par for the doubting person, who might find some alternatives more plausible or preferable than others, without being in a position to exclude the less attractive ones from consideration. Small wonder if this may lead to some cognitive distress.

A third question to ask is how fine-grained the attitudes in question are.

3. Do ignorance and doubt come in degrees?

Knowledge and belief differ in this respect, as almost all epistemologists would testify. Belief may come in degrees whereas knowledge does not. We may believe X strongly or weakly, or entertain a full belief in X when we are certain about X. Knowledge is different: we either know that X or we don't know that X. There is nothing in-between.[7] The same goes for ignorance, which like knowledge is an absolute notion: a person is either ignorant as to X or not ignorant as to X. She cannot be more or less strongly ignorant, or be ignorant to a higher or lower degree.[8] Doubt is like belief in admitting of graduation. If you doubt that X, it can be sensibly asked how much you doubt that X, that is, whether your doubt is strong or weak.

As mentioned before, an adequate formal rendering of attitudes such as belief and doubt may not capture all their features, but it should at least do justice to the more salient ones and, moreover, explain how the attitudes in question relate to each other. Preferably, a formal account should also leave room for introducing a more elaborate analysis at a later stage, implying that it should allow for a certain amount of conceptual modularity and flexibility. In the next section we will introduce the language of possible worlds as a framework in which these issues can be fruitfully addressed.

----

[7] Hetherington (2001) is an exception. According to Hetherington, knowledge, just like belief, comes in degrees.

[8] Colloquially, we may say that a person's ignorance is "considerable," "gross" or "total," signaling that we are assessing the imperfection of her knowledge on a fine-grained scale. However, the object of ignorance in such cases is plausibly not a single a proposition or issue but a whole domain of propositions or issues. Roughly, a person's ignorance of a domain of inquiry is considerable if she is ignorant about many or even most propositions or issues in that domain.

3   The Framework of Possible Worlds

The Leibnizian notion of a possible world (developed in various essays contained in Leibniz [1989]) has been widely applied as a formal tool in logical analysis to shed light on the meaning of modal notions such as necessity, possibility, obligations, tenses and, last but not least, knowledge and belief. Two major works are Hintikka (1962) and Fagin et al. (1995). Paraphrasing Carnap (1947), a possible world may be thought of as a complete description of how things are, specifying for each atomic proposition whether it or its negation is true. An atomic proposition may be thought of as expressing an elementary (not further analyzable) fact, for example, "Joe is 1.75 m tall." Given a single proposition, there are at least two possible worlds, one in which the proposition "Joe is 1.75 m tall" is true and one in which this proposition is false. The number of different state descriptions depends on how many atomic propositions are given in the language. In the following, we use "proposition," "sentence" and "formula" interchangeably.

It is important to stress that, despite what some vivid prose may suggest, possible worlds can be pragmatically thought of as mere conceptualizations rather than as real entities "out there."[9] For example, if we are talking about possible outcomes of a specific coin toss we may restrict attention to two atomic propositions: H for "the coin landed heads" and T for "the coin landed tails" and leave everything else out. There are only two possible worlds here: H and T. It is for their usefulness in representing possible states of affairs that possible worlds have become an indispensable part of the language of philosophical logic and computer science. It is perhaps more adequate, but less suggestive, to talk about "alternatives" instead of "possible worlds." We shall henceforth use both terms interchangeably.

In order to understand how possible worlds can be used to clarify epistemic notions, let us focus on our coin toss example. Suppose that the coin landed heads so that the actual world is H. How should we describe the epistemic state of an agent, at the actual world H, who has no prior expectations and cannot actually see how the coin landed? A natural choice is to say that, at H, both possible worlds H and T are alternatives that are

---

[9] Looking at possible worlds as at mere conceptualizations also neutralizes some ontological commitments that atomic propositions seem to carry. Although atomic propositions are the building blocks of a possible world, this fact does not commit us to the metaphysically controversial view that there are "atomic facts." If possible worlds are viewed as mere conceptualizations, reference to atomic propositions just entails that the language we use is (recursively) constructed over some primitives, which does not beg any substantial metaphysical questions. For the debate relative to the metaphysics of possible worlds semantics the reader may consult Menzel (2015).

Figure 4.1: The accessibility relation between possible worlds for an agent without prior expectations. The edge between H and T is bidirectional, meaning that the agent considers T as an alternative at H and, vice versa, H as an alternative at T. The loops mean that both at H and T the agent considers the actual situation an open alternative.

open or, to use the standard term, "accessible" to the agent. This relation is called the accessibility relation and it is visually represented by edges between possible worlds as in Figure 4.1. More accessible worlds correspond to more open alternatives and hence to greater uncertainty for the agent. Importantly, we will consider defining not just one but several accessibility relations over the same set of alternatives. Before defining knowledge and belief in this framework we need to introduce some additional concepts.

The formal language of standard epistemic and doxastic logic is defined over a set *Prop* of atomic propositions P, Q and so on. Starting with atomic propositions as building blocks we construct our set of formulas (complex propositions) using the Boolean connectors $\neg$ ("it is not the case that"), $\wedge$ ("and"), $\vee$ ("or"), $\rightarrow$ ("if... then") and operators for propositional attitudes B ("I believe that") and K ("I know that") according to the following rules:

1. Every atomic proposition is a formula.

2. If X is a formula, then $\neg X$, BX and KX are formulas.

3. If X and Y are formulas, then $X \vee Y$, $X \wedge Y$ and $X \rightarrow Y$ are formulas.

This allows us to express, in an unequivocal manner, complex attitudes such as $BP \wedge BQ$ ("the agent believes that P and also believes that Q"), $K(P \vee Q)$ ("the agent knows that P or Q"), $B(P \wedge KQ)$ ("the agents believes that P and that he knows that Q") and so on.

A possible worlds model $M = (W, R_1, \ldots, R_n, V)$ is a mathematical structure where:

- W is a set of possible worlds, representing the set of all alternatives for the agent (whether they are accessible or not). One of them, say w_α, represents the actual world.
- For every i such that $1 \leq I \leq n$, R_i is a relation, that is, a set of ordered pairs (w_1, w_2) of possible words such that w_2 is accessible from w_1. The relation R_i can be graphically represented by edges between possible worlds in W. The set $R_i[w]$ of possible worlds that are accessible

from the world w represents the set of alternatives that are R_i-accessible for the agent at w, i.e. R_i [w] = {v ∈ W | (w,v) ∈ R_i}.

- V is a propositional valuation (i.e. a function from atomic propositions to sets of worlds) stating, for each atomic proposition P, in which possible worlds P is true.

Given a possible worlds model, we can define truth at a possible world w for all Boolean formulas in the standard way, where P stands for an arbitrary atomic proposition, X and Y stand for arbitrary formulas and "iff" abbreviates "if and only if":

- P is true at w iff $w ∈ V(P)$
- $¬X$ is true at w iff X is not true at w
- $X ∧ Y$ is true at w iff X is true at w and Y is true at w
- $X ∨ Y$ is true at w iff X is true at w or Y is true at w
- $X → Y$ is true at w iff: if X is true at w, then Y is true at w

The conditions under which a proposition involving propositional attitudes such as "I know that X" (formally, KX) is true are specified by making reference to the alternatives R_K-accessible to the agent for a given relation R_K. More precisely,

- KX is true at w iff X is true at all v such that wR_Kv.

The idea behind this clause is that, at a given w, the agent knows a given proposition when no accessible (open) R_K-alternative falsifies it. The truth of "I believe that X" (BX) is defined in the same way as for KX but with reference to a different relation R_B, that is:

- BX is true at w iff X is true at all v such that wR_Bv.

The use of two distinct accessibility relations for defining knowledge and belief may seem puzzling at first sight.[10] However, different accessibility relations are useful to capture the fact that an agent may consider alternatives "under different aspects." Let us consider again our coin tossing example. Figure 4.1 depicts a situation where the agent has no expectations regarding the alternatives. This is encoded by the special features of the accessibility relation: both alternatives are accessible from H and from T. Suppose instead that, for some reason, the agent considers only the alternative T as available (even if the coin actually landed heads). To model this situation we should consider a different accessibility relation consisting only of two edges, one from H to T and one from T to itself. Both

---

[10] This impression is reinforced by the fact that logics of knowledge and belief have mostly been studied separately in which case, obviously, only one accessibility relation is needed.

accessibility relations may coexist in the same model, indicating two different aspects under which the agents consider the available alternatives.[11]

In general the accessibility relation for knowledge, contrary to that for belief, should be a reflexive relation whereby every world is accessible from itself: wR_Kw for all w. This secures the entailment from KX to X, that is, knowledge becomes "factive." For if KX is true at w, then, by the truth conditions stated above, X is true at all v such that wRv. Since R is reflexive, wR_Kw. Hence X is true at w. The corresponding principle clearly does not hold for belief.

Now there are at least two different ways of combining epistemic and doxastic logics in a coherent framework, and they can both be of use when analyzing doubt and ignorance. A first option (e.g., van Benthem 2007; Baltag and Smets 2008) consists in using sphere representations originally introduced by Lewis (1973) for the semantics of counterfactuals and by Grove (1988) as a basis for belief revision theory. Sphere representation provides an intuitive subdivision, from the point of view of a given world w, of an agent's space of alternatives W into a set of concentric spheres, also called a *sphere system*. At a given world w alternatives are all considered R_K–accessible but more or less relevant depending on whether they belong to the innermost or to the outermost spheres. We may think of the innermost sphere as containing those alternatives that are seriously possible from the agent's perspective at a given world. For example, consider the alternatives as described by the atomic propositions "the coin landed heads" (H) and "penguins fly" (F). The collection of possible worlds (epistemic alternatives) contains both H-worlds and $\neg H$-worlds. However, in normal conditions someone would rank differently $H \wedge F$-worlds and $H \wedge \neg F$-worlds, viewing the latter as more plausible than the former. In sphere semantics this distinction can be implemented by putting $H \wedge \neg F$-worlds in the innermost spheres of the agent's epistemic space and the $H \wedge F$-worlds in the outermost spheres. And the same reasoning applies to $\neg H$-worlds.

Given a sphere system, "I believe that X" is defined as X being the case in all alternatives in the innermost sphere, representing the alternatives that are accessible through R_B, i.e.

- BX is true at w iff X is true at all alternatives v such that $R_B(w,v)$, that is to say, true in the innermost sphere of W,

---

[11] As suggested in Lewis (1996), even a single attitude like knowledge may come in different forms and may, therefore, be modeled by distinct accessibility relations. For example, in an everyday context we may know things like "this table is flat" that we do not know in a scientific context, for example, a class in molecular physics, because the latter context includes a wider range of alternatives, including falsifying ones. See Hendricks (2006) for a throughout discussion of this point.

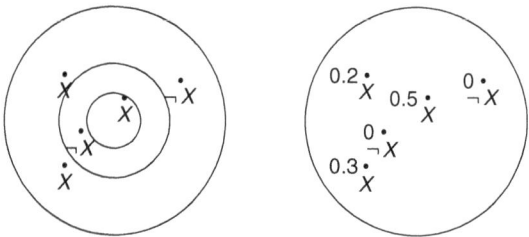

Figure 4.2: Two representations of knowledge and belief: (a) system of spheres, (b) probabilities.

whereas knowing that X is equivalent to X being the case all over the sphere system, representing the alternatives that are accessible through R_K, that is:

- KX is true at w iff X is true at all alternatives v such that $R_K(w,v)$, that is to say, true at all possible worlds in W.

Thus, here R_K is constituted by the full set of epistemic alternatives (from all the spheres) and R_B by just the innermost sphere (see Figure 4.2[a]). It is crucial here that R_B is contained in R_K. This has the intuitive consequence that the agent may be believing that X without knowing that X but not the other way around. This corresponds to a case in which all the most relevant alternatives are X-alternatives but some farther ones are not.

Following a similar line of thought one may use probabilities instead of a sphere system as discussed above. In its simplest form, this approach consists in assigning (for each possible world w in W) to all the alternatives v a probability $f(v)$ between 0 and 1, with the total summing to 1 as shown in Figure 4.2(b).

Based on this approach, we can assign degrees of belief as follows:

- The agent believes X to degree x at w iff the sum of the $f(v)$'s, for all the v where X is true, is x.

We may furthermore define full belief (or certainty) and knowledge in the following way:

- The agent fully believes X at w iff the sum of the $f(v)$'s for the v's where X is true is 1.
- The agent knows that X is true at w iff X is true at all v's, noticing that this approach, too, does not make full belief and knowledge equivalent concepts, given that we may have $f(v) = 0$ for some possible world v where X is false (see Figure 4.2[b]).

Probabilistic frameworks as the one presented here are often named "quantitative" approaches as opposite to "qualitative" ones (which include sphere representations). Both approaches have their advantages and disadvantages. The most significant drawback for us, as we shall see in Section 4.2, is that there are certain salient features of doubt that neither is able to account for.

4   Defining Doubt and Ignorance

The question is now how to analyze ignorance and doubt using possible worlds. Following Hoek and Lomuscio (2004), "being ignorant as to X" may be understood as acknowledging the presence of both X and $\neg X$ as alternatives in the epistemic space of the agent. This amounts to the following definition where IX stands for "the agent is ignorant about X":

$$IX =_{\text{def}} \neg KX \wedge \neg K \neg X$$

This is, in a sense, a minimal definition of ignorance. We may easily check that IX is consistent with BX (and also with $B\neg X$).[12] The present account is coherent with the properties of ignorance that we stressed in the previous sections. First, ignorance is a state (i.e., a particular configuration of the epistemic space). Second, ignorance is a passive attitude, insofar as whether the agent is ignorant may depend on remote epistemic alternatives to which the agent does not pay attention. Third, ignorance does not come in degrees: a single $\neg X$-alternative succeeds in making the agent ignorant about X. Note that ignorance does not come out as simply the absence of knowledge. In other words, being ignorant about X does not reduce to not knowing that X.

What about doubt? What seems clear is that "doubting that X" refers to a stronger kind of indecision among X and $\neg X$-alternatives. Our preliminary analysis suggests that doubting may be viewed as "being ignorant + something else." What are these additional ingredients? Can we try to capture them by adding conditions on top of our analysis of ignorance?

---

[12] In a sphere system both IX and BX ($B\neg X$) are true in case all most relevant alternatives are X-alternatives ($\neg X$-alternatives) but there is also some $\neg X$-alternative (X-alternative) in the epistemic space. Analogously, in a probabilistic model full belief in X may coexist with ignorance when all $\neg X$-alternatives have zero probability.

4.1   Doubt as Ignorance + Plausibility of Opposing Alternatives

Doubting requires something more than simple ignorance insofar as, when doubting whether X, our indecision is among contrasting alternatives which are both somehow relevant. A first option to express such relevance is to define doubt referring to the "plausibility of opposing alternatives." In the framework of spheres one may interpret doubting that X as having both X and $\neg X$-alternatives in one's innermost sphere. This boils down to the following proposal (where DX stands for "the agent is in doubt about X"):

$$DX =_{\text{def}} \neg BX \wedge \neg B \neg X$$

It follows that $DX \rightarrow IX$: doubt entails ignorance. Construing doubt in this way allows us to see why doubt is considered a "hot" cognitive state. This is because when the agent is in doubt, as opposed to being simply ignorant, she entertains two opposing alternatives which are both relevant in the sense of being seriously possible and attended to, meaning that the indecision is "real and living," to use Peirce's famous characterization of genuine doubt.

This analysis still does not allow us to explain how doubt may come in degrees and why, for instance, a person may be strongly doubting that X while being almost certain that $\neg X$. Using probabilities squares better with this idea. We may then, alternatively, define doubting that X as both X and $\neg X$-alternatives having a certain degree of probability. Strongly doubting that X would then be analyzed as being almost certain that $\neg X$ is the case or, more generally, as assigning a high probability to $\neg X$-alternatives and a low probability to X-alternatives.

4.2   Adding Goal Relevance and Awareness

We noted before, in connection with Thagard's characterization of doubt, that it is essential to doubt that it concerns something that is relevant to the agent's goals. This aspect – goal relevance – is not captured in the proposed definitions we have explored thus far. Consider the following example adopted from Olsson and Westlund (2006):

Suppose you believe that the National Lottery is fair. Now you are informed that the wife of the organizer has won the highest price. This is not inconsistent with your belief that the lottery is fair, but you decide nonetheless that you cannot take it for granted that the lottery is fair. [...] It seems that, given that you care about the fairness of the lottery in the first place, your retracting your belief that it is fair should be accompanied by a reopening of the question as to its fairness.

The point here is that it is constitutive of the agent doubting that X by retracting the belief that X that she asks herself whether X is true. This question – the question whether X – should now be on her "research agenda," to borrow Olsson and Westlund's expression. The research agenda of an agent is the set of questions that the agent aims to resolve in the process of inquiry.

It seems that neither sphere systems nor probabilistic approaches in their standard formulation can account for this special feature of doubt. To see why let us consider a simple example. Suppose that Alice is rolling a die. If the outcome of the roll is an even number she will win, otherwise she will lose. Now, Alice may very well doubt whether or not the outcome of a specific roll was an even number without therefore doubting whether or not it was six: she does not care what the specific outcome is, so long as it is an even number. However, assuming that all alternatives are on a par for Alice, neither of our previous attempts to define doubt within sphere systems can account for this intuition. There, doubting whether or not the outcome was an even number entails a fortiori a doubt as to whether or not the outcome was a six, which is an incorrect prediction in this case. Doubting that X implies "focusing on X" or "entertaining the issue whether X" notions that neither sphere systems nor probabilistic models seem able to capture in their standard form.

Also the process of starting to doubt something does not seem to fit with probabilities and sphere semantics. When I start doubting something, for example, that I have two hands, it does not mean that I have to revise the probability of the proposition in question or that I readjust any preference ordering I may entertain in my epistemic state. It rather seems that I am simply taking the proposition "I have two hands" into account, a proposition I may have been unaware of before.

Different refinements of epistemic and doxastic logic can deal with the issue just mentioned. Justification logic (see Artemov and Fitting 2012) and awareness logic (see Fagin and Halpern 1988) should be mentioned in this respect. However, for our present purpose we find it more appropriate to frame our proposal in terms of a framework for interrogative (question-based) belief revision (Enqvist 2009; 2011). The idea is to extend our vocabulary with the means to speak about research agendas, that is, sets of propositions that an agent is focusing on.

The most straightforward way to represent research agendas would be to extend the language with expressions of the form

$$(X1, ..., X_n)?$$

where $X_1, ..., X_n$ are sentences of our formal language. The interpretation of such an expression is that the question represented by the set of potential answers $X_1, \ldots, X_n$ is on the agent's research agenda. To give a semantics for this language, we could extend the models of the logic we started with by a representation of the research agenda. The natural way to do that would be to identify the agent's agenda at a world w with a collection *Agenda(w)* of sets of subsets of W (the set of all possible worlds). Each member Q of the agenda would be a set of subsets of W, and each X in Q would be a set of possible worlds that represents some proposition. We could then say that an expression of the kind $(X_1, \ldots, X_n)$? is true at a world w if and only if the corresponding sets of propositions are in *Agenda* (w). Details can be found in (Enqvist 2009, 2011).

We can now define doubt in the following way:

$$DX =_{\text{def}} \neg BX \wedge \neg B \neg X \wedge (X \wedge \neg X)?$$

In other words, the agent does not believe either X or $\neg X$ and the question whether X or $\neg X$ is on her research agenda. On this characterization, doubt is a state yet one with a dynamic component represented by the reference to a question to be resolved through the process of inquiry.

Returning to our previous example, it is now easy to see how to account for the fact that Alice may doubt whether the outcome of the roll of a die is even without doubting whether it is six. Assuming that there are six possible worlds, the question whether the outcome is an even number partitions W into two sets, both containing three different worlds. By contrast, the question whether the outcome is a six leads to a different partition: one world (six) on one side and five worlds on the other side. These are clearly different questions that, given our definition, do not need to belong to the same agenda. As in our previous analysis, we may supplement this analysis with a notion of degree of belief. A strong doubt in X would be represented as doubting that X, in the sense just defined, with the addition that X is assigned a low probability. Finally, on both analyses of doubt, doubting that X does not come out as the simple negation of believing that X.

A further objection may be raised which is considerably more difficult to address. What about two sentences that represent the same propositions but have different linguistic forms? Sentences such as "the outcome is an odd number" and "the outcome is either one or a prime number different from two" are made true by the same epistemic alternatives in our example, that is, they are coextensive. In our framework we cannot distinguish between these sentences and therefore we cannot doubt one without also doubting the other. This point would require a further refinement where questions are not represented by sets of propositions but by their syntactic form, that is, by the sentences that express them.

A similar problem is well-known in epistemic logic: that of "logical omniscience." Briefly put, in the basic framework of epistemic logic, an agent is required to know every logical consequence of propositions he or she knows, which implies that, when two sentences are coextensive, he or she knows both or neither. Solutions to this problem have been proposed in different forms (see Fagin et al. 1995). For instance, the aforementioned justification and awareness logics may be of relevance in this connection. Making headway on this issue would require further refinements of our framework and is outside the scope of this chapter.

5   Conclusion

Our point of departure was this observation: while the concepts of ignorance and doubt occupy central roles in epistemology as well as in philosophy generally, there have been surprisingly few attempts to give detailed analyses of these notions and to show how they differ, if at all. We raised the further question whether ignorance and doubt are simply the negations of knowledge and belief, respectively. To get clearer on these matters, we undertook to identify the main conceptual ingredients of ignorance and doubt, relying on pre-systematic considerations from C. S. Peirce and P. Thagard. This investigation informed a semi-formal account of ignorance and doubt within the possible worlds framework of epistemic and doxastic logic.

In response to the first problem, concerning the nature of the target concepts, we noted that while ignorance can be construed as the absence of knowledge of any of the alternatives, doubt is a very special kind of ignorance. We presented two, not necessarily mutually exclusive, proposals for how to capture this special feature in our framework. One centered on the notion of doubt, as opposed to ignorance, requiring maximum plausibility of opposing alternatives. According to the other, which highlighted the goal-relative character of doubt, for an agent to doubt a proposition he or she must entertain the question whether that proposition is true on his or her research agenda, which was here construed as the set of questions that he or she aims to answer. Our inquiry into the nature of ignorance and doubt suggested a solution to our second problem as well: while ignorance and doubt, as those notions are most naturally understood, are closely related to knowledge and belief, respectively, the relationship is less straightforward than one might think, going beyond that of the former being the mere negations of the latter.[13]

[13] The authors would like to thank Rik Peels and Emanuel Rutten for valuable comments on earlier versions of this article.

5   Ignorance and Epistemic Contextualism[1]

Michael Blome-Tillmann

1   Ignorance and Scepticism

In this chapter I shall take ignorance with respect to p to consist in the absence of knowledge whether p. If you don't know whether p – that is, if you neither know that p nor that $\neg p$ –, then you are ignorant as to whether p. The notion of ignorance can, in other words, be reduced to the notion of knowledge. Scepticism in epistemology is the view that we are ignorant about the external world. According to the sceptic, this ignorance is universal and ubiquitous. *Prima facie* convincing arguments have been produced in support of scepticism and a lively philosophical debate has emerged ever since Descartes introduced such an argument in his *Meditations*. This chapter will consider one such argument for our ignorance about the external world and outline how *Epistemic Contextualism* – a contemporary view about the semantics of 'knowledge'-attributions – aims to resolve the threat posed by the argument.

To begin our discussion consider the following argument:

> **Sceptical Argument**
> (i)   If I know that I have hands, then I'm in a position to know that I'm not a handless brain in a vat.
> (ii) I'm not in a position to know that I'm not a handless brain in a vat.
> (iii) I don't know that I have hands.[2]

The above argument is valid: if we accept its premises, we must accept its conclusion, too. Moreover, the above sceptical argument leaves us with

---

[1] I am indebted to Martijn Blaauw, Aidan McGlynn, Rik Peels and René van Woudenberg for discussion and comments on earlier versions of this article. Parts of this paper build on Blome-Tillmann (2015).
[2] Here is a formalized version of the argument, where '*sh*' is shorthand for 'sceptical hypothesis' and where '*op*' ranges over ordinary *p*ropositions about the external world:

(i) $Kp \rightarrow \Diamond K\neg sh.$ –   A
(ii) $\neg \Diamond K\neg sh.$ –   A
(iii) $\neg Kp.$ i, ii   *MT*

a philosophical puzzle: its premises are highly plausible while its conclusion – that we are ignorant with respect to everyday propositions such as the proposition that we have hands – is highly implausible. One way to bring this out in more detail is to consider the negation of its conclusion:

(iv) I know that I have hands.

The propositions (i), (ii) and (iv) form an inconsistent set, and so at least one of them has to be rejected. However, merely rejecting one of the members of our set doesn't amount to a satisfactory resolution of our puzzle. As Stewart Cohen (1988, p. 94) has pointed out, an intellectually satisfying resolution of the sceptical puzzle doesn't merely block the argument by identifying the culprit. Rather, a satisfactory resolution of the sceptical puzzle must, in addition, offer us an explanation of why the false member of the set appeared so plausible at first glance (see also Cohen 1999, p. 63). Why is it that our intuitions about the truth-values of at least one of the propositions at issue are misguided? And what exactly is the mistake we have made when we find ourselves puzzled by the sceptical argument? Epistemic Contextualism (EC) is a recently popular view in epistemology that promises a solution to the puzzle pertaining to our ignorance about the external world.

In what follows I shall, in Section 2, begin our discussion by motivating EC independently of the sceptical puzzle. I shall then, in Section 3, consider evidence for EC and elaborate on the question whether ascriptions of 'ignorance' are context-sensitive. In Section 4 I review the Cartesian sceptical argument, sketch the contextualist's response to that argument in Section 5, and discuss objections to EC and its stance towards closure principles for knowledge in Sections 6 and 7. Section 8 is devoted to criticisms of EC while Section 9 summarizes and concludes the paper.

2   What Is Epistemic Contextualism?

Imagine schoolteacher Jones in the zoo explaining to her class that the animals in the pen are zebras.[3] Tom is unconvinced and challenges Jones: "Are you sure those aren't antelopes?" After Jones has explained the difference between antelopes and zebras, Tom assures his classmates:

(1) She knows that the animals in the pen are zebras.

Has Tom spoken truly? Surely, Jones's epistemic position seems good enough for satisfying the predicate 'knows that the animals in the pen are

---

[3] The following example is derived from the zebra case in Dretske (1970).

zebras' (henceforth 'knows Z'): Jones has visual experiences of a black and white striped horse-like animal, she can discriminate reliably between zebras and antelopes, she has read the sign on the pen that reads 'Zebra Pen' and so on. Thus, Tom's utterance of (1) seems to be a paradigm case of a true 'knowledge' attribution.

Next, imagine a couple, Bill and Kate, walking along. Bill, a would-be postmodernist artist, gives details of his latest ideas: he envisions himself painting mules with white stripes to look like zebras, putting them in the zebra pen of a zoo and thereby fooling visitors. Our couple randomly considers Jones, and Kate claims, at the same time as Tom is asserting (1):

(2) She doesn't know that the animals in the pen are zebras.

In Kate's mind, for Jones to 'know Z', she must have better evidence or reasons in support of Z than are momentarily available to her. In particular, Kate has it that Jones's evidence must eliminate the possibility that the animals in the pen are painted mules. As long as her evidence, however, is neutral with respect to whether or not the animals are cleverly painted mules, Kate claims, Jones doesn't qualify as 'knowing Z'.

What is going on in our little example? According to our intuitions, an utterance of (1) is true in the context of the school class, while an utterance of (2) is true in the context of the artistic couple. Moreover, (2) is the negation of (1): it doesn't differ from (1) except for containing the verbal negation 'doesn't'. And since the personal pronoun 'she' refers in both contexts to Jones, it seems that the schoolteacher satisfies the predicate 'knows Z' in the context of the school class but not so in the context of the artists.

How are we to account for these phenomena? Firstly, note again that Tom and Kate are talking about one and the same person – Jones – at exactly the same time. Thus, we cannot resolve the situation by claiming, for instance, that Jones 'knows Z' in one context but not the other because she believes Z in one context but not in the other. Similarly, we cannot plausibly respond that Jones has certain visual experiences in one context that she is lacking in the other, or that she has the ability to discriminate reliably between certain scenarios in one context but not the other, or, finally, that she has read the sign on the zebra pen in one context but not in the other. All factors pertaining to the subject are identical with respect to both contexts, as the speakers in both contexts – Tom and Kate – are talking about one and the same subject at one and the same time.[4]

---

[4] Similarly, it follows that we cannot plausibly explain the phenomena by pointing out that Jones is in a different practical situation (has different practical interests, for instance) with

Thus, what the above example suggests is that the mentioned factors – Jones's visual experiences, her discriminatory abilities and so on – are sufficient for her to satisfy 'knows Z' in one context, but not so in the other. And it is this view that *epistemic contextualism* (EC) takes at face value: how strong one's *epistemic position* towards p must be for one to satisfy 'know(s) p' may vary with the context of utterance. In the artists' conversational context, Jones needs to be in a stronger epistemic position – she needs more evidence in support of Z – than in the school class's conversational context in order for her to satisfy 'knows Z'. In fact, some contextualists describe the situation by claiming that contexts of utterance are governed by so-called *epistemic standards*.[5] Given this terminology, the epistemic standards in our example are lower in the context of the school class than in the context of the artists' conversation. In fact, in the former context, the standards are low enough for Jones to satisfy 'knows Z', while in the latter they are too high: Jones does not, in the artists' context, satisfy 'knows Z' but, rather, satisfies 'does not know Z'. Now, the notion of an epistemic standard can be explicated in a number of different ways. On the most popular way, which is inspired by *relevant alternatives* approaches to contextualism, epistemic standards are said to be higher in the school class's context because, as David Lewis (1996) puts it, satisfying 'knows Z' in that context does not require the elimination of the possibility that the animals are painted mules, while this is required in the context of the postmodernist artists: more alternatives must be eliminated in the context with the higher standards than in the context with the lower standards.

Given the hypothesized context-sensitivity of the predicate 'know(s) p', it is in general possible that a subject satisfies the predicate in one conversational context but does not do so in another, or, in other words, that somebody in a given context speaks truly when uttering a sentence of the form 'x knows p' while somebody in a different context speaks falsely when uttering the very same sentence – even though both speakers are speaking about the same subject x at the same time of utterance t. Epistemic contextualism is, as a consequence, a linguistic or a semantic view – namely, the view that 'knowledge'-ascriptions – sentences of the form 'x knows p' – may express different propositions in different contexts of utterance. According to EC, 'knowledge'-ascriptions are, as Stanley

respect to the two contexts: she isn't. This fact about the above example provides problems for so-called *Subject-Sensitive Invariantist* accounts of knowledge. See, for instance, Fantl and McGrath (2002), Hawthorne (2004), Stanley (2005).

[5] Cf. Cohen (1988), DeRose (1995), Lewis (1996).

(2005, p. 17) puts it, context-sensitive in a distinctively epistemological way: the content of a sentence *S* containing the predicate 'know(s) *p*' can change with context, independently of whether *S* contains further index-icals, is ambiguous, or is context-sensitive in any other way.

In a first approximation, we can thus define 'epistemic contextualism' as follows:

> (EC′) Knowledge ascriptions may express different propositions relative to different contexts of utterance, where this difference is traceable to the occurrence of 'know(s) *p*' and concerns a distinctively epistemic factor.

Given semantic compositionality – the view that the content or semantic value of complex expressions is a function of its ultimate constituents and the way in which they are combined – (EC′) entails (EC):

> (EC) The content of the predicate 'know(s) *p*' may vary with the context of utterance in a distinctly epistemic way.

According to EC, the predicate 'know(s) *p*' *adds* context-sensitivity to a sentence it occurs in, and this context-sensitivity is distinctly epistemic – that is, it goes over and above the context-sensitivity that the verb con-tributes to the sentence by virtue of its tense.[6]

The exact details as to how to semantically model the context-sensitivity of 'know(s) *p*' shall not concern us in this chapter. However, it is worth noting that EC is not a lexical ambiguity theory – that is, it does not claim that 'know(s) *p*' is assigned multiple conventional meanings in English, as are the lexically ambiguous expressions 'bank' or 'orange'. On the contrary, contextualists have commonly compared 'know(s) *p*' to indexical expres-sions, such as 'I', 'that' and 'today', or to gradable adjectives, such as 'flat' and 'empty': these expressions are widely taken to have only one conven-tional meaning – what Kaplan (1989) calls their 'character' – but different contents or semantic values in suitably different contexts of utterance.

While there are several distinct ways to semantically model the context-sensitivity of 'know(s) *p*', contextualists have often stressed an analogy between the semantics of 'know(s) *p*' and the semantics of gradable adjectives such as 'flat', 'empty' or 'tall': just as what counts as satisfying 'flat', 'empty' or 'tall' may vary with context, contextualists have argued, what counts as satisfying 'know(s) *p*' may vary with context, too.[7] Given this analogy, EC can be construed as claiming that (1) and (2) in our example in this section stand in a relation similar to the relation between

[6] Cf. Schaffer and Szabó (2014) for the definition of EC in this section.
[7] For this analogy see Unger (1975), DeRose (1995), Lewis (1996), Cohen (1999, 2004).

a basketball coach's utterance of 'MB-T isn't tall' and a jockey coach's utterance of 'MB-T is tall': while the surface syntax of these sentences suggests a contradiction, the propositions expressed are compatible, as the semantic value of 'tall' changes with the context of utterance. Ordinary usage of 'tall' and 'know' seem to be similar: both expressions seem to be context-sensitive.[8]

Before moving on, consider the question whether the predicate 'is ignorant' in English is context-sensitive. According to what we may call the standard account of ignorance, ignorance with respect to p is the absence of knowledge whether p. Thus, on the standard account, (3) is synonymous with (4):

(3) *S is ignorant with respect to p.*

(4) *S neither knows that p nor that ¬p.*

Now, given EC, the truth-conditions of (4) vary with the context of ascription in a specifically epistemic way. If (3) is synonymous with (4), however, it also follows that the truth-conditions of (3) vary with the context of ascription in a specifically epistemic way. Given the standard account of ignorance, contextualism about 'knowledge' entails contextualism about 'ignorance'.

It is noteworthy, however, that the entailment from contextualism about 'knowledge' to contextualism about 'ignorance' does not hold on certain alternative accounts of the semantics of 'ignorance'. According to the absence-of-true-belief account championed by Goldman (1986, p. 36) and Peels (2010), for instance, 'ignorance'-attributions of the form in (3) are to be analysed as in

(5) *S doesn't believe truly that p.*

On this view of the semantics of 'ignorance', the verb 'is ignorant' is not context-sensitive in a specifically epistemic way. Ignorance, on the view at hand, just boils down to the absence of true belief and is, in fact, an entirely non-epistemic notion. Thus, whether 'ignorance'-attributions are context-sensitive in a specifically epistemic way depends partly on their semantic relations to 'knowledge'-attributions. In what follows I shall assume what I have called the standard view about ignorance and sketch the contextualist's response to arguments for our universal ignorance about the external world.

---

[8] Not all contextualists endorse the analogy to gradable adjectives (see, for instance, Schaffer and Szabó (2014), but it is at this point helpful in illustrating the general concept of context-sensitivity underlying the view.

3   Evidence for Contextualism

The main evidence for EC derives from our intuitions about the truth-values of 'knowledge'-ascriptions in examples such as the above zebra case. However, there are further, more familiar examples that have been presented in support of EC in the literature. Consider, for instance, Stewart Cohen's (1999, p. 58) *Airport Case*:

Mary and John are at the L.A. airport contemplating taking a certain flight to New York. They want to know whether the flight has a layover in Chicago. They overhear someone ask a passenger, Smith, if he knows whether the flight stops in Chicago. Smith looks at the flight itinerary he got from the travel agent and responds, 'Yes I know – it does stop in Chicago.' It turns out that Mary and John have a very important business contact they have to make at the Chicago airport. Mary says, 'How reliable is that itinerary? It could contain a misprint. They could have changed the schedule at the last minute.' Mary and John agree that Smith doesn't really know that the plane will stop in Chicago. They decide to check with the airline agent.

As Cohen's example suggests, the sentence 'Smith knows that the flight stops over in Chicago' seems true as uttered in Smith's context but false as uttered in Mary's and John's context. Moreover, it seems as though the practical interests and goals of the conversational participants or how high the stakes are with regard to the proposition that the flight will stop over in Chicago influence the respective contexts' epistemic standards, and thus whether Smith satisfies 'knows': in Smith's own context he satisfies 'knows that the flight will stop over in Chicago', but in Mary's and John's context, where the stakes are significantly higher, he doesn't.

Here is another example reinforcing this point – namely, Keith DeRose's (1992) famous *Bank Cases*, as presented by Stanley (2005, pp. 3–4):

Low Stakes
Hannah and her wife Sarah are driving home on a Friday afternoon. They plan to stop at the bank on the way home to deposit their paychecks. It is not important that they do so, as they have no impending bills. But as they drive past the bank, they notice that the lines inside are very long, as they often are on Friday afternoons. Realizing that it isn't very important that their paychecks are deposited right away, Hannah says, "I know the bank will be open tomorrow, since I was there just two weeks ago on Saturday morning. So we can deposit our paychecks tomorrow morning."

High Stakes
Hannah and her wife Sarah are driving home on a Friday afternoon. They plan to stop at the bank on the way home to deposit their paychecks. Since they have an impending bill coming due, and very little in their account, it is very important that they deposit their paychecks by Saturday. Hannah notes that she was at the

bank two weeks before on a Saturday morning, and it was open. But, as Sarah points out, banks do change their hours. Hannah says, 'I guess you're right. I don't know that the bank will be open tomorrow.'

Similar to Cohen's example, DeRose's case suggests that it is more difficult to satisfy 'knows' in a context in which the stakes are higher: in *Low Stakes* Hannah satisfies 'knows that the bank will be open tomorrow', whereas in *High Stakes* she does not, even though she is in exactly the same epistemic position in both cases. And, again, the defender of EC argues that the difference in our intuitions in the two bank cases is due to the fact that the relevant 'knowledge'-ascriptions are made in different conversational contexts: in the context of *High Stakes*, the argument goes, it is considerably more difficult to satisfy 'knows that the bank is open on Saturday' than it is in the context of *Low Stakes*.[9]

The above examples and others like them have attracted a large amount of critical attention in recent years. Note, for instance, that the argument in support of EC emerging from the above data amounts to an inference to the best explanation: in evaluating the support EC receives from the examples, we must therefore compare EC's account of the data with competing explanations of rival theories. Such comparisons of explanatory virtue in philosophy, however, are usually rather difficult and complicated. A further challenge to EC's account of the above data pertains to the data's evidential status: some practitioners of experimental philosophy have, in recent studies, aimed to undermine the contextualists' case by arguing that the professional philosopher's intuitions about the above cases do not coincide with the intuitions of the more general public. While the above issues present interesting and legitimate challenges to EC, we shall, in this article, leave them to one side and focus our attention on a topic that is commonly taken to provide an important philosophical motivation for EC: sceptical puzzles.[10]

Before moving on to the issue of sceptical puzzles, however, let us briefly consider the question whether examples of the above type can be employed in determining whether ascriptions of 'ignorance' are context-sensitive. One immediate worry with respect to the relevant examples

---

[9] Note that since the relevant 'knowledge'-ascriptions in DeRose's bank cases as presented above are made from the first person perspective – they are so-called *self-ascriptions* – the data from DeRose's example are not suited to support EC over certain rival accounts such as *Subject-Sensitive Invariantism* (SSI): according to SSI, whether one knows *p* depends in part on one's own and thus the subject's (as opposed to the ascriber's) epistemic standards (see Hawthorne (2004); Stanley (2005); Fantl and McGrath (2009) for versions of this view). A straightforward subject-sensitive invariantist explanation, however, is not available for Cohen's Airport Case and the Zebra Case in paragraph 1 of this paper.

[10] See DeRose (2011) for a critical discussion of some experimental philosophy papers in the area.

concerns the idiomaticity of 'ignorance'-ascriptions in examples such as High Stakes. It would, I take it, seem somewhat odd for Hannah in High Stakes to assert:

> (6) I guess you're right. I'm ignorant as to whether the bank will be open tomorrow.

Despite the non-idiomaticity of (6), however, it should be noted that (6) doesn't appear outright false as uttered by Hannah in High Stakes. In fact, I take it that our intuitions are rather firmly leaning towards the view that it expresses a truth – despite being somewhat clumsy. Whatever the consequences of these data are for the potential context-sensitivity of 'is ignorant', it should be noted that our amended version of High Stakes spells significant trouble for the absence-of-true-belief account of ignorance mentioned earlier. Remember that, according to Goldman (1986, p. 36) and Peels (2010), one is ignorant with respect to p just in case one doesn't believe truly that p. It then follows that Hannah's utterance of (6) in High Stakes expresses a falsehood, for Hannah believes, we may assume, that the bank won't be open tomorrow.[11] But such a verdict is clearly not confirmed by the data. Moreover, note that, given the absence-of-true-belief account of ignorance, Hannah's utterance of (6)'s negation – that is, her utterance of 'I am not ignorant as to whether the bank will be open tomorrow' – shouldn't seem false in High Stakes: according to the absence-of-true-belief account, such an utterance expresses the truth that Hannah believes truly that the bank will be open tomorrow. It is not a trivial task for the defender of the absence-of-true-belief account to explain the datum that Hannah's utterance of (6)'s negation appears false in High Stakes. In summary, it is doubtful whether the absence-of-true-belief account of ignorance is confirmed by the data emerging from amending the above cases to involve ascriptions of 'ignorance'.[12]

4   Cartesian Sceptical Puzzles

We have seen so far that EC receives some *prima facie* support from certain linguistic data – namely, the examples discussed in the previous

---

[11] Hannah believes that the bank won't be open tomorrow, even though she does not outright believe it: she believes that the bank won't be open tomorrow while at the same time believing that she doesn't know that proposition. Those who disagree that Hannah believes that the bank will be open tomorrow can consider the third person ascription from Section 2 with respect to which there is no doubt that the subject believes the proposition in question.

[12] Other troublesome examples for the absence-of-true-belief account include lottery-style examples, in which there is a strong intuition that the subject is ignorant as to whether her ticket is a loser, despite the fact that she truly believes that it is a loser.

sections. Traditionally, however, contextualists have also claimed that besides the above empirical evidence in favour of their views there is also an independent, philosophical motivation for EC. More specifically, contextualists have argued that the context-sensitivity of 'know(s) p' suggested by the above examples provides us with an attractive resolution of sceptical puzzles.

To begin our discussion of the contextualist response to scepticism, reconsider the sceptical argument, reproduced here from Section 1:

Sceptical Argument
(i) If I know that I have hands, then I'm in a position to know that I'm not a handless brain in a vat.
(ii) I'm not in a position to know that I'm not a handless brain in a vat.
(iv) I don't know that I have hands.

Note again that the argument is valid: if we accept its premises, we must accept its conclusion, too. Moreover, together with the eminently plausible (iv), the argument constitutes a paradox:

(v) I know that I have hands.

The propositions (i), (ii) and (iv) form an inconsistent set; and so at least one of them has to be rejected. But which one are we to reject, and on what grounds? What exactly is the mistake we have made when we find ourselves puzzled by the Sceptical Argument?

5   The Contextualist Solution to Sceptical Puzzles

The traditional contextualist's response to the sceptical puzzle is to claim that the Sceptical Argument is unsound in conversational contexts that are governed by our moderate everyday epistemic standards but sound in contexts with artificially high, sceptical epistemic standards.[13] In everyday contexts, the argument goes, I satisfy 'knows that he isn't a handless brain in a vat' and premise (ii) of the sceptical argument expresses a falsehood: if I satisfy, in ordinary contexts, 'knows that he isn't a handless brain in a vat', then I also satisfy, in ordinary contexts, 'is in a position to know that he's not a handless brain in a vat'. Consequently, the Sceptical Argument is unsound in ordinary contexts, and its conclusion doesn't follow: relative to ordinary contexts, I satisfy

---

[13] The following is a description of standard contextualist views on sceptical puzzles, as it can be found – more or less explicitly – in all major writings of contextualists. See, for instance, DeRose (1995) and Cohen (1999).

'knows that he has hands' and the conclusion of the sceptical argument expresses a falsehood.

However, as indicated already, things are different in so-called sceptical contexts in which we practice epistemology and consider and discuss sceptical scenarios such as the brain-in-a-vat scenario. In such contexts, the argument goes, the epistemic standards are considerably higher – in fact, outrageously high – to the effect that premise (ii) expresses a truth in such contexts. For instance, contextualists have argued that because sceptical possibilities are epistemically relevant in sceptical contexts, premise (ii) of the Sceptical Argument expresses a truth: sceptical possibilities are, after all, uneliminated by our evidence, and we therefore do not, in sceptical contexts in which they are relevant, satisfy the predicate 'is in a position to know that she or he is not a handless brain in a vat'. Consequently, when the sceptic asserts, in her sceptical context, 'MB-T doesn't know that he has hands', she asserts a truth. However, it is crucial to emphasize that the truth of the sceptic's assertion does not affect the truth-values of my positive 'knowledge'-ascriptions in ordinary contexts.

To illustrate this view further, it is worth noting that traditional contextualists aim to resolve the tensions between our anti-sceptical intuitions on the one hand and the intuition that sceptical arguments are sound (and their conclusions, therefore, true) on the other. We can represent these intuitions as follows:

Anti-Sceptical Intuition (ASI)
People often speak truly when they assert 'I know p'.

Sceptical Intuition (SI)
People sometimes speak truly when they assert 'Nobody knows p' in contexts in which sceptical arguments are discussed.

The traditional contextualist claims that both of these intuitions are correct and only seemingly contradictory: they are correct because the semantic value of 'know(s) p' varies with the context of utterance; so when we claim in everyday contexts that we 'know p', our utterances are not in contradiction to our utterance of 'Nobody knows p' in sceptical contexts. Thus, it is crucial to note that, according to the traditional contextualist, it is not (iv) which is shown to be true or (iii) which is shown to be false. Rather, the traditional contextualist emphasizes that our sceptical and anti-sceptical intuitions are exclusively intuitions about the truth-values of *utterance tokens*, which are by their very nature situated in particular conversational contexts. Our intuitions are not about the truth-values of sentences as considered more or less in the abstract in a philosophical essay or discussion. Once we appreciate this point and take into account the context-sensitivity of 'knowledge'-attributions, the sceptical puzzle is – the traditional contextualist argues – easily dissolved: the argument is sound in contexts with exceedingly high or sceptical epistemic standards, but unsound in contexts with ordinary or everyday epistemic standards.

6   Error Theory and Contextual Shifts

An important question arises at this point: if the semantic value of 'know' can in fact change in a way allowing for both (ASI) and (SI) to be true, why, then, are we initially puzzled by sceptical arguments? Shouldn't we be somehow sensitive to or aware of the context-sensitivity of 'know(s) p' and avoid making the mistake the contextualist ascribes to us? If EC is true, why, in other words, are sceptical arguments puzzling in the first place?

To account for the puzzling nature of sceptical arguments, the contextualist is committed to the view that we sometimes lose sight of the context-sensitivity of epistemic terms, and in particular that we do so when confronted with sceptical arguments.[14] Therefore, according to the traditional contextualist, we do not recognize that the sceptical conclusion is true in the context of discussions of sceptical arguments while false in everyday contexts. Thus, the traditional contextualist argues that, when we are puzzled by sceptical arguments, we fail to realize that the propositions expressed by the arguments' conclusions are perfectly compatible with the propositions expressed by our everyday 'knowledge'-claims. Contextualists accordingly pair their semantics of 'know(s) p' with the view that we are sometimes unaware of or tend to overlook the context-sensitivity of 'know(s) p'. Stephen Schiffer, in an important paper criticizing this view, aptly calls this element of standard contextualism its *error theory* (see Schiffer 1996). Ultimately, it is, of course, entirely due to this error theory that EC can claim to be able to account for both the plausibility of sceptical arguments and our intuition that our everyday 'knowledge'-ascriptions express truths.

We shall return to the plausibility of EC's error theory later on in this chapter (in Section 7). In the meantime, however, note that the contextualist's resolution of sceptical puzzles makes crucial use of the intuitive notion of a shift in or variation of epistemic standards between contexts. It is important to note at this point, however, that arguing for the context-sensitivity of 'know(s) p' on the basis of the claim that the Bank Case, the Airport Case and our Zebra Case involve contextual variation of epistemic standards is one thing, while claiming that epistemic standards are 'shifty' in precisely the way required for a resolution of sceptical puzzles is

---

[14] Cf. Cohen (1988, p. 106); DeRose (1995, p. 40).

quite a different proposition. In fact, for the contextualist's resolution of sceptical puzzles to be credible, we need to be told more about what exactly the mechanisms underlying contextual shifts and variations are. In other words, we need to be told more about what epistemic standards are and how they are determined by context: why is it that epistemic standards are high in so-called sceptical contexts, and why are they lower in everyday situations?

Different contextualists have different stories to tell about what epistemic standards are and about how they shift and vary. But it is fair to say that the original approaches defended by early contextualists (such as DeRose [1995] and Lewis [1996]) are highly problematic and must be refined and amended substantially before we can grant the contextualist that her view offers a resolution of sceptical puzzles. However, a detailed discussion of the more recent literature on epistemic standards is beyond the scope of this chapter.[15]

7   Closure

Another important aspect of the contextualist resolution of sceptical puzzles to be mentioned here is that the contextualist resolves sceptical puzzles while fully respecting our intuition that one can extend one's knowledge by competent deduction. To see what I have in mind here, consider the following principle, which is familiar under the label *Single-Premise Closure*:

> (CL) If x knows p and x knows that p entails q, then x is in a position to know q.

Here is an instance of (CL) for illustration: if, firstly, I know that the animal outside my window is a fox and if, secondly, I know that its being a fox entails that it's not a cat, then I am also in a position to know that the animal outside my window is not a cat. Of course, I am in a position to know that latter proposition because I can competently deduce it from (i) my knowledge that the animal is a fox and (ii) my knowledge that its being a fox entails that it is not a cat. Single-premise closure captures fairly precisely the intuition that one can extend one's knowledge by means of deductive reasoning.

---

[15] Lewis's (1996) 'Rule of Attention' and DeRose's (1995) 'Rule of Sensitivity' offer accounts of contextual shifts that, on the face of it, are useful for the resolution of sceptical puzzles, but that turn out to be problematic for independent reasons. For criticism of DeRose's approach, see Blome-Tillmann (2009a), and for a refinement of Lewis's relevant alternatives approach to contextualism that avoids a number of problems, see Blome-Tillmann (2009b, 2014).

Now, while some epistemologists have argued that giving a response to the sceptic requires us to give up (CL), the contextualist resolution gets by without any such move.[16] How does the contextualist avoid rejecting closure? Note that, according to EC, every semantic value that the verb 'knows' can express in a given context is, loosely speaking, closed under 'known' entailment. Here is a more precise and contextualized formulation of the single-premise principle to illustrate the idea:

> (CLC) If x satisfies 'knows p' in context C and satisfies 'knows that p entails q' in C, then x is in a position to satisfy 'knows q' in C.

(CLC) is a meta-linguistic principle. Loosely speaking, (CLC) says that (CL), its non-contextualized cousin, expresses a truth as long as the conversational context is kept fixed.[17] Thus, unlike Nozick (1981) and Dretske (1970), who reject (CL) in giving a response to the sceptic, the contextualist, by ascending semantically, merely modifies and clarifies (CL) in a way that respects our intuitions about the validity of the closure principle. Contextualists have traditionally taken this to be a great comparative advantage of their theories over epistemological theories that advocate closure failure.

8   Criticisms of Contextualism

Epistemic contextualism has been criticized for a number of reasons. In this paper, we shall focus on two criticisms of EC that have figured most prominently in the recent literature. Firstly, Ernest Sosa has wondered what the epistemological relevance of contextualism is, given that EC is a linguistic view – that is, a view about the predicate 'know(s) p' and its content rather than about knowledge. Considering the contextualist's resolution of sceptical puzzles sketched above, this worry may appear

---

[16] Note also that the sceptic uses (CL) when motivating premise (i) of her argument: she reasons from the assumption that I know that my having a hand entails that I am not a handless brain in a vat to the conclusion that if I know that I have a hand, then I am in a position to know that I am not a handless brain in a vat, i.e., to premise (i) of the *Sceptical Argument*. The precise reasoning is as follows:

Closure Argument for (i)
(1) $(Kp \land K(p \to \neg sh)) \to \Diamond K \neg sh.$ from CL
(2) $K(p \to \neg sh) \to (Kp \to \Diamond K \neg sh).$ 1   *Exp*
(3) $K(p \to \neg sh). -$ A
   (i) $Kp \to \Diamond K \neg sh.$ 2, 3   *MP*

Note that there are other ways to motivate (i), but I shall ignore them in this paper (see, for instance, Brueckner [1994]).

[17] See DeRose (1995); Lewis (1996); Cohen (1999).

somewhat surprising. However, Sosa thinks that EC, even though true, has only little epistemological relevance, if any at all:

> The main thesis of [EC] has considerable plausibility as a thesis in linguistics or in philosophy of language. In applying it to epistemology, however, it is possible to overreach ... (Sosa 2011, p. 98)

What, then, is Sosa's objection? To see what Sosa has in mind, let us introduce some technical language. Let 'KE' express the content of 'know' in *everyday* contexts and let 'KS' express the content of 'know' in *sceptical* contexts. Now consider (7), which we derive from (ASI) by disquotation:

(7) People often speak truly when they assert that they know p.

Depending on whether the epistemic standards of our present context are those of everyday contexts or those of sceptical contexts (7) expresses the content of either 0 or (9):

(8) People often speak truly when they assert that they KE p.

(9) People often speak truly when they assert that they KS p.

Since Sosa assumes that contexts of epistemological enquiry are inevitably sceptical contexts, Sosa thinks that (7), in the context of this article, expresses the proposition expressed by (9). Now, the alleged problem for EC is that (9) is clearly false, for it suggests that people in quotidian contexts assert that they KS p. However, when people in quotidian contexts use the word 'know', its semantic value is always KE rather than KS. Thus, Sosa complains that contextualists convey a falsehood, when they assert (7) in a context of epistemological discussion.

   How serious an objection is this to EC? The obvious reply to Sosa's objection is, of course, that the contextualist ought to distinguish more carefully between the mention and the use of 'know' and thus only assert (ASI) instead of the disquoted (7): Sosa's objection rests on a conflation of the use/mention-distinction.[18] Moreover, it is worthwhile noting that more recent contextualists have developed accounts according to which contexts of philosophical and epistemological enquiry are by no means automatically sceptical contexts.[19] On these more moderate views (7), in the context of this paper, expresses the content of 0 rather than that of (9), and I therefore speak truly when, in the context of this paper and the epistemology classroom more generally, asserting (7). As a consequence,

---

[18] See Blome-Tillmann (2007) for more details on this line of reasoning.
[19] See Blome-Tillmann (2009b, 2014) and Ichikawa (2011a, 2011b).

there are several ways the contextualist can respond to Sosa's charge that EC is epistemologically irrelevant.

Another recently influential type of objection to EC proceeds by highlighting disparities between certain linguistic properties of 'know-(s) p' on the one hand and more recognized context-sensitive expressions on the other. Remember that, for instance, contextualists compare 'know(s) p' to gradable adjectives, such as 'flat', 'empty' and 'tall'. However, as Jason Stanley (2005, chapter 2) has pointed out, 'know(s) p' has very different syntactic properties from gradable adjectives: as Stanley shows in great detail, 'know(s) p' is not syntactically gradable and doesn't accept a large number of constructions that gradable adjectives can be felicitously combined with. Similarly, it has been pointed out that our semantic blindness towards the context-sensitivity of 'know(s) p' – discussed above under the label of EC's *error theory* – is not observed in connection with recognized indexicals such as 'I', 'here' and 'today'. This fact is illustrated by the following principle:

> (10) If an English speaker E sincerely utters a sentence S of the form 'A knows that p', and the sentence in the that-clause means that p and 'A' is a name or indexical that refers to a, then E believes of a that a knows that p, and expresses that belief by S.

As John Hawthorne (2004, p. 101) points out, (10) seems entirely natural. But, of course, (10) is false if 'know(s) p' is context-sensitive: since E's context might be governed by epistemic standards that are different from those operative in this paper, the disquotation of 'knows' in (10) is illegitimate. Since the possibility of an asymmetry between E's and our own epistemic standards is largely hidden from competent speakers, the contextualist must accept that the context-sensitivity of 'knows' is non-obvious: it is not as readily detected by competent speakers as the context-sensitivity of core indexicals.

Interestingly, however, similar phenomena are not observed with respect to 'I'. Consider (11), a disquotation principle for 'I':

> (11) If an English speaker E sincerely utters a sentence S of the form 'I am hungry', then E believes that I am hungry, and expresses that belief by S.

Clearly, it is not the case that every English speaker who utters 'I am hungry' believes that I, MB-T, am hungry.

What is worth emphasizing in response to Hawthorne's worry, however, is that the gradable adjectives 'flat' and 'empty' display somewhat similar behaviour with respect to disquotation. Consider the following disquotation principles for 'flat' and 'empty':

> (12) If an English speaker E sincerely utters a sentence S of the form 'A is flat', and 'A' is a name or indexical that refers to a, then E believes of a that a is flat, and expresses that belief by S.

> (13) If an English speaker E sincerely utters a sentence S of the form 'A is empty', and 'A' is a name or indexical that refers to a, then E believes of a that a is empty, and expresses that belief by S.

As the intuitive plausibility of (12) and (13) demonstrates, the context-sensitivity of 'flat' and 'empty' is just as non-obvious or hidden from competent speakers as the context-sensitivity of 'knows'. Thus, on the assumption that gradable adjectives are in fact context-sensitive, the context-sensitivity of 'know(s) p' has been shown to be no more puzzling or mysterious than the comparatively humdrum context-sensitivity of 'flat' and 'empty'. It is due to data such as these that there is a growing consensus in the literature that the semantic blindness objection is not all that damaging to contextualism.

Finally, it is worth emphasizing that, even if 'know(s) p' varies in certain linguistic respects – whether semantic, syntactic or pragmatic – from other recognized context-sensitive expressions, it is not clear whether the contextualist should be worried about such a discovery. For why shouldn't we accept that 'know(s) p' is linguistically exceptional? Let us not forget, after all, that 'know(s) p' combines a number of fairly interesting and unique properties: 'know(s) p' is a factive verb that accepts a sentential complement, and its satisfaction at a context is, arguably, the norm of assertion, practical reasoning, and belief at that context.[20] Moreover, 'know(s) p' gives rise to sceptical puzzles, which surely makes the predicate rather unique. This combination of properties is no doubt unique, and we should therefore not expect 'know(s) p' to function in each and every linguistic respect exactly like other context-sensitive expressions. Thus, if EC should in fact commit us to the uniqueness of 'know', then this shouldn't worry us too much, as long as a coherent, illuminating and systematic account of this uniqueness can be given.

---

[20] See Blome-Tillmann (2013, 2014) for a discussion of the knowledge norms in a contextualist account.

9   Conclusion

In summary, epistemic contextualism not only offers an interesting approach to sceptical puzzles but is also motivated by a large set of empirical data. To be sure, the philosophical jury is still out on epistemic contextualism: the view is, after all, still rather contentious and hotly debated in the literature. However, it is undeniable that EC is nowadays rather popular, not only amongst epistemologists but also amongst philosophers more generally.[21] And as we begin to achieve an increasingly better understanding of natural language semantics in general and linguistic context-sensitivity in particular, contextualists may hope that EC will someday become one of the progressively more standard views in philosophy. At least to the author's mind, the prospects are rather bright that EC will one day be considered as making a lasting and important contribution to our understanding of scepticism and sceptical puzzles.

---

[21] See Chalmers et al. (2014), whose data suggest that EC is the most widely accepted view in the semantics of 'knowledge'-attributions.

6   Anti-Intellectualism and Ignorance

Jessica Brown

1   Introduction

Two of our most important sources of knowledge are testimony and memory. Thus, it would be problematic for any view of knowledge if it were in tension with the idea that these sources yield knowledge. For, it would leave us much more ignorant than we ordinarily take ourselves to be. But, this is precisely the objection levelled against anti-intellectualism on which whether a subject knows that p depends not only on traditional truth-conducive factors but also on the stakes for her. Suppose that a subject, Hi, is in a high stakes context and so, by anti-intellectualism, needs a very strong epistemic position in order to know that p. As a result, even if a subject in a low stakes context, Lo, knows that p and testifies that p to Hi, Hi might not thereby acquire knowledge. Further, it seems that, on an anti-intellectualist view, Hi ought to check whether there is a problematic difference of stakes between herself and Lo. But, it has been claimed that hearers do not exhibit any such stakes-sensitivity. In this way, anti-intellectualism has been thought to make it problematic how we gain knowledge by memory and testimony and leaves us much more ignorant than we ordinarily take ourselves to be.

In this chapter, I defend anti-intellectualism against this objection. In Section 2, I consider the objection that anti-intellectualism is incompatible with intuitive principles concerning the transmission of knowledge. In response, I will argue that the allegedly intuitive principles are in fact very controversial, and that anti-intellectualism may well be compatible with plausible formulations of transmission principles. In Section 3, I turn to the distinct objection that our testimonial and memorial practices do not exhibit the kind of sensitivity to stakes which would be required if anti-intellectualism were true. I argue that there is a plausible reading of the sensitivity requirement which is compatible with anti-intellectualism and

Thanks to audiences at Cambridge, Copenhagen and Vienna for useful discussion of versions of this paper and to Cohen, Egan, Sosa, Weatherson and colleagues at St. Andrews for useful comments.

imposes no more work on producers and consumers than would likely be imposed on them by the rival intellectualist view (Sections 4–6). I conclude that, despite its popularity, the objection that anti-intellectualism is incompatible with our practices of testimony and memory is incorrect.

2   A Clash with Intuitive Principles for Transmission?

According to anti-intellectualism about knowledge, whether a subject knows a proposition p depends not only on truth-conducive factors but also on the stakes for her. Thus, of two subjects who both truly believe a proposition on the same basis, only one of the subjects may know the proposition because of a difference in the stakes they face (e.g., see Fantl and McGrath 2002, 2009; Hawthorne 2004; Stanley 2005; Weatherson 2011). It has been argued that anti-intellectualism is inconsistent with intuitive principles governing the way we acquire knowledge by testimony and memory, or 'transmission principles'. For instance, MacFarlane (2005) complains that anti-intellectualism is inconsistent with the following principle governing the transmission of knowledge by testimony:

> T) If B knows that p, then if B asserts that p and A accepts B's testimony without doxastic irresponsibility, then A knows that p[1].

MacFarlane explains that in T), 'without doxastic irresponsibility' is 'meant to exclude cases in which A disregards evidence for the falsity of the speaker's claim or the untrustworthiness of the speaker' (p. 133). For the purposes of later argument, it is important to note that the negative requirement that one not disregard evidence of falsity or untrustworthiness does not amount to the positive requirement that one have positive reasons to trust the testifier, or testimony in general.

MacFarlane argues that anti-intellectualism is incompatible with T) by considering a case in which a speaker, Lo, in a low stakes situation testifies to a hearer, Hi, in a high stakes situation. Suppose that Lo knows that p on the basis of evidence which the anti-intellectualist holds is sufficient for knowledge in Lo's low stakes situation but would not be sufficient for knowledge if Lo instead faced the high stakes in fact faced by Hi. Suppose that Lo testifies that p to Hi who accepts what Lo says without doxastic irresponsibility. By T), it follows that Hi knows that p on this basis. But, this is to allow that Hi can escape the stringent demands on knowledge due to her high stakes situation by getting her knowledge second hand

---

[1] Proponents of versions of this thesis include Austin (1979), Welbourne (1979), Fricker (1987), Coady (1992) and Adler (1996).

from Lo who is in a lower stakes situation. So, the anti-intellectualist should reject T) (MacFarlane 2005).

A first worry with MacFarlane's argument is that transmission principles for testimony are highly controversial given the disagreement between reductionists and non-reductionists in the epistemology of testimony. Reductionists hold that a hearer is not justified in accepting the word of a speaker without positive epistemic reasons to trust; whereas non-reductionists reject this requirement. Thus, MacFarlane's principle, T), would be rejected by reductionists. For, as we have seen, his condition 'without doxastic irresponsibility' does not require that the hearer has positive epistemic reasons to trust. His principle would also be rejected by many non-reductionists who hold that the transmission of knowledge by testimony may be undermined in ways not mentioned in MacFarlane's principle. To give just one example, Lackey (2008) argues that even if the conditions in the principle are met, a non-reductionist should allow that the hearer would not gain knowledge by testimony if the hearer is in a Gettier-style case in which, by chance, she asks the one speaker out of the group present who would reliably testify to her (pp. 164–167; for other alleged necessary conditions for transmission, see Lackey's complex formulation of a non-reductionist position below).

Given that many participants in the debate about the epistemology of testimony would reject T), it is not an uncontroversial principle inconsistency with which would be a serious objection to anti-intellectualism. Further, since formulating plausible transmission principles requires substantial theoretical work, the anti-intellectualist may argue that, when properly formulated, transmission principles are not incompatible with anti-intellectualism. In particular, an anti-intellectualist may argue that a difference in stakes would violate some necessary condition in a plausible formulation of the conditions for acquiring knowledge by testimony.

To illustrate, consider Lackey's formulation of a non-reductionist account of testimony:

For every speaker, A, and hearer, B, B knows that p on the basis of A's testimony if and only if:

1. B believes that p on the basis of the content of A's testimony;
2. B has no undefeated defeaters for A's testimony;
3. It is true that p;
4. A's testimony is reliable or otherwise truth-conducive;
5. B is a reliable or properly functioning recipient of testimony[2];

---

[2] She explains that condition (5) amounts to the requirement that the hearer is suitably sensitive to defeating information. (6) is designed to overcome Gettier-style cases discussed in the main text above.

6. The environment in which B receives A's testimony is suitable for the reception of reliable testimony. (p. 167)

To see how more complex forms of transmission conditions for testimonial knowledge might be compatible with anti-intellectualism, let us focus on conditions (2) and (4). An anti-intellectualist may suggest that a suitable difference in stakes between speaker and hearer constitutes a defeater for the speaker's testimony, and so fails Lackey's condition (2). It is standard to allow that defeaters may include conditions of which the subject is not aware (e.g., Lehrer 1965). So, the fact that the hearer may be ignorant of the problematic difference of stakes presents no obstacle to regarding this difference as constituting a defeater. It is less standard to use a difference of stakes as a defeater. But, the idea that stakes may constitute a defeater has recently been suggested in Weatherson (2011) independently of concerns with testimony.

Alternatively, an anti-intellectualist may claim that a problematic difference of stakes between speaker and hearer undermines Lackey's condition (4) that the speaker's testimony be reliable or truth conducive. This condition is motivated by her idea that we should replace the traditional focus on the speaker's beliefs and whether they constitute knowledge with a focus on the speaker's testimony and whether it is reliable (2008, chapter 2). However, this condition raises the question of what level of reliability is enough for the acquisition of knowledge by testimony. An anti-intellectualist might say that the condition is naturally interpreted as requiring that the speaker's testimony be as reliable as the hearer requires, given her stakes. In this way, if the speaker's reliability is less than what is required by the hearer's situation, then condition (4) for the acquisition of knowledge by testimony is not met.

Similar points affect the claim that anti-intellectualism is incompatible with plausible principles concerning the acquisition of knowledge by memory. For instance, consider the following principle which Blaauw suggests:

If S acquires the knowledge that p at t1, then S is in a position to know that p at T2 on the basis of memory, provided that i) at T2, S's memory is functioning as it should; and ii) S has not acquired at T2 compelling, but misleading, evidence to the effect that not-p. (Blaauw 2008, p. 320)

An anti-intellectualist might hope to respond to the suggestion that their position threatens this principle about memory in a way similar to their response to the parallel point about testimony. First, they may argue that transmission principles for memory are controversial. Second, an anti-intellectualist may argue that, when properly formulated, transmission principles for memory are compatible with anti-intellectualism. For instance, she may argue that any reasonable transmission principle should include a no-defeaters clause understood so that a difference in stakes can count as a defeater. Alternatively, she may argue that the condition that memory be 'well-functioning' be broadened to exclude cases of a problematic difference of stakes.

In conclusion, it is not clear that anti-intellectualism is incompatible with plausible formulations of the principles governing the way in which knowledge is transmitted by memory and testimony. In the rest of the chapter, I examine the different objection that our testimonial and memorial practices do not exhibit the kind of sensitivity to stakes that would be required if anti-intellectualism were true.

3   Sensitivity to Stakes

As we have seen, anti-intellectualism allows that a difference of stakes can undermine the transmission of knowledge by testimony and memory. For, a hearer may be at higher stakes than the speaker and so might fail to gain knowledge that p from the speaker's assertion that p even though the speaker knows that p. It is not enough to deal with this issue that one simply modifies transmission principles for knowledge by testimony and memory in the way discussed in the Section 2. In addition, it is arguable that if anti-intellectualism were true, then our testimonial and memorial practices should be sensitive to such differences in the stakes. In particular, we would expect that speakers and/or hearers would check to see whether there is a problematic divergence of stakes between them so as to ensure that the hearer doesn't trust the speaker's word inappropriately, that is, when the speaker's epistemic position is not good enough for the hearer to know given her stakes. For, otherwise, a subject in a high-stakes scenario might trust a speaker's assertion that p and so act on the basis that p even though the speaker's epistemic position is not good enough for the speaker to know that p given her stakes. However, it has been argued, our testimonial and memorial practices do not exhibit the required sensitivity. As Schaffer (2006, p. 97) puts it, the practice of testimony 'proceeds without needing to know what may be at stake for the testifier'.

In order to examine this objection, we need to see just what kind of sensitivity to stakes would be required if anti-intellectualism were true. For example, in the case of testimony, whose role is it to try and avoid situations in which the hearer trusts the speaker's word that p although the speaker's epistemic position is not good enough for the hearer to thereby know that p because of her stakes? Is it the job of the speaker, the hearer, or a mix of both? Similarly, in the case of memory, we can ask whether the sensitivity must be exhibited at the time the memory is laid down, or when it is later recovered, or a mix of both? In the next few sections, I consider the suggestion that all of the required sensitivity is achieved by the work of 'producers' of information (speakers, or subjects laying down propositions in memory); or by 'consumers' of information (hearers, or subjects retrieving propositions from memory); or a mix of both.

4   The Producer Alone

According to the producer-only picture, the required sensitivity to a difference of stakes is achieved by the work of the producer of information alone. However, we can quickly see that the producer-only picture is very implausible for memory. In the case of memory, the producer is the subject at the time of laying down the memory. But, at the time a memory is laid down, the subject has no idea at what future point she might exploit this memory and what stakes she will be in at that time. Indeed, she might exploit a memory on numerous future occasions, which differ widely in the stakes. Thus, she cannot ensure that she lays down a proposition in memory at a time t only if her strength of epistemic position at that time meets that required on later occasions of use.

In the case of testimony, the producer-only picture claims that the required sensitivity is achieved wholly by the work of the speaker. In more detail, a speaker would ensure that she asserts a proposition only if her epistemic position is strong enough that she would know the proposition if she were to face the stakes in fact faced by the hearer. On a few occasions, speakers do exhibit something like the sensitivity required. For instance, I am usually happy to assert straight out that the bank is open on Saturday having been there recently myself on a Saturday. However, if an enquirer makes it clear that she stands to lose her house if she is wrong about the opening hours of the bank, then I would be more likely to say something qualified, such as, 'Well, I think it is open on Saturday. I was there just a couple of weeks ago and it was open on Saturday.' Usually, when hearers make it clear that they face extraordinarily high stakes, cooperative speakers make more qualified assertions. However, this fact does not show that all the required sensitivity is done by speakers alone. Frequently, speakers have no idea what stakes are faced by their hearers. They may be talking to several conversational participants (plus potential eavesdroppers), for whom the stakes are different. Further, even if speakers have a view about the stakes faced by hearers, their view may be inaccurate. Thus, speakers lack the epistemic information required to ensure that they assert a proposition only if their epistemic position is sufficient for the requirements of the hearer(s). More generally, if sensitivity to difference of stakes is to be achieved by the producer alone, then this condition cannot be met.

5   The Consumer Alone

Applied to the case of memory, the consumer-only picture amounts to the view that the required sensitivity to stakes is achieved by the consumer of memories alone. On occasion, consumers of memories exhibit some sensitivity to stakes. For example, consumers in very high stakes are unlikely just to rely on apparent memory and would instead check, or even double-check, a proposition before acting on it. However, this is not enough to show that consumers of memory exhibit the required sensitivity. Even a subject in moderate stakes is at risk of acting on a proposition which was laid down in memory at a time when her epistemic position was not strong enough for the situation she now finds herself in. But with the exception of very high-stakes situations, it seems that we typically rely on propositions laid down in memory without checking the details of the situation in which they were laid down, the stakes obtaining then, or the particular strength of epistemic position we then had. Indeed, although we may occasionally be able to remember such details, this does not seem to be typically the case. Memory seems to function primarily to record contents, not the details of the situations in which those propositions were laid down. In many cases, I merely remember that p, without having any idea of the particular situation in which I first laid down this memory. Given this, when subjects retrieve a proposition from memory, they have little ability to check whether the epistemic position responsible for the storage of the proposition in memory is good enough for their current purposes. So, the consumer-only model is very implausible for the case of memory.

The consumer-only model also faces difficulties in the case of testimony. On the consumer-only view of testimony, the work in ensuring that testimonial practice is sensitive to stakes is undertaken by hearers. Hearers do occasionally undertake some such work. For instance, if the hearer faces extraordinarily high stakes, she wouldn't just take the word of any speaker on the matter in question, but would check or double-check. However, that agents facing extraordinarily high stakes check and double-check before acting on a proposition is not enough to show that hearers exhibit the required sensitivity. Even a subject in moderate stakes is at risk of accepting the word of a speaker whose epistemic position is so weak that she (the speaker) would not know were she to occupy the stakes facing the hearer. But, outside extraordinarily high stakes cases, we frequently accept the word of others without enquiring into the stakes facing them, and without enquiring into the strength of epistemic position they possess with respect to the asserted proposition. Further, in the case of written testimony, we frequently have no opportunity to enquire into the stakes and/or epistemic position of the testifier at the time of her testimony. For, the testifier may not be epistemically accessible, say if she is in the distant past, or in a geographically remote location.

6   The Combined View

In light of the difficulties facing the producer-alone and consumer-alone pictures, the anti-intellectualist may try a combined view according to which the work of ensuring that our testimonial and memorial practices are sensitive to the stakes is undertaken by a combination of work by producers and consumers. However, the combined view faces difficulties due to the limitations we have already seen in the ability of consumers (producers) to adjust their behaviour to the epistemic position of producers (consumers). As we have seen in Section 4, producers cannot always adjust the production of information to fit consumer's stakes since speakers are often ignorant of the stakes faced by the relevant hearers, and there is no mechanism available by which a later consumer of memory can make known her high stakes to her earlier self at the time the memory was laid down. In addition, as we saw in Section 5, outside very high-stakes situations, consumers often fail to check the stakes and/or the epistemic position of producers. Indeed, in the case of memory, and some written testimony, consumer access to the details of the conditions in which the memory or testimony was produced is often severely limited.

The limits on the extent to which producers (consumers) have access to the details of the epistemic position of consumers (producers) suggests that there is little plausibility in the suggestion that activities on the part of producers and consumers ensure a fine grained adjustment of production to consumption conditions on a case-by-case basis. Despite this, a more coarse-grained approach might be suggested. On the envisaged view, production conditions would not be matched to the particular requirements of each consumption occasion. Instead, producers would make information available only if a certain threshold of epistemic position is met. The threshold could not be so high as to meet the needs of a consumer in any stakes, no matter how high. The effect of such a tough requirement would be to ensure that unqualified propositions are almost never asserted or stored in memory. So, instead, let us suppose that the production requirement is merely that one should assert a proposition, or lay it down in memory, only if one meets a certain threshold, T, of strength of epistemic position which will enable consumers with a variety of low to moderate stakes to appropriately rely on the proposition. If producers do as much work as this, then there will still be some work for consumers to do. When a consumer is in stakes such that an epistemic position of less than or equal to the threshold would not be enough for her requirements, then she should not simply accept a proposition on the basis of testimony or memory, but rather seek further evidence for the proposition before relying on it in her practical reasoning.

The picture sketched of a threshold for production combined with care in consumption when the stakes are high enough is a more plausible one than the producer-only or consumer-only pictures examined so far. However, defending this hybrid picture requires addressing two further issues. First, it may be suggested that the hybrid picture undermines key elements of the anti-intellectualist view, in particular the claim that knowledge is the norm of practical reasoning. Second, an intellectualist may argue that while the hybrid picture is the best option for the anti-intellectualist, it still places unrealistic demands on testimonial and memorial practices, and that the intellectualist picture of testimony is more plausible. I consider each of these objections in turn.

6.1   The Threshold Norm and the Knowledge Norm

The idea that knowledge is the norm for practical reasoning has been central to one main line of argument for anti-intellectualism made explicit in Fantl and McGrath (2009). According to the knowledge norm for practical reasoning in its sufficiency direction (or *Sufficiency*), if a subject knows that p, then she is in a good enough epistemic position to rely on p in her practical reasoning (e.g., Fantl and McGrath 2009; Hawthorne 2004; Hawthorne and Stanley 2008). Fantl and McGrath's argument starts from the assumption that, by raising the stakes, one can shift a subject from a situation in which she knows that p and is in a good enough epistemic position to rely on p in her practical reasoning to one in which she is not in a good enough epistemic position to rely on p in her practical reasoning. Assuming *Sufficiency*, it follows that she doesn't know in the second situation. Thus, we have a difference of knowledge generated by a difference in stakes.

Since *Sufficiency* is a premise in one of the major arguments for anti-intellectualism, it would be problematic if responding to the objections from testimony and memory required an anti-intellectualist to reject *Sufficiency*. But the suggested threshold rule for producers may seem to undermine *Sufficiency*. According to the rule, a producer should produce information for consumption only if her epistemic position exceeds a certain threshold, T. Thus, a subject who knows that p should neither assert that p, nor store the proposition that p in memory, unless it is also the case that her epistemic position exceeds the threshold T. Since asserting a proposition is a kind of action, this might seem to amount to denying *Sufficiency*.

However, the impression that the anti-intellectualist needs to reject *Sufficiency* is not borne out. The knowledge norm for practical reasoning is only concerned with whether one is in a good enough epistemic position to rely on a proposition in one's practical reasoning, not with whether one ought to act on it in some particular way. So, even if knowledge places one in a good enough epistemic position to rely on a proposition in one's practical reasoning, it does not follow that one should act on that proposition by asserting it. To take one example, even if I know a juicy piece of gossip about a colleague, g, so that I am in a good enough epistemic position to rely on g in my practical reasoning, it does not follow that I should assert it. To take another, even if I know where the nuclear device is hidden so that I am in a good enough epistemic position to rely on that proposition in my practical reasoning, it doesn't follow that I should tell the terrorists where it is hidden. Similarly, if assertion is governed by a threshold rule as suggested, then if I know a proposition p but do not meet the threshold for assertion, the knowledge norm for practical reasoning does not have the consequence that I ought to assert that p. For instance, if testimony is governed by the suggested threshold norm, then a subject who knows that p and is asked whether p might reason as follows:

1. p.
2. Cooperation enjoins that I should assert a proposition in response to an enquiry whether p only if my strength of epistemic position exceeds the threshold.
3. My strength of epistemic position with respect to p does not exceed the threshold.
4. Thus, I should not assert that p straight out, but say something more qualified, say 'I believe that p'.

Thus, it seems that it is compatible for an anti-intellectualist to endorse the suggested threshold rule for producers while also accepting the sufficiency direction of the knowledge norm for practical reasoning.

Despite this, it is worth noting that the threshold rule is incompatible with another norm sometimes endorsed by anti-intellectualists, namely the sufficiency direction of the knowledge norm for assertion. By *Sufficiency for assertion*: if a subject knows that p, then she is in a good enough epistemic position to assert that p (e.g., Hawthorne 2004). That the threshold rule is incompatible with *Sufficiency for assertion* is not problematic for the anti-intellectualist since, as we will see, *Sufficiency for assertion* is not used in any of the main lines of argument for anti-intellectualism and is questionable on independent grounds.

According to the sufficiency direction of the knowledge norm for assertion, if a subject knows a proposition then she is in a good enough epistemic position to assert it. But, according to the suggested threshold rule, a subject who knows a proposition might not meet the relevant threshold and so might not be in a good enough epistemic position to assert that proposition. Thus, the suggested threshold rule seems incompatible with *Sufficiency for assertion.*[3] However, even if the anti-intellectualist needs to abandon *Sufficiency for assertion*, this does not seem very problematic for the position. For, *Sufficiency for assertion* is not used as a premise in any of the main arguments for anti-intellectualism. Further, the main data used to support the knowledge norm for assertion in fact most clearly supports its necessity direction rather than its sufficiency direction, such as the impropriety of lottery propositions and Moorean propositions, and the way in which assertions are challenged and defended. In addition, there are well-known putative counterexamples to the sufficiency direction of the knowledge norm for assertion (e.g., Lackey 2007; Brown 2008).

Anti-intellectualists more frequently appeal to the necessity direction of the knowledge norm for assertion rather than the sufficiency direction. According to the necessity direction, a subject is in a good enough epistemic position to assert a proposition only if she knows it. Note that the suggested threshold rule is compatible with the necessity direction of the knowledge norm for assertion. For, it could be that an appropriate assertion requires both that the speaker knows what she says, and that her strength of epistemic position meets the required threshold. The compatibility of the threshold rule and the necessity direction of the knowledge norm for assertion is fortunate since anti-intellectualists have appealed to the necessity direction to support their view. For example, anti-intellectualists have appealed to the necessity direction to explain why attributers in a high-stakes situation are reluctant to ascribe knowledge to a subject who is in a low stakes situation (Hawthorne 2004; Stanley 2005). Hawthorne (2004) also argues that his subject sensitive

---

[3] There seems no way to suggest that the threshold rule is compatible with *Sufficiency for assertion* in the way that, for example, rules of propriety, etiquette or professional norms are. For, first, the way in which somebody who knows that *p* but does not meet the threshold would be inappropriate to assert that *p* is that their epistemic position is not strong enough. Second, the threshold rule is not supposed to govern assertions only in certain circumstances (say certain professional circumstances), but all assertions whatsoever. So, it seems to amount to a general rejection of *Sufficiency for assertion.*

invariantism is better able than contextualism to accommodate the intuitive links between knowledge, assertion and practical reasoning. However, although Hawthorne appeals to biconditional versions of the knowledge norm for assertion and practical reasoning, he could make his points merely by relying on the necessity direction. For example, exploiting the necessity direction, Hawthorne could complain that contextualism has the result that an attributer in a high stakes context could truly make the following assertion about a subject in a low stakes context 'You don't know that p, but it's appropriate for you to assert that p and rely on it in your practical reasoning'.

In conclusion, the suggested threshold norm for assertion is compatible with the sufficiency direction of the knowledge norm for practical reasoning that is used as a premise in a central line of argument for anti-intellectualism. Such a threshold norm is compatible with the necessity, but not the sufficiency, direction of the knowledge norm for assertion. But that is not problematic given that the sufficiency direction is not exploited in central arguments for anti-intellectualism and is independently questionable.

6.2   The Plausibility of the Hybrid Picture

On the proposed hybrid picture, the work of ensuring the required sensitivity to stakes is split between producers and consumers. Even if this picture is more plausible than the consumer-alone or producer-alone pictures considered earlier, an intellectualist may suggest that it still places implausible work on the shoulders of producers and consumers. Let us consider this objection by first considering the work assigned to consumers and producers in the hybrid model.

On the producer side, the proposed hybrid solution requires that if a subject knows that p in virtue of the combination of a very weak epistemic position and the fact that she's in very low stakes, then she would not testify that p, or store p in memory. Instead, she would do these things only if her strength of epistemic position is over the relevant threshold. It seems relatively plausible that producers behave in this way if the threshold is not set too high.

Now let us consider the consumer side. Even if producers assert a proposition or store it in memory only if their strength of epistemic position meets the relevant threshold, then this still leaves consumers in high enough stakes at risk of relying on a producer concerning a proposition p when the producer does not have the strength of epistemic position required for the consumer's circumstances. For instance, suppose that Sally faces a practical reasoning decision with moderate stakes which turns on whether p is the case. And let us assume with anti-intellectualists the biconditional knowledge norm for practical reasoning. Sally intends to visit her bank to conduct some business on her way home from work on Friday. However, as she approaches the bank, she sees that there is a huge line-up inside. She prefers to avoid this queue if she can. But she needs to do this business within a week and it would be very inconvenient for her to go to the bank during the next working week (Monday–Friday).

Since Sally faces moderate stakes, it seems plausible that she would rely on testimony in deciding what to do without launching positive enquiries into the particular epistemic position of the testifier. But, if the threshold is set at a low enough position, then by trusting testimony she is at risk of relying on the word of a testifier whose epistemic position is not in fact strong enough for her requirements. So, we may worry that Sally, and subjects like her who are in moderate stakes positions, simply do not do enough work to ensure sensitivity to stakes. For, plausibly, they accept the word of others without further investigation.

A defender of the threshold view could reply to this kind of worry by saying that, in fact, the threshold is set such that any subject who is in a moderate stakes situation runs no risk of accepting the word of someone whose epistemic position is lower than she requires. If, in reply, an intellectualist were to suggest that, at slightly higher stakes, Sally would run such a risk, the anti-intellectualist could reply that, at such raised stakes, Sally would undertake positive investigation into the epistemic position of the testifier. It seems hard, then, to show that consumers do not do the work envisaged by the hybrid account offered by the anti-intellectualist. For, in reply to any putatively problematic case, the anti-intellectualist can always claim that the threshold is set at a higher point, and/or that when the stakes get high enough, consumers are disposed to double-check.

I have argued that the requirements placed on consumers and producers by the hybrid model are not implausible. Indeed, an anti-intellectualist may argue that there is little prospect of an intellectualist showing that the required work is not done since similar work will be required even on an intellectualist account of testimony. Of course, for the intellectualist, there is no problem of the failure of transmission of knowledge across testimony or memory generated by a difference of stakes. Nonetheless, intellectualists face a related if distinct problem, namely that the consumer of information may be at risk of acting on information from a producer even though the producer's strength of epistemic position is less strong than she, the consumer, requires. This problem arises because, on any view, whether intellectualist or anti-intellectualist, the strength of epistemic position a subject needs to act on a proposition depends on the stakes. So, if a consumer who is in a very high stakes situation relies on the word of an informant or an earlier memory, she runs the risk of acting on a proposition even though the testifier, or her earlier self at the time the memory was laid down, did not have an epistemic position strong enough for her current requirements. So, even intellectualism faces the problem of a potential mismatch between the epistemic position of producers and consumers. Further, to the extent that the intellectualist faces the same menu of options as the anti-intellectualist, whatever problems there are in dealing with testimony and memory affect both positions equally.

In order to see what kind of mismatch problem arises on intellectualism, let us start with a case in which a producer is in a low stakes situation, and has a relatively weak epistemic position with respect to the proposition that p, whereas the relevant consumer is in a high stakes situation and so requires a very strong epistemic position to rely on p in her practical reasoning. For the anti-intellectualist, the producer may well know that p. They deal with such cases by appeal to the idea that a threshold norm governs both assertion and memory in addition to the knowledge norm. By contrast, intellectualists can deal with such cases without appeal to a threshold norm over and above the knowledge norm. Suppose that the producer's epistemic position is so weak that she doesn't count as knowing by the lights of the intellectualist. Assuming that knowledge is necessary for appropriate assertion/storage in memory, and that the producer follows this knowledge norm, she would neither assert that p nor store it in memory. Thus, it seems that both intellectualists and anti-intellectualists place similar work on the shoulders of producers. Both take assertion to be governed by norms according to which subjects whose epistemic position with respect to a proposition is very weak should not assert that proposition (either because of the knowledge norm, or because of a threshold norm over and above the knowledge norm). Since each view imposes similar work on the part of producers, it is hard to defend one view over the other on this basis.

Now let us consider a case in which the producer has a stronger epistemic position, one meeting the intellectualist's conditions for knowledge. Unless the intellectualist sets the conditions for knowledge implausibly high, there will still be some consumers who are at such high stakes that there is a mismatch between their needs and the epistemic position of the producer. Suppose that the producer knows that p and asserts that p. On intellectualism, if the consumer accepts that p then even though she is in a higher stakes situation than the producer, this does not affect whether she knows that p. There is no problem of failure of transmission of knowledge due to a difference in stakes. Still, intellectualism faces the problem that the consumer may act on the word of the producer, even though the producer's epistemic position is weaker than what the consumer requires, given her high stakes. How can an intellectualist avoid this result?

On the producer side, the intellectualist's options look similar to those of the anti-intellectualist. She could attempt to impose some further cooperative norm on assertion in addition to the knowledge norm. But, any such additional norm would plausibly leave certain mismatch cases unaddressed in which the producer does meet this further cooperative norm, but her strength of epistemic position is still short of what is required by a consumer in high stakes. So, instead, the intellectualist could attempt to avoid the mismatch by requiring work of the consumer. Again, her options look remarkably similar to those of the anti-intellectualist. She would need to require that, whenever the consumer's stakes are such that a producer meeting the requirements on assertion could still fall short of the consumer's requirements, the consumer would not rely on their word in her practical reasoning, but would enquire further. Of course, on the intellectualist view, if the consumer were to accept the producer's word, the consumer would plausibly acquire knowledge. Nonetheless, it remains the case that, were the consumer to act on the relevant proposition, then she would do so even though the producer whose word she trusts has an epistemic position weaker than what she, the consumer, requires.[4] To avoid this, it seems that the consumer facing a high-stakes practical reasoning decision should not accept the word of another or an earlier memory without further checks.[5]

In summary, it seems that both intellectualists and anti-intellectualists must assume that similar work is done by producers and consumers of information to prevent consumers taking propositions on trust from producers, even though the epistemic position of those producers is weaker than what the consumer requires. The most plausible solution seems to have roughly the same shape whether one is an intellectualist or an anti-intellectualist. First, one must place a norm on production so that

---

[4] Thus, the sketched intellectualist position is likely to deny that knowledge is sufficient for being in a good enough epistemic position to rely on a proposition in one's practical reasoning, for example, Hill and Schechter (2007), Lackey (2007), Brown (2008), Reed (2010).

[5] Alternatively, it may be suggested that it is appropriate for the consumer to accept the producer's word that p but that she ought to undertake further checks before acting on p. But, notice this does not remove the need for extra checking but just relocates it to a different point. So, it does not undermine the overall message of the section that an intellectualist will need to require similar work to the anti-intellectualist to avoid a consumer acting on the word of a producer when the producer's epistemic position is not good enough for the consumer's purposes.

producers with a very weak epistemic position with respect to p violate the norms of assertion or memory if they assert that p or store it in memory. For an intellectualist, this will likely be achieved by a combination of an intellectualist account of knowledge, and the requirement that one should assert that p, or store p in memory, only if one knows it. For an anti-intellectualist, this will be achieved by holding that assertion and memory are subject to some threshold requirement over and above knowledge. Second, both intellectualists and anti-intellectualists must suppose that consumers take extra care when they are in stakes high enough that a producer meeting the norms of production may have an epistemic position short of what the consumer requires. Given the overall similarity in intellectualist and anti-intellectualist approaches to the problem of mismatch, it seems unlikely that one could criticise the hybrid view on the grounds that it is implausible that producers and consumers undertake the work it places on their shoulders.

Despite this, an intellectualist might suggest that even though anti-intellectualism is strictly consistent with our practices of memory and testimony, the intellectualist view is to be preferred to the anti-intellectualist view because it is simpler. In particular, she may say that, on her account, production of information is governed only by the knowledge norm. By contrast, as we have been imagining it, on the anti-intellectualist view, production is governed both by the knowledge norm and the threshold norm.[6] Thus, on the anti-intellectualist view, a producer should assert that p or lay it down in memory only if she knows that p and her epistemic position meets the threshold T.

Note, first, that this intellectualist objection is rather different from the original formulation of the testimony and memory objection to anti-intellectualism, namely that anti-intellectualism is inconsistent with our testimonial and memorial practices, either because it is inconsistent with transmission principles, or because it requires a sensitivity to stakes which those practices do not instantiate. Indeed, the imagined intellectualist objector simply concedes the main point at issue in this paper, namely that anti-intellectualism is compatible with our practices of testimony and memory. Second, to fairly assess the charge that the anti-intellectualist

---

[6] On an alternative way of implementing the hybrid view, only the threshold norm governs assertion and memory so that it can be appropriate for a high-stakes producer to assert that p or lay it down in memory even though she does not know it. However, this implementation of the hybrid view makes it hard to explain the data supporting the necessity direction of the knowledge norm for assertion, such as lottery data, the infelicity of utterances of the form 'p but I don't know that p', and the fact that assertions are often defended and challenged by appeal to knowledge. As we saw previously, anti-intellectualists have appealed to the necessity direction of the knowledge norm for assertion in their dialectic with contextualists.

picture is more complex than the intellectualist one, we need to look not just at the testimony/memory debate, but at a broader set of data. The various options in the debate about knowledge – anti-intellectualism, contextualism and traditional invariantism – need to account for a large array of different data. This data might reasonably be taken to include, inter alia, the shiftiness of knowledge attributions (both first and third person), retraction and disagreement data, data concerning modal claims and the theoretical role of knowledge for instance in testimony and memory. Different positions in the debate do better in accommodating some of this data than others. So a relative evaluation of the different positions needs to take an overall view of how it deals with all this data, not just testimony/memory.

Such a global comparison is outside the scope of this paper. But it is worth illustrating the point that the greater complexity of an anti-intellectualist account of memory and testimony may be compensated for by greater simplicity elsewhere by considering the comparison of anti-intellectualism and one of its rivals, traditional invariantism. As we have seen, anti-intellectualism offers a slightly more complicated account of testimony and memory than does intellectualism. However, on the other hand, it is arguable that anti-intellectualism offers a simpler account of the shiftiness of first-person knowledge attributions.

In more detail, anti-intellectualism treats our shifty intuitions about first-person knowledge attributions as reflecting truth values. For example, in a first person bank case it treats the intuition that it is appropriate for DeRose to self-attribute knowledge in the low context as reflecting the fact that such a self-attribution would be true, and it treats the intuition that it is inappropriate for DeRose to self-attribute knowledge in the high context as reflecting the fact that such a self-attribution would be false. While an anti-intellectualist can offer a particularly simple explanation of the shiftiness of first person knowledge attributions, traditional invariantism faces a greater challenge here. Since she denies that the truth value of knowledge attributions changes with the stakes, a (non-sceptical) traditional invariantist will claim that it would be true for DeRose to self-attribute knowledge in both the low and high contexts. Furthermore, she must claim that even though it seems appropriate for DeRose in the high context to deny that he knows, this denial would be false. So, she must offer either a pragmatic or error theoretic treatment of our intuitions about whether DeRose knows in the high context. A variety of both pragmatic and error theoretic accounts have been offered, yet there are difficulties and challenges for either strategy. For instance, a pragmatic account needs to appeal to independently motivated pragmatic general principles. In addition, there is the issue of whether a literally false attribution may seem appropriate by conveying a truth.

Here is not the place to resolve these difficult issues. Rather, the point is that we should assess the relative strengths and weaknesses of anti-intellectualism and its intellectualist rivals, whether contextualism or invariantism, by looking at how they deal with the large array of relevant data. Thus, the fact that the anti-intellectualist offers a slightly more complicated account of memory and testimony is not a fatal blow against the account. For, it may be compensated for by the fact that the anti-intellectualist can offer a more simple account of some other data than its rivals.

7   Conclusion

I have been considering the suggestion that there is a conflict between anti-intellectualism about knowledge and two of our most important sources of knowledge, namely testimony and memory. Memory and testimony are so central to our intellectual lives that if anti-intellectualism were inconsistent with our gaining knowledge from these sources, it would result in a problematic ignorance. I have considered two versions of this objection to anti-intellectualism. According to the first version of this challenge, anti-intellectualism is incompatible with intuitive principles governing the transmission of knowledge by testimony and memory. But, we have seen that testimonial and memorial transmission principles are in fact highly contentious. In addition, the anti-intellectualist may argue that, when such principles are properly formulated, they are compatible with anti-intellectualism.

According to the second version of the challenge, our testimonial and memorial practices do not exhibit the sensitivity to stakes which would be required if anti-intellectualism were true. By carefully distinguishing different ways of understanding the sensitivity requirement, we saw that there is a plausible hybrid understanding of this requirement on which the work of ensuring that practices are sensitive to a potential difference of stakes is split between the producer and consumer of testimony and memory. Further, we saw that even an intellectualist will plausibly need to suppose that similar work is done by producers and consumers to ensure that consumers do not rely on a proposition from a producer whose epistemic position falls short of what they, the consumer, require. So, there is little prospect of an intellectualist arguing that the anti-intellectualist account of memory and testimony places unrealistic demands on producers and consumers. I conclude that the fact that testimony and memory are important sources of knowledge does not constitute a knockdown consideration against anti-intellectualism.

7   Ignorance and Epistemic Value

Duncan Pritchard

1   Epistemic Value/Disvalue

Recent years have seen a huge upsurge of interest in the topic of epistemic value, particularly with regard to the value of knowledge in contrast to other positive epistemic standings such as justified belief and understanding.[1] The questions raised for positive epistemic standings such as knowledge can, however, equally be posed with regard to negative epistemic standings such as ignorance, which we will simply take to be the lack of knowledge.[2] Interestingly, as we will see, it does not follow from the fact that ignorance is a negative epistemic standing that it is thereby a disvaluable epistemic standing.[3] For just as we can imagine positive epistemic standings being sometimes disvaluable, so we can likewise conceive of negative epistemic standing being valuable.

Before we get to this point, however, we first need to flag an ambiguity in the very notion of epistemic value, one that is often overlooked but that is, as we will see, very important to evaluating the putative epistemic value of ignorance. The most natural way to understand the notion of epistemic value is as picking out a particular kind of value that is distinctively epistemic, just as we might suppose that aesthetic value picks out a particular kind of value that is distinctively aesthetic. But there is also a secondary usage of this notion in the literature, often not kept apart from the first, whereby it is taken to also cover the value of a particular epistemic standing, whether that value is distinctively epistemic or otherwise.

---

[1] As Riggs (2008) has put it, this reflects the so-called 'value turn' in epistemology. For some key works on epistemic value, see Jones (1997), Kvanvig (2003), Zagzebski (2003), Greco (2009) and Pritchard, Haddock and Millar (2010). See also Pritchard (2009, 2011, 2014, forthcoming b). For two useful recent surveys of the literature on epistemic value, see Pritchard (2007) and Pritchard and Turri (2011).

[2] For a prominent recent defence of this account of ignorance, see Le Morvan (2011). For a spirited defence of an alternative conception of ignorance, such that ignorance is lack of true belief rather than knowledge, see Peels (2012).

[3] Note that, for the sake of simplicity, I will here treat value and disvalue as exhaustive categories. Thus, a lack of positive value will equate to a disvalue. This is, of course, contentious, but I don't think anything of substance hangs on this point for our purposes.

It is common in the literature, for example, to explore the 'epistemic value' of knowledge by appealing to its practical utility.[4] But since no one thinks that practical utility is a distinctively epistemic kind of value, it is clear that we are here using the phrase 'epistemic value' in an importantly different way.[5] In particular, 'epistemic value' here means not a distinctively epistemic kind of value but rather instead the value of the epistemic (which may itself be either distinctively epistemic or otherwise).[6] Henceforth, we will keep these two notions of epistemic value apart, and do so by only using 'epistemic value' to refer to the distinctively epistemic kind of value.

One reason why this distinction is so important to the debate about the value of epistemic standings is that while it is very easy to conceive of positive epistemic standings that sometimes have negative value – and, indeed, negative epistemic standings which sometimes have positive value – it is not so easy to conceive of positive epistemic standings that sometimes have negative epistemic value (and, likewise, mutatis mutandis, for negative epistemic standings). Take knowledge, for example. Coming to know that one was adopted may cause one great unhappiness, such that one wished one had never found out. In such a case, one might reasonably regard this knowledge as highly disvaluable from the practical

---

[4] A good example of this can be found in Goldman and Olsson (2009).

[5] Of course, there are those in the literature who argue that there is no hard-and-fast distinction to be drawn between practical and epistemic value, and there are also those who maintain that practical factors can have a significant impact on epistemic standing, but these views are some remove from the claim that practical value just is a variety of distinctively epistemic value. For an example of the former, see Wright (2008), who offers a conception of epistemic normativity that draws on both classically epistemic and prudential considerations. For an example of the latter, see the literature on pragmatic encroachment in epistemology. A good overview of this literature is offered in Fantl and McGrath (2010).

[6] I draw this distinction, and explain its import to the debate about the epistemic value, in a number of places. See, for example, Pritchard, Millar and Haddock (2010, chapters 1–4), and Pritchard (2011, 2014, 2015, forthcoming b). Note that there is a related distinction in the vicinity here – due to Geach (1956) – between what he calls 'predicative' as opposed to 'attributive' expressions. Here is an example that he uses to illustrate the distinction. To say that a fly is big is to say that it is big *for a fly*; it is not to say that it is both a fly and big (i.e., big *simpliciter*). This is thus an attributive expression. In contrast, to say that a book is red is not to say that it is red *for a book*, but rather to say that it is both red and a book. This is a predicative expression. The contrast that Geach makes relates to the distinction that we have drawn since in effect we can read the expression 'epistemic value' either attributively (i.e., as pertaining to a kind of value which is specifically epistemic) or predicatively (i.e., as pertaining to something which is both epistemic and valuable). That said, note that one should be wary about completely equating the distinction we have drawn with Geach's distinction, in that when we talk of the 'value of the epistemic' we leave it open that it may be a particularly epistemic kind of value which is at issue – the point is rather that this is not being demanded, as it is when 'epistemic value' is being read attributively.

point of view of what promotes, or undermines, one's own happiness. But that this knowledge is practically disvaluable in this way does not entail that it lacks epistemic value, as this is to evaluate that knowledge along an entirely different axis of evaluation.

This issue is important to our discussion of ignorance, since if ignorance is lack of knowledge, and knowledge can sometimes be disvaluable, then it follows that ignorance can sometimes be valuable.[7] In the case just offered, for example, concerning the knowledge that one is adopted, it would be more valuable to have not known that this was the case. Thus, ignorance of this fact will be valuable. But since the kind of value in play here is just practical value, this is not yet to say that ignorance is epistemically valuable. Accordingly, if we want to argue that ignorance can have epistemic value, we will need to supply additional grounds.

2   The Epistemic Efficacy of Ignorance

Let us grant for the sake of argument that positive epistemic standings such as knowledge are generally both epistemically valuable and valuable simpliciter. There is of course a lively debate in epistemology about whether this really the case, and in particular about the different relative value, epistemic or otherwise, of particular epistemic standings (e.g., the value of knowledge as opposed, say, to understanding). But it would take us too far afield to get into these issues here.[8] If the claim that knowledge is generally both epistemically valuable and valuable simpliciter is true, then ignorance, qua lack of knowledge, will generally be both epistemically disvaluable and also disvaluable simpliciter. We have already noted, however, that the general value, epistemic or otherwise, of knowledge, does not exclude cases in which knowledge is disvaluable, as in the case described in the last section. And where knowledge is disvaluable, so ignorance will be valuable. We noted too, however, that the kind of value/disvalue in play here is not specifically epistemic. So if we want to defend the more interesting claim that ignorance can have epistemic value, then we have further work to do. On the plus side, we have identified one way of determining such value, which is to look for cases in which knowledge is epistemically

---

[7] Is ignorance just lack of knowledge? While I think this is broadly correct, there are some difficult cases involving well-grounded true belief which does not amount to knowledge (e.g., which has been Gettierized). Would we really class such a person as *ignorant*? I am not so sure, though we clearly would class them as lacking knowledge. In any case, in order to keep our discussion manageable I will set this complication to one side I what follows. For a helpful recent discussion of these kinds of cases, and the problems they pose for the view of ignorance as lack of knowledge, see Peels (2012).

[8] I explore these issues at length in Pritchard, Millar and Haddock (2010, chapters 1–4). See also Pritchard (2007) and Pritchard and Turri (2011).

disvaluable, since they will be instances in which ignorance, qua lack of knowledge, is epistemically valuable.

Before we can do that, however, we first need to say something about what epistemic value is, specifically. For our purposes, we can characterise epistemic value in terms of the distinctive truth-directed goal characteristic of good inquiry. In short, our distinctively epistemic goal is to get at the truth, and so, in the broadest terms, what promotes this goal has epistemic value. The acquisition of true belief, and the avoidance of false belief, are thus two core epistemic goods which determine epistemic value, in that whatever promotes truth in one's beliefs, and the avoidance of error, will have epistemic value. So, for example, this is why it is epistemically valuable to have good evidence in support of one's beliefs, since good evidence is a guide to the truth (i.e., will lead to true beliefs), and will generally steer you away from error (i.e., away from false beliefs).

More generally, whatever promotes not just true belief and the avoidance of error, but also accuracy in one's propositional attitudes in general – where applicable anyway – will be epistemically valuable. So, for example, consider the propositional attitude of accepting that p. Accepting that p comes apart from believing that p at least to the extent that one can accept a proposition without believing it.[9] For example, a scientist working in a highly controversial and theoretical domain might accept a certain theory because she recognises that it is by far the best current theory available even though she is sufficiently unsure of its truth that she does not actually believe it. Just as we would want a good inquirer's beliefs to be responsive to the truth-relevant considerations available to her, so we would want her acceptances to be similarly responsive to these considerations. In this case, for example, the scientist should not accept the theory unless the available evidence really does pick out that theory as the best available.[10] That said, henceforth in what follows we will focus, for the sake of simplicity, on the goals of promoting true belief and avoiding false beliefs.

We can now rephrase our question about whether there are cases in which possessing knowledge is epistemically disvaluable in terms of whether such an epistemic standing can either lead one to error or at

---

[9] On most views, acceptance and belief are also different in that they come apart in the other direction too. Since all that is important for present purposes is that they are not the same propositional attitude, we can set this further difference to one side. For a classic discussion of the notion of acceptance in contrast to belief, with specific reference to the context of philosophy of science, see van Fraassen (1980). See also Cohen (1992).

[10] Of course, one option here is to treat our epistemic evaluation of what the scientist accepts as being derivative on the goal of promoting true belief and avoiding false belief, in that epistemically good acceptances are precisely those acceptances which promote these epistemic goals. Thanks to Rik Peels for pressing me on this point.

least prevent one from gaining true beliefs. So construed, there is one straightforward type of case which fits the bill – misleading defeaters. A defeater is a consideration that undermines one's knowledge. So, for example, finding out that one has recently ingested a hallucinogenic drug can undermine one's perceptual knowledge about one's environment, since it follows that the deliverances of one's perceptual faculties are no longer reliable. A misleading defeater is a specific kind of defeater which, as the name suggests, points one away from the truth rather than towards it. So, for example, being falsely told that one has recently ingested a hallucinogenic drug will no less undermine one's perceptual knowledge about one's environment than being truly told that this is the case. Crucially, however, in the former case, since one has not in fact ingested the hallucinogen, then it follows that one is not in fact forming one's perceptual beliefs unreliably. Defeaters, whether misleading or otherwise, defeat one's knowledge until they are in turn defeated by further evidence (e.g., finding out that one hasn't in fact ingested the hallucinogen, or else discovering that while one has ingested this hallucinogen, it has been ineffective in this case).

What is interesting about misleading defeaters is that while one cannot rationally ignore them once one is made aware of them, there is a perfectly good sense in which one is epistemically better off if one does not come into contact with them. Consider, for example, two identical agents who occupy otherwise identical environments except that only agent one is regularly subject to misleading defeaters. Imagine, for example, that both agents are plagued by an 'epistemic joker' who keeps ensuring that there are misleading defeaters in play – who, for instance, puts it about that our agent has ingested an hallucinogen when in fact she has not, and so forth. The difference between the two agents, however, is that only agent one is in fact affected by the epistemic joker, and hence has her knowledge defeated. In contrast, agent two is never affected by the epistemic joker because she is in addition protected by an 'epistemic helper' who, knowing that the epistemic joker is planting these misleading defeaters, ensures that agent two never encounters them. For example, she ensures that agent two doesn't receive the misleading testimony that she has ingested a hallucinogen, and so continues to (rightly) trust her perceptual faculties as before.

Here is the crux of the matter: agent two seems to be epistemically better off than agent one, in that she knows lots of things that agent one, who is subject to the misleading defeaters, is unable to know.[11] Crucially,

---

[11] Though note that in saying that agent two is epistemically better off than agent one, we are in effect buying into a certain conception of epistemic value, as will be explained below. After all, there is a sense in which agent one does know some propositions that agent two doesn't know (e.g., about the presence of the defeater). As explained below, the

however, agent two knows more than agent one, all things considered, by also in a certain sense knowing less – i.e., by being ignorant of the misleading defeaters (on account of the fact that they have been neutralised by the epistemic helper). The upshot is that having knowledge of a misleading defeater can be epistemically disvaluable. This means, in turn, that being ignorant of a misleading defeater can be epistemically valuable. We have thus identified at least one plausible sense in which there is an epistemic efficacy in being ignorant.[12]

3   Weighing Epistemic Value

The phenomenon of misleading defeaters thus offers one straightforward way in which ignorance can be epistemically valuable. As we will see, this phenomenon points towards a more general, and also more interesting, way in which ignorance can be epistemically valuable, but in order to see this we first need to think a little more about how we 'weigh' epistemic value.

We noted above that epistemic value is concerned with what enables us to get at the truth, and hence avoid error. Insofar as we focus on beliefs in this regard, this means that epistemic goodness is about what promotes the acquisition of true beliefs (and the avoidance of false beliefs). With this point in mind, a very natural picture emerges of how to 'weigh' epistemic goodness. This is that we further our epistemic aims insofar as we maximise the number of true beliefs that we hold while minimising the number of our false beliefs. Accordingly, if belief system X has more true beliefs than belief system Y, but they have an equal number of false beliefs, then X is epistemically more valuable than Y.

Now one issue we might raise about this conception of how to weigh the epistemic good is how to manage the trade-off between maximising the

point is that one should not 'weigh' epistemic value purely in terms of the number of true propositions believed.

[12] Note that it should not be inferred from the discussion of this case that merely being ignorant of a misleading defeater suffices to ensure that it does not undermine one's knowledge. This is because there can be what are known as *normative defeaters*, which are defeaters which one ought to be aware of (but which one might in practice not be aware of). Accordingly, the mere fact that the epistemic helper has ensured that agent two does not encounter the misleading defeater does not suffice to ensure that agent two retains her knowledge, since it may nonetheless be the case that this is a defeater that agent two ought to be aware of (e.g., perhaps she ought to be more attentive to the fact that there are people in her environment who believe that she has ingested the hallucinogen). For our purposes, we can set this complication to one side by stipulating that not only is agent two unaware of the misleading defeater, but she is also *quite rightly* unaware of it. For a useful recent discussion of normative defeaters, in this case with regard to the specific issues raised by such defeaters in the epistemology of testimony, see Lackey (2005).

number of true beliefs and minimising the number of false beliefs. This is clearly going to be a vexed question, with several competing strategies available, depending on what kind of premium, if any, is placed on accuracy over error. But this is not the issue that I want to engage with here, interesting though it is. Instead, I want to suggest that this conception of how to weigh epistemic goodness is faulty in a fundamental respect, regardless of how one settles the more parochial question, in comparison, of how to manage the trade-off between maximising accuracy and minimising error within this general picture. As we will see, realising that this conception of how to weigh epistemic goodness is fundamentally mistaken will help us to recognise one important sense in which ignorance can be epistemically valuable.

Here is the crux of the matter. In saying that epistemic goodness is essentially about the acquisition of true rather than false beliefs, we are not thereby saying that the epistemic good is equally served by the acquisition of any particular true belief. We can bring this point out by considering a fallacious kind of reasoning which is unfortunately quite common in epistemology. Epistemologists often reason something like as follows:

The Trivial Truths Problem

(P1) If acquiring true belief is always epistemically good, then we should value all true beliefs, even the trivial ones.

(P2) We rightly do not value trivial true beliefs.

(C) So, acquiring true belief is not always epistemically good.

So, for example, if the epistemic good is furthered by maximising true belief, then adding any additional true belief to our stock of true beliefs should be an epistemically good thing to do, no matter how trivial that belief might be – for example, even if this is a true belief about the number of grains of sand on a beach. Clearly, however, we do not think it is epistemically valuable to add additional trivial true beliefs to our stock of true beliefs. So hence there must be more to our evaluations of epistemic value than just a concern to acquire true beliefs.[13]

Here is another way of putting this problem. Suppose one is faced with a situation where we can acquire one true belief or another (but not both). If we hold that acquiring true belief is always equally epistemically good, no matter which proposition is in play, then from a purely epistemic point

---

[13] Versions of this general line of argument abound in the contemporary epistemological literature. For a sample of high-profile endorsements of this kind of reasoning, see DePaul (2001), Sosa (2001) and Goldman (2002b). (The 'sand' example is due to Sosa.)

of view we should be indifferent between which of these true beliefs that we acquire. And yet it seems that if one of these beliefs is about a trivial matter, such as how many grains of sand are on a given beach, while the other belief is about something of great consequence, such as a truth of fundamental physics, then we should not be indifferent between these two beliefs. In particular, even from a specifically epistemic point of view where we set aside any practical implications of acquiring the beliefs in question – for example, the truth of fundamental physics, as it happens, has no more practical utility than the truth about the number of grains of sand on the beach – it still seems that as a good inquirer one should prefer the 'weightier' truth about fundamental physics over the trivial truth about the number of grains of sand on a beach. Hence it seems that it is not, or at least is not just, the acquisition of true belief that we really care about when it comes to epistemic value.

This is the so-called *trivial truths problem*, which on the face of it seems to call for a fairly fundamental reappraisal of the notion of epistemic value. While this style of reasoning is admittedly very appealing, it does not stand up to close scrutiny. The fallacy in this reasoning is the idea that if we epistemically value true belief then it follows that we should episte-mically value all true belief equally. But the latter does not follow from the former. As Nick Treanor (2013, 2014) has pointed out in some excellent recent work on this problem, if this reasoning were sound then it would follow from the fact that gold mining aims at acquiring gold that it there-fore treats all gold that is acquired as being of equal value, whether it is a small nugget of gold or a large block of the stuff. Since this obviously is not the case, the upshot would be that gold mining is not aimed at acquiring gold, which is of course absurd. The crux of the matter is that just as two lumps of gold could be of different value, because one is larger than another, so two true beliefs can be of different epistemic value, because one of the beliefs has more content than the other, and hence captures more of the truth.

This last point can look mysterious at first blush, but once one reflects on the matter one can see that it actually reflects a fairly mundane point about propositional content. If I am told (truly) that <something has fallen down the cellar>, I am given far less of a grip on what has actually happened than if I am told (truly) that <your brother has pushed your mother and she has fallen down the cellar>. Even setting aside the greater practical utility of the second true proposition (e.g., one knows in the latter case that an ambulance needs to be called, and also that one needs to be wary of one's brother!), there is also a perfectly straightforward sense in which the second true proposition gives one a more comprehensive grip on reality than the first true proposition. If one's epistemic goal in inquiry is to get at the truth, then one ought to be motivated, ceteris paribus, towards truths with more content over truths with less. Hence, aiming at the truth does not entail epistemically valuing all true beliefs equally.[14]

Indeed, once we recognise this point, then we can start to see other ways in which from a purely epistemic point of view we might value two propositions very differently. Suppose one is building a comprehensive theory regarding some subject matter, but is missing some crucial ingredient, some fact which has yet to be unearthed. This truth, in isolation, may seem relatively uninteresting, at least to the impartial observer anyway, but given one's current epistemic state it could well prove momentous. Clearly, as a truth-seeker, one should prefer this truth over an alternative truth that lacks this momentous import, even insofar as one grants that the alternative truth is roughly equal in terms of its content.[15] After all, this particular momentous truth, while perhaps not epistemically weighty in and of itself, is of great epistemic weight when it comes to one's own epistemic position, in that it will enable one to gain a far more comprehensive grip on the nature of reality than would be otherwise available to one.[16]

With these points in mind, we can see how the epistemic value of ignorance when it comes to misleading defeaters is really a special case of a more general phenomenon whereby one's wide epistemic goals are served by ignorance. Motivated only by purely epistemic concerns, a good inquirer may nonetheless focus her attention on acquiring a truth of substance – for example, a truth that will enable her to gain a comprehensive understanding of a particular subject matter, say—as opposed to focussing on even a large body of truths which don't open up such an epistemically valuable vista. This is why a good inquirer, whose goal is to get at the truth, will tend to favour a set of true beliefs that includes a true belief about fundamental physics rather than a true belief about the number of grains of sand on a beach. To choose to know the

---

[14] This solution to the problem of trivial truths is expertly discussed in Treanor (2013, 2014). I also further explore this proposal in Pritchard (2014).

[15] How does one 'measure' content? I do not pretend to have a developed theory of this (though the general idea that interests us is clearly to measure it along broadly information-theoretic lines – that is, in terms of the amount of information contained within the content). Fortunately, this does not matter for our purposes, since all that concerns us is whether the subject regards these truths as carrying roughly equal amounts of content (for example, they are not like the two statements about the object that fell down the cellar that we encountered earlier, which were clearly containing very different amounts of information).

[16] Note that this is not to say that our only epistemic interest is in gaining a scientific grip on the nature of reality. Truths about the human condition might be of no less epistemic interest, for example, and yet gain one no purchase at all on the nature of (physical) reality.

latter, rather than the former, would be an epistemically disvaluable course of action. Accordingly, a good inquirer may well eschew the possibility of acquiring knowledge of a large body of true beliefs about grains of sand in favour of acquiring knowledge of a single truth about fundamental physics. In doing so, our inquirer is not disavowing the epistemic goal of truth, but rather better satisfying this goal. Moreover, in pursuing this particular kind of inquiry she is also furthering the epistemic good by being ignorant of certain truths. Indeed, our agent, in pursuit of the epistemic good, is actively choosing to be ignorant of these truths. We have thus captured an important sense in which ignorance can be epistemically valuable.

4   Ignorance and Intellectual Humility

A final issue I want to explore in this regard is the epistemic utility of a particular kind of attitude to one's own epistemic standing and epistemic capacities, what we might term *intellectual humility*. By this I have in mind a sensitivity to one's own epistemic limitations, and hence a standing disposition not to overestimate one's epistemic grip on the facts. Intellectual humility is often thought to be at least generally valuable, to the extent that it is a component part of a virtuous life of flourishing.[17] But is intellectual humility of epistemic value, specifically? If so, then what is interesting about this from our perspective is that such humility seems to involve awareness of one's ignorance. To this extent, then, the epistemic value of intellectual humility seems to suggest, at least in a rather indirect way, a potentially new way in which ignorance can be epistemically valuable.

We should note from the outset off that it is not at all obvious that intellectual humility is epistemically valuable. It could be, for example, that focussing on one's epistemic limitations could undermine one's confidence in one's judgements such that one's inquiries are stymied, and hence never lead to fruitful conclusions. Does not good inquiry sometimes involve boldness rather than diffidence? Perhaps, but I think the proponent of the idea of intellectual humility as epistemically valuable has ways of accommodating this idea.

To begin with, note that boldness in one's inquiries should be differentiated from dogmatism. One might boldly put forward a scientific conjecture that runs counter to current thinking and then proceed to test that conjecture. If the conjecture is found to be true, one might thereby come to gain a deep understanding of a subject matter that

---

[17] See, for example, Roberts and Wood (2007) and Baehr (2011).

might not have otherwise have been available. Boldness in inquiry is here seen to be delivering the epistemic good. But this bold inquiry, so described, does not implicate any dogmatism – the bold conjecture was, after all, confirmed by the tests run, and hence was eventually supported by evidence. Suppose that, instead, the tests did not support the conjecture, and that this is a stable feature of the tests run. To continue to press the conjecture would now be to embrace dogmatism, in that one is now inquiring without concern for the evidence, and hence for the truth. Here we have gone beyond mere boldness of inquiry. Moreover, such dogmatism is clearly not serving the epistemic good, but leading one down an intellectual dead end, and one would expect the intellectually humble inquirer, who will not be prone to dogmatism, to not be lead astray in this fashion. So long as we can keep boldness and dogmatism apart, then, there seems to be a way of making the epistemic goodness of intellectual humility compatible with bold inquiry.[18]

The point is that being intellectually humble does not require one to avoid being bold. Rather, what it requires is that, in being aware of one's epistemic limitations – in being aware of the general level of one's ignorance – one is appropriately sensitive to the possibility of error, and so revises one's beliefs accordingly. Indeed, we can think of intellectual humility as an intellectual virtue, and hence as a mean between two epistemically viceful extremes. One of these extremes is the epistemic vice of dogmatism that we just witnessed. The other extreme would be an epistemic vice that we can call intellectual diffidence, where this involves a complete lack of faith in one's judgements, one that is entirely unresponsive to the evidence to the contrary. The virtuous believer will have the practical wisdom to steer between these two extremes and in the process manifest her intellectual virtue. In doing so, she will appropriately employ her knowledge of her general level of ignorance in order to better track the epistemic good.

Now that we have set out what intellectual humility, qua intellectual virtue, involves, however, then it becomes clear that it does not entail that ignorance can be epistemically valuable. It is, after all, one's knowledge of one's ignorance that is servicing the epistemic good when it comes to

---

[18] Another point to bear in mind when we epistemically evaluate the potentially intellectually virtuous behaviour of the intrepid scientist who proposes bold conjectures is that we would not expect her commitment to these conjectures to be anything more than provisional. In particular, we would not expect her to believe these propositions to be true, given their conjectural nature. Thus the very character of her propositional commitments in this regard is revealing a sensitivity to the evidence in play, and hence a lack of dogmatism. (Indeed, it could well be that the scientist's commitment to theoretical claims in general is not one of belief, but rather a weaker propositional attitude, such as acceptance. See, for example, van Fraassen [1980]).

displays of intellectual humility, rather than the ignorance itself. Hence, despite first appearances, intellectual humility does not offer us another way, albeit a tangential one, in which ignorance could be epistemically valuable.[19]

5   Concluding Remarks

Our focus here has been on the epistemic value of ignorance in a very specific sense. In particular, our concern has not been the general value of the epistemic standing of being ignorant, but rather the specifically epistemic value of ignorance. As we have seen, while it is much harder to demonstrate that ignorance is valuable in the latter sense than the former sense, there are some plausible candidates in this regard. The most straightforward of these is misleading defeaters, as it seems that one is epistemically better off in being ignorant of them.

A more interesting kind of case is exposed once we reflect on the best way of 'weighing' epistemic value, since if we do not treat all true beliefs as being of equal epistemic value, then we can accommodate a sense in which one might be epistemically better off in believing some truths rather than others, and thus capture a further way in which ignorance might be epistemically valuable. Finally, we examined intellectual humility, and the idea that this both serves the epistemic good while at the same time incorporating an awareness of one's ignorance. It thus seemed to potentially capture a further, albeit rather indirect, sense in which ignorance could be of epistemic value. As we saw, however, the epistemic value of intellectual humility, properly understood, lies in one's knowledge of one's ignorance rather than in the ignorance itself, and hence this is not a further instance of how ignorance can be epistemically valuable.[20]

---

[19] I am grateful to Rik Peels for discussion on this topic. I discuss intellectual virtue and intellectual humility in more detail in Pritchard (forthcoming a), Carter and Pritchard (forthcoming), and Kallestrup and Pritchard (forthcoming).

[20] This paper was written as part of a research project hosted by the University of Edinburgh's *Eidyn* Philosophical Research Centre: the Templeton Foundation-funded 'Virtue Epistemology, Epistemic Dependence and Intellectual Humility' project. I am grateful to the Templeton Foundation for their support of this research. Thanks to J. Adam Carter, Jesper Kallestrup, and Nick Treanor for helpful discussion on related topics. Special thanks to Rik Peels for detailed comments on an earlier version of this paper.

8   Ignorance and the Religious Life

Justin McBrayer

> For Life is a fire burning along a piece of string – or is it a fuse to a powder keg which we call God? – and the string is what we don't know, our Ignorance, and the trail of ash, which, if a gust of wind does not come, keeps the structure of the string, is History, man's Knowledge ...
>
> ~Robert Penn Warren, *All the King's Men*[1]

1   Ignorance and Religion

There is debate over the nature of ignorance. Some philosophers argue that ignorance is a lack of knowledge (e.g., Le Morvan 2011, 2012, 2013). This is the knowledge view of ignorance. On this view, ignorance is compatible with true belief. Others argue that ignorance is a lack of true belief (e.g., Peels 2010, 2011a, 2012). This is the truth view of ignorance. On this view, ignorance is incompatible with true belief. Since a lack of true belief entails a lack of knowledge, any mental state that counts as ignorance on the truth view will also count as ignorance on the knowledge view. But it is possible for a mental state to count as ignorance on the knowledge view but not on the truth view. For example, one might have a true belief but have arrived at the truth in a Gettier case.

Which of these two conceptions of ignorance we employ will affect our thinking about the relation between religion and ignorance. For example, on the truth view, if it is true that God exists, then it will follow that many religious believers are not ignorant of that fact. Indeed, it will be the non-theists who are ignorant for they shall lack true beliefs about divine reality. These religious believers may not *know* that God exists, but if that's not required to avoid ignorance, then they can meet the test.

The ideas in this paper benefitted from several conversations with Dan Howard-Snyder and Jon Kvanvig at the Nature of Faith conference in St. Louis, Missouri, in November of 2014. That conference was generously funded by the John Templeton Foundation. Gijsbert van den Brink, Dugald Owen, Rik Peels, and Martijn Blaauw provided very helpful comments on an earlier draft of this paper.
[1] Warren (1946, p. 151).

There is more likely to be a deep and pervasive religious ignorance on the knowledge view. This is because there are more conditions that have to be met to avoid ignorance. For this reason, this chapter assumes the more traditional, knowledge view of ignorance. Ignorance is a lack of knowledge. On this conception, it is at least initially plausible that many religious people are ignorant: they believe a great many religious propositions that they do not know. These propositions may be true. The religious likely have faith that these propositions hold. They might even have some justi-fication for the religious propositions in question. But, given the presence of defeaters, the reliance on untrustworthy testimony, and so on, it is likely that a great many of these beliefs will fall short of the higher standards required for knowledge.

How does this ignorance affect the religious life? A careful investigation would reveal the role played by ignorance in both religious theory and religious practice. The point of the chapter to sketch a broad taxonomy of the various roles that ignorance plays in the religious life. This is impor-tant since the religious life is shaped as much by what we do *not* know as by what we do.

2   Ignorance and Religious Theory

Plato's cave is an image of ignorance. We live underground and confront the mere shadows of reality. Enlightenment requires a painful and diffi-cult struggle of breaking free and seeing the light of day for the first time. The questions investigated by philosophy are not prone to easy answers, leaving us in ignorance much of the time. This is even more so the case with philosophy of religion. If there is a supernatural reality, it is plausible that it would be far removed from our everyday experiences. As such, our theoretical grasp on the divine is bound to come up short. For example, if there is a God, it is plausible that we would be deeply ignorant of many of his reasons for acting in the world. This section surveys the role that ignorance has played in theorizing about the *existence* of a divine reality, the *nature* of divine reality, and the *relation* between humans and divine reality.

2.1   Ignorance and the Existence of Divine Reality

Is there a supernatural reality or is the natural world all that there is? Not surprisingly, human ignorance plays a key dialectical role in the evalua-tion of arguments both for and against the existence of the divine. This is especially clear in the development of philosophy of religion in the West where philosophers have been preoccupied with arguments for and

Table 1 *Utility Calculus*

	God exists	God does not exist
Believe that God exists	Infinite gain	Wash
Do not believe that God exists	Infinite loss	Wash

against the existence of God. Without making a claim to a comprehensive survey, here are two examples of ignorance being invoked in favor of theism or atheism and two examples of ignorance being invoked to block arguments for theism or atheism.

Example 1: From ignorance to theism.

Historically, one of the most common ways of justifying the existence of the divine has been through what has been derogatorily called the "God-of-the-Gaps" strategy. This strategy finds some data that cannot be explained (e.g., lightning, the seasons, the existence of life) and then posits God as the explainer. It is obvious how ignorance plays a role in this sort of justification for the divine. It is also obvious that this strategy will commit an illicit appeal to ignorance unless the inference is framed in a careful way (more about this below vis-a-vis fine-tuning arguments).

However, ignorance also plays a key role in "making room" for one of the most contentious arguments for theistic belief, namely Pascal's Wager (e.g., Jordan 2006). Pascal's Wager (and similar prudential arguments for theistic belief) purports to show that it is in our best interest to believe in God regardless of the available evidence. While there are many ways to read the cryptic passages that give rise to the Wager, a standard rendering of the argument is in the form of a utility calculus (see Table 1).

The idea is that if God exists, theists will receive all of the goods of the afterlife whereas non-theists will not. On the other hand, if God does not exist, there is no substantial difference between the goods secured by a theist versus a non-theist. And even if we are ignorant of the existence of God, as long as there is a finite chance that he exists and infinite rewards to be gained, it makes sense to bet on God. So even in the absence of evidence for the existence of God, there is still a powerful, prudential reason to be a theist.

Example 2: From ignorance to atheism.

Some philosophers seem to think that human ignorance renders atheism the dialectical *status quo*. In other words, they think that our ignorance is a reasonable basis to deny the existence of the divine (e.g., Flew 1976;

Mion 2012). However, this kind of move would not be accepted in many other contexts. For example, the status quo should not be to disbelieve that there is life elsewhere in the universe until we get evidence otherwise. In our ignorance, the most reasonable position is to be agnostic on whether or not there is life elsewhere in the universe. For this reason, most philosophers seem to think that agnosticism about the divine is a more reasonable *status quo* and that the dialectical burden is on those who would either affirm or deny the existence of the divine.

The argument from divine hiddenness is the most sophisticated argument that invokes human ignorance as a premise in an argument for atheism (e.g., Schellenberg 1993). The gist of the argument is that the absence of evidence for God constitutes evidence for the absence of God. A very basic version of the argument proceeds as follows:

1. If there were a God, reasonable people would not be ignorant about his existence.
2. But reasonable people ARE ignorant about the existence of God.
3. Therefore, there is not a God.

The defense of premise one rests on the idea that a relationship with God would be among the very highest goods achievable and a relationship with someone requires belief in that person's existence. So given that God is both perfectly loving and perfectly powerful, he would ensure that all reasonable persons would have enough evidence so that belief in God is reasonable. The defense of premise two appeals to the apparent fact that there are many reasonable, thoughtful people who are capable of belief in God and yet are ignorant about his existence due to a shortage of evidence. These people may even have true belief concerning God, but this belief doesn't amount to knowledge and hence is ignorance. And according to the argument from divine hiddenness, this ignorance about the existence of God provides us with a reason to think that there is no such being.

Example 3: Using ignorance to block an argument for theism.

Not only can ignorance be invoked as a reason to be a theist or atheist, it can also be used as a defensive maneuver in the face of arguments for theism or atheism. One prominent example in the current literature concerns cosmic versions of the argument from design (e.g., Swinburne 2004, chapter 8). Sometimes called the fine-tuning argument, this argument starts from a premise about the fine-tuning of the universe and concludes that a powerful designer like God is the best explanation of the fine-tuning data. Very roughly, the fine-tuning data is a collection of all of the facts discovered by scientists working in cosmology regarding the life-permitting parameters of the physical cosmos. It appears that there are many variables that, had they been any other way, would not have allowed for life in the universe. Robin Collins (1999) provides a standard example of this sort of data:

> If the initial explosion of the big bang had differed in strength by as little as one part in 10^{60}, the universe would have either quickly collapsed back on itself, or expanded too rapidly for stars to form. In either case, life would be impossible. (p. 49)

How can we explain the fine-tuning data? Only three possibilities are salient: chance, necessity, or design. The fine-tuning argument attempts to show that design is the best option.

However, design arguments of this sort are often countered by appeals to human ignorance. The idea is that we know too little about the basic structure of the universe or about the conditions for life to make any grand pronouncements about how best to explain the fine-tuning data. Here are two examples of this strategy. First, the design argument relies on the claim that the parameters of the universe could have been different. But perhaps this appearance of contingency is really just our ignorance of deep facts about the parameters of the universe. If it turns out that the parameters of the universe could not have been different, then the design hypothesis is undermined. Second, the design argument relies on the claim that only a handful of universe parameter combinations are life-permitting. But perhaps we are not entitled to this assumption. It if turns out that radically different life forms are possible, perhaps the range of universes that is life-permitting grows substantially. In either case, our ignorance of the deep facts about the universe and life offer avenues to undermine fine-tuning arguments.

Example 4: Using ignorance to block an argument for atheism.

One of the most common arguments for atheism is the argument from evil (e.g., van Inwagen 2006). Suppose the world is governed by a perfectly good and perfectly powerful deity like God. It would be surprising to find that world occupied by the amount, kind, and distribution of evil that we find in the actual world. A very basic version of the argument proceeds as follows:

1. If there were a God, the world would not contain gratuitous evil.
2. But the world DOES contain gratuitous evil.
3. Therefore, there is not a God.

While the argument can be made more sophisticated, something very much like this underlies the atheism of many people in the West.

However, theists have responded to the argument in a number of ways. Relevant to our purposes here is a family of responses termed "skeptical theism" (e.g., McBrayer 2010). In brief, the skeptical theist is a theist who thinks that no one is justified in believing that any given instance of evil is gratuitous. The idea is that we are simply ignorant of too much of moral reality to draw an inference as to whether an evil is necessary for some compensating good. Skeptical theists sometimes rely on analogies to make this point: just as a novice chess player watching a match should not assume that a particular chess move is worthless, so, too, humans looking around at the world should not assume that a particular evil is pointless. In both cases, if there is a master in control of the pieces, there would be many moves/evils that seemed pointless that were not. And if this general line of thought is correct, ignorance appears to undermine the second premise of a general form of the argument from evil.

2.2   Ignorance and the Nature of Divine Reality

The previous section canvassed attempts to invoke ignorance in premises for or rebuttals to arguments for divine reality, specifically God. Just as ignorance plays a key role in arguments for the *existence* of a divine reality, so too does ignorance play a key role in theorizing about the *nature* of that divine reality. For example, in the Christian tradition, St. Paul acknowledges our current ignorance of divine reality when he writes that "for now we see through a glass, darkly; but then face to face . . ." (I Corinthians 13:12). This section explores two prominent examples of the role of ignorance in shaping our thought about the nature of divine reality.

Example 1: The Apophatic Tradition.

Virtually every major world religion includes a strand of theology known collectively as apophatic theology (*apophanai* is Greek for "to say no"). The basic idea is that human concepts fall short of the true nature of the divine. As a result, we cannot speak (or believe) truly about what the divine IS. Instead, we are limited to saying what the divine is *not*. In short, our ignorance of the true nature of the divine is utterly complete. The best we could ever come to know is what the divine is not. However, just as dust might show the form of an invisible man, so, too, might our claims about what the divine is not illuminate the form of the divine. We know indirectly through our ignorance.

Several Western religious thinkers turned toward apophatic theology in the wake of what they saw as blatant anthropomorphism in the theology of the Greek pantheon. Prominent examples of early church fathers include Pseudo-Dionysius, Saint Cyril of Jerusalem, and the Cappadocian fathers. For example, Gregory of Nazianzus wrote that "the only thing that could be comprehended about the incomprehensible divine nature was its 'boundlessness' – what it was not rather than what it was" (Pelikan 1993, p. 42).

The pendulum away from affirmative theology reached a peak in the Medieval period where apophatic reasoning was termed the *via negativa* (Latin for "the negative way"). While those working in the *via affirmativa* tradition attempt to say what God is really like, thinkers in the *via negativa* tradition demur and restrict themselves to claims about what God is not. The idea is that God in his true form is ineffable, and the application of finite concepts to an infinite being only results in confusion.[2]

This negative tradition claims a grounding in the Jewish scriptures at least as early as Moses and the burning bush. When Moses asks who is sending him back to Egypt, the answer is "I am who I am" and nothing more. Maimonides, perhaps the greatest Jewish thinker in the medieval period, writes that:

Know that the negative attributes of God are the true attributes: they do not include any incorrect notions or any deficiency whatever in reference to God, while positive attributes imply polytheism, and are inadequate ... [w]e cannot describe the Creator by any means except by negative attributes. (1956, p. 81)

And while many mystical strains of Christianity are obviously apophatic, the *via negativa* can still be found in contemporary theology (e.g., Marcus Borg's *The God We Never Knew*). Despite this presence, it's also probably fair to say that it plays a larger role in Orthodox Christian theology as compared to Roman Catholic or Protestant theology.

Apophaticism shows up in Eastern religions, too. Hindu philosophers are cagey about their descriptions of Atman and Brahman. On the one hand, Brahman is recognized as the ultimate reality. But what that reality is like becomes hard to say. Those working in the Advaita Vedanta tradition of Hinduism explicitly endorse our ignorance of divine reality by naming reality *Nirguna Brahman*: reality indescribable by human predicates. Similarly, philosophers working in Taoist tradition insist that our understanding of the divine is shrouded in ignorance. The first lines of the *Tao Te Ching* are as follows:

> The Tao that can be told of is not the eternal Tao;
> The name that cannot be named is not the eternal name.
> The Nameless is the origin of Heaven and Earth;
> The Named is the mother of all things.   (Chan 1963, p. 97)

As soon as you apply a human concept to the divine, you're guaranteed to have gotten it wrong. Ignorance is at the heart of our theorizing about the nature of the divine.

---

[2] There are, of course, theologians in the Medieval period who draw from both the *via affirmativa* and *via negativa* traditions. One anonymous reviewer suggests that St. Thomas is an example of this blend.

Example 2: Divine Reality as the Noumenon.

Kant famously argues that we cannot have unmediated metaphysical knowledge. Thus we are ignorant of reality as it exists outside of our own concepts. While we can know a great deal about how the world *appears* to us (the phenomenal realm), we know next to nothing about the world *as it is in itself* (the noumenal realm). In short, Kant insists that a perceived situation owes as much to the perceiver as to the world outside of the perceiver.

Several philosophers of religion have applied this insight to our understanding of divine reality. John Hick is the foremost contemporary example to have exploited this comparison (Hick 1989). According to Hick,

... the realization that the world, as we consciously perceive it, is partly our own construction leads directly to a differentiation between the world *an sich*, unperceived by anyone, and the world as it appears to, that is as it is perceived by, us. (p. 241)

As applied to divine reality, we might say that the divine being as it is exists *an sich* may be different from the divine being as it appears to us. The result is that " ... the great post-axial faiths constitute different ways of experiencing, conceiving and living in relation to an ultimate divine reality which transcends all our varied visions of it" (pp. 235–236). Divine reality is the noumenon. The perceptions of the divine are the phenomena. In each case, the Christian, Jew, Muslim, Hindu, and Buddhist are responding to the same ultimate divine reality, albeit this reality is perceived in radically different ways. So on the one hand, our grasp of the divine is steeped in ignorance. Our knowledge of the divine *as it exists in itself* is restricted to logical or formal properties like "exists." On the other hand, our grasp of the divine *as it is perceived* by humans is much deeper, although obviously relative to different religious communities. In this sense, our knowledge of the divine-as-perceived will include the attribution of a range of substantive properties such as "is good," "created us."

2.3   Ignorance and the Relation between Humans and Divine Reality

The last two sections canvassed major roles that ignorance plays in arguments for the existence of a divine reality and arguments about the nature of divine reality. This final section on ignorance in religious theory will highlight two prominent cases in which ignorance plays a theoretical role in the relation between humans and divine reality.

Example 1: Freedom and Foreknowledge Debate.

At least in the West where the divine is portrayed as a person, the question of human freedom looms large in the face of divine foreknowledge. If acting freely requires the possibility to do otherwise and if infallible foreknowledge eliminates the possibility of acting otherwise, how can humans ever act freely given the existence of an omniscient being like God? Many philosophers, both historical and contemporary, have agreed that foreknowledge threatens genuine freedom (e.g., Hasker 1985).

While there are many purported solutions to the problem, one of the most serious contenders in contemporary philosophy of religion is a view known as open theism (e.g., Hasker 2004). According to open theism, God is ignorant of our future actions that are not necessitated by current states of affairs plus the laws of nature. In other words, there are a great many things about the future that God does not know, and since he does not foreknow these things, all possibilities remain open for the human actors in question. Of course, it would be a very good thing to know what would happen in the future, so open theists owe an explanation for why a perfect, omniscient being would fail to have this knowledge. One standard explanation is that an omniscient being will know all that there is to know. However, when it comes to future actions, these facts are contingent upon human choices and so there is no fact yet to be known. To use Aristotle's example, it is neither true nor false that there will be a sea battle tomorrow. But since knowledge implies truth, there is nothing to be foreknown about the sea battle. Other open theists grant that future contingents have a truth value but insist that God remains ignorant of these truths in order to preserve the possibility of free action. This is a perfect example of ignorance being invoked to solve problems in religious theorizing.

Example 2: The Nature of Salvation.

While European explorers of the New World undoubtedly had many different motivations, chief among them was a desire to evangelize the native peoples. This religious drive continues to the present day. For example, the Mormon (LDS) Church claims to have almost 100,000 missionaries in the field at any time.[3] Why?

Theories of salvation vary widely among world religions, but historically a centerpiece in many of these religions is the view that ignorance is inimical to salvation. To be truly saved, one must truly believe. As long as one remains ignorant of divine reality, salvation is impossible. Thus the

[3] www.mormonnewsroom.org/facts-and-stats

chief good that a missionary could deliver is the information needed to reach salvation. Knowledge (or at least true belief) is a requirement for avoiding damnation or achieving the beatific vision. And so ignorance plays a major theoretical role in religious theories of the afterlife.

In Christianity this understanding is motivated in no small part by "the Great Commission" in the gospel of Mark:

And [Jesus] said to them, "Go into all the world and preach the gospel to all creation. He who has believed and has been baptized shall be saved; but he who has disbelieved shall be condemned." (Mark 16:15–16)

This verse, among others, has been used by Christians to argue that true belief is necessary for salvation. This explains the preeminence of creeds and the attendant importance of orthodoxy in many religious traditions: heaven or hell hang in the balance.

However, just as some philosophers have defended the necessity of true belief for salvation, others have criticized it. The core critique is that praise and blame are typically reserved for features of one's life that are under one's control. For example, it makes sense to praise someone for his hard work but not for the color of his hair. Paired with the uncontroversial claim that we do not exercise direct voluntary control over our beliefs, this common sense moral principle implies that we cannot be praised or blamed for our religious ignorance. Of course, this is not to deny that we often have *indirect* control over our beliefs. If I want to learn the capital of Kenya, I can consult an authoritative source. But whether my experience of the source gives rise to a belief about the capital of Kenya is beyond my control. The same goes for religious propositions: perhaps we can be held accountable for whether we carefully considered the evidence available. But whether these experiences give rise to religious belief is out of our control. And so, according to some philosophers, it is problematic to give ignorance a prominent role in determining afterlife goods.

On a related issue, just as ignorance of certain propositions might bar one from heaven, it might also be required to remain in heaven. For example, on the Christian conception of the beatific vision, the saved experience eternal bliss in the presence of God. But many philosophers of religion have wondered whether this eternal bliss were possible in the face of certain kinds of knowledge (e.g., Talbott 1990). For example, how could one be happy and content in heaven on the assumption that many of one's former friends and relatives are suffering the torments of hell? One popular response to this objection is that the saved are purposefully kept ignorant about the fates of those consigned to hell (e.g., Craig 1991).

And so while ignorance may play a theoretical role in determining where one exists in the afterlife, it may also play a theoretical role in determining the quality of that afterlife.

3   Ignorance and Religious Practice

We have seen that ignorance plays many key roles in religious theory. How might ignorance affect religious practice? As with religious theory, ignorance is important both for the communal lives of religious people and also the lives of religious individuals as they live out their faiths.

3.1   Ignorance in Communal Religious Life

Religious communities have often employed the ignorance of others to their advantage. In some cases, ignorance is essential for the survival of the communities in question. Easy examples include the early Christian church's efforts to keep the Roman authorities in ignorance and 18th–20th century efforts by Jewish communities in Europe to stay under the radar of anti-Semitic governments.

But in at least some cases, religious communities inculcate an ignorance even among their own congregations. Again, the early Christian church is an obvious example. Like something out of the *Da Vinci Code*, early church leaders sought to keep both outsiders and newly initiated Christians in the dark about many of the church's rituals and practices. This practice was much later termed the *disciplina arcani*: the arcane disciplines. According to the Catholic encyclopedia New Advent, the practice has its roots in the Christian scripture[4]: "Do not give dogs what is sacred; do not throw your pearls to pigs. If you do, they may trample them under their feet, and turn and tear you to pieces" (Matthew 7:6). Some scholars have argued that this practice of concealing certain rituals and services led rather naturally to the growth of Christian mysticism in the early medieval period (e.g., Stroumsa 2005).

3.2   Ignorance in the Individual Religious Life

What role might ignorance play in the life of individual religious people? It is initially plausible that ignorance is an impediment to living a religiously virtuous life or a life of genuine religious faith. The virtuous religious person is not a person of doubt. The faithful religious person, it might be supposed, is a knower, not a doubter. But this initial

---

[4] www.newadvent.org/cathen/05032a.htm

presumption is too quick. This final section canvasses the role of ignorance in a life of religious virtue and a life of religious faith.

Regarding religious virtue, the *pro tanto* case against ignorance is based on an isomorphic case against ignorance with regard to moral virtue. In ethical theory, it is commonplace to assume that knowledge is a prerequisite for exercising the moral virtues. Aristotle claims that, "[the virtuous agent] must be in a certain condition when he does [the virtuous action]; in the first place he must have knowledge; secondly he must choose the acts, and choose them for their own sakes; and thirdly his action must proceed from a firm and unchangeable character" (*Nicomachean Ethics* II.4.1105a 31–34). So it appears that knowledge is a necessary condition for virtuous action. Since religion is at least partly a normative endeavor, it is inevitable that there are certain character traits that function as virtues and others that function as vices. And just as ignorance is bad for the practice of ethical virtues, so, too, is ignorance bad for the practice of religious virtues.

But philosophers have challenged this picture of moral virtue as overly-intellectualized. Julia Driver (2001) argues that not only is knowledge not required for the exercise of all moral virtues but in fact knowledge is inconsistent with certain moral virtues. She argues for an entire class of virtues that she terms "virtues of ignorance" that include things like genuine modesty, blind charity (roughly seeing the best in others while ignoring their faults), impulsive courage, and a sort of forgiveness. In each case, she claims that full disclosure would eliminate the virtuous disposition. At least some recent experimental philosophy backs up this picture (e.g., Feltz and Cokely 2012). It turns out that ignorance does not rule out our attributions of virtue in many cases, and, even more surprisingly, ignorance can boost the odds of ascriptions of virtue in certain cases. Especially regarding cases of modesty and impulsive courage, respondents are somewhat more likely to attribute the virtue in question to an actor when it is stipulated that the actor is ignorant of certain facts.

Perhaps the same goes for religious virtues. As recounted in the Jewish and Christian traditions, Adam and Eve were expelled from the Garden of Eden for eating from the tree of the knowledge of good and evil. God had created them with an ignorance that rendered them better off to at least some extent. A loss of that ignorance left them shamed and homeless. Is that true for religious virtues in general? A full examination of the topic would require an account of religious virtue and vice and a discussion of whether ignorance preempts the "activation" of such virtues. For present purposes, a brief illustration is sufficient. In the Christian tradition, there are three theological virtues that have traditionally been offered as primary religious virtues: faith, hope, and love (sometimes termed "charity"). Since faith is considered separately below, does ignorance impair the exercise of hope or love?

It is quite clear that religious belief can be a *source* of hope. For example, empirical research suggests that religious belief in those who are ill boosts a hope in recovery (e.g., McBrayer 2014). And there are famous examples of religious believers whose belief sustained almost unbelievable efforts in the face of dismal odds. As a singular example, recall the trials of Father Trocme and his fellow villagers in the French town of Le Chambon as they struggled to locate and save Jews from the Nazis during World War Two. The townspeople managed to save literally thousands of lives over the course of the war. Philip Hallie, the philosopher who chronicled the effort, concludes that "in all certainty ... [father] Trocme's belief in God was at the living centre of the rescue efforts of the village" (1979, p. xxi).

But can this sort of hope obtain in the absence of religious belief? It seems so. Louis Pojman's famous paper "Faith, Hope and Doubt," argues that faith does not require belief (see below) and further that something like hope could serve as a substitute for belief. In his description of hope, he makes a persuasive case for the claim that we can hope for things that we do not believe. As an easy example, I can hope that I win the lottery even though I do not believe that I will win the lottery. There is no apparent reason why religious hope would be any different than hope *simpliciter*. And if so, then it makes perfect sense to conclude that religious people might be able to exercise the virtue of religious hope even in the presence of a deep and abiding religious ignorance. The religious individual might have to believe that P in order to know that P, but she doesn't have to believe that P in order to hope that P.

The same might be said of charity. Take an example familiar to anyone who has spent time in a large city: panhandling. When faced with a destitute stranger asking for money, what would the virtuous person do? There is ample evidence that in at least some cases the donated funds are used for illicit purchases like drugs that harm the stranger's welfare in the long run. But this is not always the case. And so we are left in ignorance about a great many things that would help us to make a wise decision. Does that ignorance eliminate the possibility of true charity? No. While the ignorance may function as an excuse that counters the duty of beneficence, it need not do so. The truly charitable person may give even in the presence of ignorance.

As applied to religious individuals, the amount of charity given by those who practice a religion is staggering. Aside from the often significant support that such religious individuals provide to their own religious communities, the religious often give more to secular causes as well (e.g., Brooks 2007). In many of these cases, the givers are ignorant not only about the relevant religious propositions but also about the full uses of the funds in question – how many supporters of the local mosque know the local budget? So it is difficult to see how any sort of general ignorance blocks the activation of religious virtues. Furthermore, the correlation between religiosity and certain virtues suggests a causal connection.

Leaving the other virtues aside, what is the relation between *faith* and ignorance? Many people are religiously faithful and practice their faith on a daily basis. Does ignorance hamper their effort, aid their effort, or neither? Answering this question requires a clear conception of the nature of religious faith, and that is highly contested ground in which contemporary philosophers of religion are expending enormous amounts of effort. Still, it is possible to give a quick survey of the field.

Some philosophers have argued that ignorance hampers faith. This view has deep roots in the development of Christian thinkers in the west. For example, John Calvin wrote that faith is "a firm and certain knowledge of God's benevolence towards us" (*Institutes* III, ii, 7, 551). For Calvin, faith is not just identified with knowledge but with certainty! Similarly, John Locke describes divine testimony as follows:

This is called by a peculiar Name, Revelation, and our Assent to it, Faith: which as absolutely determines our Minds, and as perfectly excludes all wavering as our Knowledge itself ... so that Faith is a settled and sure Principle of Assent and Assurance, and leaves no manner of room for Doubt or Hesitation. (*An Essay Concerning Human Understanding*, Book IV, Chapter XVI and 14; Nidditch 1975, p. 667)

And so for Locke, faith excludes doubt and ignorance in the same way that knowledge does. At least some prominent contemporary philosophers endorse this view that faith is either identical with or presupposes knowledge (e.g., Plantinga 2000).

Other thinkers claim the very opposite: faith requires ignorance. St. Thomas Aquinas writes that "you can't know what you simultaneously put faith in, because knowledge sees and faith doesn't" (*Summa Theologiae* 1989, p. 329). Bishop (2010) makes a similar point by citing Kant: "I have ... found it necessary to deny *knowledge*, in order to make room for *faith*" (preface to the second edition of *The Critique of Pure Reason*). Additionally, William James' work on what he calls the "will to believe" presupposes a great deal of ignorance (e.g., James 1912). For James, we can be within our intellectual rights in endorsing one hypothesis over another even if we are ignorant of which of the two hypotheses holds. And, in fact, it's only in the face of such ignorance that the will to believe "kicks in." In other words, without ignorance, there is no will to believe. There are contemporary philosophers who endorse this incompatibility. Clegg (1979) opens with what he takes to be an obvious admission: ". . . we all recognize that we can have faith only in what we do not know – in an uncertain future, for instance, but not in an obvious past" (p. 225). For philosophers in this camp, faith that X precludes knowledge that X.

Finally, some philosophers reject both of these views. These philosophers deny both that faith requires knowledge and that faith requires ignorance. Faith is compatible with either. Many of these views of faith are non-cognitive in the sense that they do not require the faithful to endorse a specific cognitive content. While there are many such non-cognitive views, what follows is a brief sample. According to Clegg (1979), faith is the emotional inverse of fear. It is an affective state that is manifested only in ignorance. Like other emotional states, "a faith may be shaken, crushed, dashed, lost, or abandoned, but not falsified" (1979, p. 232). Other philosophers think of faith as a kind of acceptance that is different from belief (e.g., Alston 1996; Howard-Snyder 2016). The idea is that one can accept a claim and act in accord with it even though one does not yet believe the claim. The acceptance model of faith is similar to a view sometimes described as a practical commitment model of faith (e.g., Kvanvig 2013). On this view, having faith is having a disposition to act in accord with an ideal even when one's evidential situation falls short of justifying a belief that the ideal will obtain. On any of these views of the nature of faith, true faith is compatible with ignorance.

While perhaps at odds with everyday intuitions, the view that faith is compatible with ignorance gains traction when we examine the lives of role models in the faith. San Juan de la Cruz writes powerfully of his "dark night of the soul" in which God deliberately pulls away from the converted Christian:

> . . . spiritual persons suffer great trials, by reason not so much of the aridities which they suffer, as of the fear which they have of being lost on the road, thinking that all spiritual blessing is over for them and that God has abandoned them . . . . For the more a soul endeavours to find support in affection and knowledge, the more it will feel a lack of these . . . (Peers 1951, pp. 71, 74)

During the dark night, ignorance reigns, even when the faithful follower wishes it would go. A contemporary example is Mother Theresa who confesses that her knowledge of God ebbed and flowed leaving her at times with the challenge of living a faithful life in her ignorance. At one point, Mother Theresa sets her goal "to live by faith and yet not to believe" (Kolodiejchuk 2009, p. 248). While it is probably true that Mother Theresa was a religious believer for much of her life, it seems equally clear that she was not a religious believer for all of her life. She wrestled with extreme periods of doubt, and hence she is an example of someone living a life of faith not just in ignorance but even without belief.

4   Conclusion

In the end, the relationship between the religious life and ignorance offers a lesson of hope. Ignorance can be marshaled as evidence both for and against theoretical conceptions of the divine, but it is not decisive in either case. Furthermore, ignorance appears compatible with a life of religious virtue and a life of religious faith. While it is surely worthwhile to improve our knowledge of the world and whatever supernatural elements it may contain, our current ignorance need not paralyze us. We can live, hope, and even worship despite, and perhaps because of, our ignorance.

9   Epistemic Injustice and the Preservation of Ignorance

Miranda Fricker

Ignorance is not always bad; far from it. Looking at the issue in its most general aspect there is the obvious point that for finite beings, massive ignorance is a precondition of having an epistemically functional life, for cognitive overload is an epistemic liability. There is an indefinite, indeed infinite, number of things that we do not have the slightest need to know – the number of hairs on your head at midnight on your next birthday, for instance. Furthermore, we actively need *not* to know most of them (or not to spend time and energy investigating them) in order to conserve cognitive capacity for those things that we do need to know. Less abstractly, there is also the point that there are many things it would be morally and/or prudentially bad to know – intimate details that are none of our business; techniques of criminality; methods of rekindling old ethnic hatreds in a population. These points are familiar from debates about 'the value question' in relation to knowledge.[1] Furthermore, as Cynthia Townley has argued, many forms of epistemic cooperation and many of the dispositions involved in epistemic virtues generally depend crucially upon our leaving some useless or harmful things unknown by passively or actively preserving others' ignorance of things they need not or should not know (Townley 2011). In short, good epistemic practice is necessarily highly selective in all sorts of ways. What matters is that we know what we *need* to know, expanding outwards to the broader aim of knowing and telling what we *should* know and tell, given our purposes and broadly ethical obligations all things considered. Good epistemic conduct needs to be understood as the maintenance of appropriate balances of knowledge and ignorance, in oneself and also in relation to others.

This opening reflection on the epistemic value of ignorance and its place in the epistemic economy directs our attention to the basic norma-

---

[1] See Sosa's example of 'trivial' knowledge (2002, p. 156); and Zagzebski's examples of prudentially and morally 'bad' knowledge (2003, p. 21).

tive ambivalence in our use of the term.[2] 'Ignorance' may refer simply to an epistemically innocent absence of knowledge (this absence being advantageous or disadvantageous, as the case may be, without any reflection on the conduct of the epistemic subject in question); or alternatively it may refer to some kind of cognitive failure, which might be non-culpable (perhaps the result of misleading evidence) or which might, on the other hand, represent a blameworthy failure to put the requisite effort or skill into knowing something one ought to know.

This paper will focus on those forms of culpable and non-culpable ignorance that are created or preserved by one or another kind of epistemic injustice that I have elsewhere labelled 'testimonial injustice' and 'hermeneutical injustice'.[3] I shall discuss the first only briefly, for it is more specifically in relation to hermeneutical injustice that new and complex issues have recently been raised concerning various different forms of ignorance that can be involved in this phenomenon. In particular I hope to say something useful about the place of 'wilful'[4] or motivated ignorance, and to thereby contribute to recent debates in which the phenomenon of hermeneutical injustice has been related to what Charles Mills has termed 'white ignorance'.[5] Ultimately I shall argue that the phenomenon Mills characterises on the whole picks out a different kind of ignorance from any that is involved in hermeneutical injustice. But I shall also argue that the two categories can overlap.

1   Preserving Patterns of Social Ignorance: Testimonial Injustice and Hermeneutical Marginalisation

When the level of credibility attributed to a speaker's word is reduced by prejudice operative in the hearer's judgement, the speaker suffers a *testimonial injustice*. Despite the specific label, the speech act in which his word is expressed need not be strictly that of testimony or telling, but might equally be the airing of an opinion, suggestion or relevant possibility. Furthermore, as Christopher Hookway has suggested, it might even be occasioned by the asking of a question that is designed to contribute to some shared inquiry.[6] The prejudice driving any case of testimonial injustice may or may not be a belief, and it operates specifically in the

---

[2] For debate about what ignorance is necessarily ignorance *of*, see for instance the exchange between Pierre Le Morven (2010, 2011) and Rik Peels (2011a).
[3] See Fricker (2007, 2013b).
[4] The term 'willful ignorance' is from Gaile Pohlhaus (2012).   [5] See Mills (2007, 2015).
[6] I am grateful to Chris Hookway for this point that someone who puts a *question* as a contribution to collective inquiry (perhaps in the classroom) might find her question passed over due to prejudice (Hookway 2010). I hope I may ultimately be allowed this as a limiting case of testimonial injustice, even though it concerns a speech act that is not an

hearer's *judgement of credibility*, where the judgement may be unreflective and spontaneous – a matter of ingrained habit. (The trained quasi-perceptual dispositions governing such judgements I have elsewhere labelled the hearer's 'testimonial sensibility'.) The influence of prejudice in judgements of credibility can make itself felt regardless of the hearer's beliefs, indeed in spite of them, for prejudice can operate unconsciously or, as we have now learned to say, at the level of 'implicit bias'.[7] Testimonial injustice's obvious connection to ignorance is that in cases where the speaker knows that *p* and the prejudice operative in the hearer's credibility judgement prevents her learning that *p* from the speaker, other things equal she thereby stays ignorant of *p*.

Testimonial injustice not only blocks the flow of knowledge, it also blocks the flow of evidence, doubts, critical ideas and other epistemic inputs that are conducive to knowledge. The free circulation of these epistemic goods is conducive to knowledge not only in the direct sense that ready-made items of knowledge may themselves be transmitted, but also in the indirect sense that such items tend also to constitute reasons to believe *other* things, so that they may have the epistemic power to convert other of the hearers beliefs into knowledge. The obstructions that testimonial injustice introduces into the circulation of such epistemic items is therefore not only bad for the person whose word is prejudicially downgraded; it is epistemically bad for the hearer, and for the epistemic system quite generally. An epistemic system characterised by testimonial injustice is a system in which ignorance will repeatedly prevail over potentially shared knowledge, despite speakers' best efforts. Where a speaker knows something the hearer does not (and where the level of credibility deficit is such that the hearer does not accept what she is told) the hearer's ignorance is conserved. Alternatively, where the speaker is offering evidence with a (positive or negative) bearing on something the hearer already

---

assertion. The label 'testimonial injustice' was always explicitly intended capaciously, to include not only the broad class of tellings but also cases where a speaker 'expresses a personal opinion to a hearer, or airs a value judgement, or tries out a new idea or hypothesis on a given audience' (Fricker 2007, p. 60). Hookway's case of the student's relevant question admittedly stretches my characterisation; but provided one can regard the asking of such a question as potentially vulnerable to a *prejudicial credibility deficit*, then it seems more or less to belong to the same category. I would certainly acknowledge that this requires us to take 'credibility' in its everyday sense, as covering the wide range of respects in which what someone says may be taken as more or less authoritative. Such a colloquial construal is supported by the fact that the object of any credibility judgement includes not only *what is said* but also *the speaker*. At any rate, I hope these considerations provide enough commonality to keep the diverse possibilities sufficiently unified under the category 'testimonial injustice'.

[7] There is a fast growing philosophical literature drawing upon empirical work in psychology on implicit bias. See, for instance, Holroyd (2012), Saul (2013), Gendler (2014), Nagel (2014), Leslie (forthcoming) and Brownstein and Saul (eds.) (2016).

believes but does not know, then the hearer misses out on reasons which (if positive) might render her belief knowledge or at least lend it greater justificatory weight; or which (if negative) might disabuse her of a false belief, or at least reveal it as less well supported than it had seemed. Either way, an opportunity for epistemic improvement is lost, and ignorance prevails.

A further, more buried, form of epistemic damage caused by testimonial injustice is that, where it is persistent and socially patterned (as anything driven by prejudice is likely to be), it will tend to create or increase *hermeneutical marginalisation*. That is to say, it will tend to create and sustain a situation in which some social groups have less than a fair crack at contributing to the shared pool of concepts and interpretive tropes that we use to make generally shareable sense of our social experiences. We might gloss this idea of a pool of concepts and interpretive tropes as 'shared social meanings', where the idea is that while this pool will surely not exhaust all the various up and running sets of social meanings that are being used locally by this or that group in a given society, the *shared* pool (elsewhere I have called this the 'collective hermeneutical resource') contains only meanings that just about anyone can draw upon and expect those meanings to be understood across social space by just about anyone else. The collective hermeneutical resource contains those concepts and conceptualisations that are held *in common*.

This means that being a member of a social group that does not contribute on an equal footing with other groups to that shared interpretive resource (a position of hermeneutical marginalisation) puts one at an unfairly increased risk of having social experiences that one needs, perhaps urgently, to understand and/or communicate to certain powerful social others—to a teacher, an employer, a police officer, a jury – but which cannot be made mutual sense of in the shared terms available. We are only now, for instance, entering a historical moment in the West at which it is increasingly possible for a young person originally assigned as 'male' to be able to say to a parent, teacher or friend that he has always felt himself to be a girl in 'the wrong body' and hope to be understood as expressing an intelligible experience. Increasingly the various concepts and conceptions of how sex, gender, sexual orientation and other deep identity affiliations may be organised and reorganised in an individual's experienced identity – notably the concept of *trans* together with its less established counterpart *cis* – are gradually entering the shared hermeneutical resource instead of staying local to the trans community. Still now, where a trans woman might attempt to describe her experience of gender identity to a social other who does not share the relevant concepts, she is unlikely to be able to make herself much understood, and this is where her remaining hermeneutical marginalisation will manifest itself in the unfair deficit of intelligibility that constitutes a hermeneutical injustice. Like testimonial injustices, this kind of hermeneutical injustice preserves ignorance, for that which remains insufficiently intelligible to the relevant social other cannot be passed on to them as knowledge.

Here we see how closely the two kinds of epistemic injustice are related: testimonial injustice can create or sustain hermeneutical marginalisation by blocking the flow of reports, ideas and perspectives that would help generate richer and more diversified shared hermeneutical resources that all can draw on in their social understandings, whether of their own or of others' experiences. Therefore the broad patterns of testimonial injustice – most likely patterns created by the operation of negative identity prejudices, inasmuch as these are the chief systematic prejudices – will tend to reproduce themselves as patterns of hermeneutical marginalisation, and it is these that give rise to systematic hermeneutical injustices. Thus we can see how the preservation of hearer-ignorance that is the likely effect of any instance of testimonial injustice can contribute directly to the hermeneutically marginalised position of the speaker. And a hermeneutically marginalised speaker is vulnerable to hermeneutical injustice. Charles Mills has noted this close connection between the two kinds of epistemic injustice in respect of race:

> Applying these concepts [of testimonial and hermeneutical injustice] to racial domination, we could say that white ignorance is achieved and perpetuated through both varieties working in tandem: a general scepticism about non-white cognition and an exclusion from accepted discourse of non-white categories and frameworks of analysis. Thus a double handicap will result—*people of color will be denied credibility and the alternative viewpoints that could be developed from taking their perspective seriously will be rejected* [italics added]... (Mills 2015 p. 222)

So the two kinds of ignorance that are preserved through the operation of the two kinds of epistemic injustice are causally connected, and this interconnection is part of why our subject-variant areas of ignorance— especially our ignorance of different areas of our shared but dramatically stratified social world—tend to display the patterns of social power.

2   Clarifying Hermeneutical Injustice: Spaces for Localised Hermeneutical Practices

Hermeneutical injustice is internally diverse in various dimensions. One internal differentiation we can usefully emphasise is between two sorts of case. The difference is between a radical case where the person concerned is at least temporarily unable to make full sense of her own experience even to herself; and a more moderate sort of case where she understands the nature of her own experience perfectly well, and, furthermore, is able to communicate it to members of a social group to which she belongs, and yet she is unable to render it intelligible across social space to some significant social other to whom she needs to convey it.

In *Epistemic Injustice* (Fricker 2007) I tried to bring out this distinction by way of a contrast between what we might call a 'maximal' and a 'minimal' case – that is, between a case where the individual was not in a position to make proper sense of her own experience even to herself; and, by contrast, a case where the individual could make perfect sense of it, and could have communicated it to almost any social other except the particular social others he specially needed to communicate it to. These two opposite extremes were intended to imply a continuum of possibilities in between – that is, a range of cases in which there is shared intelligibility across an increasingly large group or groups. The maximal example – drawn from Susan Brownmiller's memoir of the US women's liberation movement (Brownmiller 1990) – was that of a woman in late-1960s North America, Carmita Wood, who was being sexually harassed at work but for whom extant hermeneutical resources did not enable her to experience this lucidly for what it was, so that while she experienced it as upsetting, intimidating, demeaning, confusing ... somehow she was also aware that these forms of understanding did not capture it. As recounted by Brownmiller, Carmita Wood remained confused about what it was she was experiencing, because there was an objective lack of available concepts with which to make proper sense of it. Her achievement was to find a community of women who together created a safe discursive space in which to explore their experiences and find a way of interpreting them that rendered them more fully intelligible. Through dialogue within the group they hit upon a critical composite label, 'sexual harassment', and they overcame their hermeneutical marginalisation in this regard by demanding that the term and the interpretation it expressed become part of the wider shared vocabulary.

In *The Epistemology of Resistance*, José Medina emphasises that marginalised groups may often have perfectly functioning and sophisticated sets of interpretive practices up and running within their social group or community, which however do not work communicatively outside the group – the non-sharedness of the requisite concepts and interpretations reflecting the fact that the 'privileged' meanings held in common are inadequate.[8] This is indeed worth emphasising, and in this connection

---

[8] Medina (2013). See also Medina (2012), Mason (2011), Pohlhaus (2011) and Dotson (2012).

I would reaffirm the idea that the concepts and meanings that are shared by all are bound to reflect, in the broad view, the perspectives and experiences of those groups with more social power generally, for the reason that those with more social power are very likely to be over-contributors to the shared hermeneutical resource. (That tendency, that alliance of hermeneutical power with other kinds of social power, is present in the very idea of hermeneutical *marginalisation*.) Accordingly, the possibility of localised hermeneutical practices is built in to the picture of how Carmita Wood and her fellow consciousness raisers overcame hermeneutical injustice. The group was of course not a *pre-existing* community, but like other such groups it swiftly developed a voice of its own, operating in a relation of dissonance and dissent as regards mainstream understandings. If we jump forward a couple of years from the time of the consciousness raising group's first meetings, we would find a fully operative localised hermeneutical practice among feminists who readily named sexual harassment for what it was, even while that concept had not yet entered the shared hermeneutical resource, recalcitrant employers and all, as later it came to do. This represents a localised well-functioning hermeneutical practice that nonetheless leaves its practitioners susceptible to hermeneutical injustice whenever they should attempt to render the experience intelligible across social space to others who are non-conversant, perhaps resistant to, the requisite modes of interpretation.

Contrasting with the maximal case exemplified by Carmita Wood, the minimal case of hermeneutical injustice presented in *Epistemic Injustice* also, and more explicitly, illustrates the possibility of a fully functioning yet insufficiently widely shared hermeneutical practice. It is already a case of such a practice, though not this time on the part of anyone generally lacking in social power. The example was that of Joe, the central character in Ian McEwan's novel *Enduring Love* (McEwan 1998). Joe is being stalked by a religious fanatic who wants to convert him. Joe is an educated, white, middle-class man, whose hermeneutical marginalisation (if any – it is the vanishingly minimal case) is highly specific, localised to the particular matter in hand, and whose experience he himself has no difficulty in understanding and would easily be able to communicate to members of almost any social group.[9] And yet when it comes to the most important social body to which he needs to be able to communicate it, namely the police, he finds they are not in a position to make proper sense of it – there is quite literally no appropriate box to tick on their form.

---

[9] That his hermeneutical marginalisation is so highly specific to one area of experience (that of being non-violently stalked) renders Joe's hermeneutical injustice, in the terminology I used in *Epistemic Injustice*, a thoroughly 'incidental' rather than 'systematic' case of the injustice (see Fricker 2007, chapter 1, p. 7).

Thus I would argue that a commitment to the existence of localised interpretive practices that may perfectly capture a given range of experiences but whose meanings are not sufficiently shared across wider social space is already present at the heart of the original account of hermeneutical injustice. I gladly acknowledge, however, the importance of centre-staging, as others have done,[10] what I am here calling *midway* cases of hermeneutical injustice – those situated somewhere between maximal and minimal in virtue of the fact that they concern existing communities who operate localised or in-group hermeneutical practices that are none-theless not shared across further social space. These are cases in which there are sophisticated interpretive practices, perhaps with their own history of internal challenge and change, which are already functionally entrenched for a given social group or groups, but not shared with at least one out-group with whom communication is needed. Members of such hermeneutically self-reliant groups are vulnerable to hermeneutical injustices whose form does not involve any confused experiences whatever, but only frustratingly failed attempts to communicate them to members of an out-group. (In the next section we shall see this midway form of hermeneutical injustice put to work in relation to a special case of white ignorance.) Medina is right to emphasise that the intersectional ignorances created by the possession and non-possession of this or that cluster of interpretive concepts growing out of this or that area of social experience tell a 'polyphonic' or multi-voiced story of power *and* resistance, societal conceptual impoverishment *and* localised interpretive sophistication and creativity. These opposing energies are present in both maximal and minimal cases, but the creative and affirming energy involved in resisting mainstream meanings and nurturing instead a set of more localised concepts and interpretations is obviously more to the fore in those cases of hermeneutical injustice that *start* from a situation in which a relatively powerless group has developed well-entrenched but localised interpretive practices of its own. In such cases, in-group intelligibility is doing just fine; and any hermeneutical injustices that arise will be strictly a matter of unfairly limited communicative intelligibility in relation to an out-group.

An illustration of such a midway case of hermeneutical injustice might be drawn from the history of post-colonial race relations in the UK. Drawing on an account of the experience of growing up in postwar Britain as the children of Caribbean immigrants to 'the mother country' – often symbolised by the *Empire Windrush* arriving at Tilbury Docks in 1948 – we find that the experience of integration into British life was not

[10] See, for instance, Mason (2011), Pohlhaus (2011), Dotson (2012) and Medina (2012, 2013).

structured in relation to the conceptual poles of 'acceptance' or 'rejection' to which the white perspective gave rise. Instead the black experience was structured in relation to the concept of *citizenship*. Mike Phillips and Trevor Phillips recount it as follows:

> We observe that the overt declarations of racist hostility which were commonplace in the fifties have, more or less, disappeared from public life in Britain. On the other hand, it is clear that racial hostility and exclusion are a routine part of British life, and few black British people can be in any doubt that the majority of their fellow citizens take the colour of their skins to be a characteristic which defines what they are and what they can do.
>
> At the same time, paradoxically, among ourselves we never interpreted the racial discrimination or hostility that we encountered as 'rejection', largely because we never believed that 'acceptance' or 'rejection' was a choice available to Britain. Far from it. Our instinct told us that such notions were merely part of a racialised idiom, describing an identity which had long ago ceased to be relevant. For us the issue was ... about our status as citizens ... (Phillips and Phillips 1998, p. 5)

What their instinct told them formed the cornerstone of their localised conceptualisation of their situation – an understanding not supplied by the shared hermeneutical resource dominated by the 'racialised idiom' that characterised the perspective of white Britain – and it delivered a mode of understanding which they were rightly concerned to insist on introducing into the common pool of understanding: an idea of black colonial immigrants as fellow British citizens. The Empire had told their parents that Britain was their mother country and it seems that they had, in part at least, believed and internalised this fact – many had signed up to fight in the war under the identity it imposed – so that those arriving in Britain on ships like the *Windrush* 'regarded their Britishness as non-negotiable' (Phillips and Phillips 1998, p. 5). The mother country had made them British, and now it was a matter of holding her to the full implications of that status. Ideas of 'acceptance' or 'rejection' may have structured white consciousness around this immigration, but the immigrant population was living an independent and novel conceptualisation according to which they were *black British citizens* – a hermeneutical trope seemingly absent from the repertoire of the white population. One could say the concept of a black British citizen had not yet taken hold in white British consciousness, and white resistance to that conceptual neologism was such that it would take some significant time to do so.

In this example, it seems the sooner the new conceptualisation could become widely entrenched in the shared hermeneutical resource the better. But it is worth remembering that there can be cases in which it may not be in the interests of an oppressed group to fight immediately for the introduction of local meanings into the wider collective hermeneutical resource. (This is a point made by Mills, quoting 'the black American folk poem, "Got one mind for white folks to see / Another for what I know is me" (Mills 2007, p. 18); and also emphasised by Medina.[11]) Sometimes there can be significant advantage in keeping things local, perhaps so that there is more time in a safe space to develop one's dissenting forms of understanding, or perhaps simply because the wider climate makes it pointless, or too dangerous to try anything else. To take an example now from the history of race in the United States, in a radio interview the writer Alice Walker describes aspects of her upbringing under segregation in the American South in terms that indicate the value of maintaining hermeneutical privacy. Confident in their own interpretations of the social world, her parents inculcated in their children a way of understanding racial oppression that might be read as incorporating a certain security in on-going hermeneutical separation:

Lucky for us we lived very far in the country. We saw very few white people. And when we went to town we followed rules about where we could go. And we just followed our parents. They basically helped us to see white people as, you know, very stunted. That was just the way they were. There was nothing you could do about it, they were just like that. (Who knew why they were like that?) And that was helpful. They were discussed as if they were the weather ... Like 'Oh well, that's how they are. You know, what we try to encourage in our children, they beat it out of their children. They don't want their children to be kind. They don't want their children to ever see a black person and think of them as human.[12]

Here the idea that white people were 'very stunted' captures a localised hermeneutical practice that embodied a clear and confident knowledge that black people were not as white people painted them, and moreover that the racial attitudes of white people only showed them up as seriously morally damaged. The moral knowledge at large in the black community could not on the whole cross the segregated social space to find intelligible expression in the white community. Thus the hermeneutical practices that produced that moral knowledge in the black community was, judging from Walker's account, highly localised. The comment about 'weather' is particularly resonant in this connection. Perhaps when the terms of segregation mean that the normal 'reactive attitudes' of moral participation can only be a losing game, it is empowering to reach instead for what P.F. Strawson identifies as the 'objective' attitude of non-engagement, so that the agency of certain others is received as weather – meaningless (if

---

[11] 'As many Latina feminists and colonial theorists have argued, colonized peoples have a long tradition of exploiting the ignorance and hermeneutical limitations of the colonizers to their advantage, which can be justified for the sake of their survival' (Medina 2013, p. 116).

[12] *Desert Island Discs*. 2013. BBC Radio 4, May 24th.

potentially dangerous) causal impacts to be managed, tolerated, avoided.[13] Keeping one's hermeneutical practices localised in a situation such as this might be a decision to leave the powerful to their pitiful ignorance, safeguarding one's localised forms of moral and social understanding as a source of in-group solidarity and strength.

3   White Ignorance and Hermeneutical Injustice

Continuing with questions of race and the different forms of ignorance that can be generated and preserved by the operation of epistemic injustice, let me now relate our discussion to a different kind of ignorance: what Charles Mills has named 'white ignorance' (Mills 2007). I would like to offer an account of the boundaries of the two phenomena.[14] I shall argue that for the most part the ignorance that is produced and maintained by hermeneutical marginalisation, and made manifest in hermeneutical injustice, is different in two key respects from the ignorance in white ignorance. First, white ignorance is normally epistemically culpable; and, second, it does not generally involve any paucity of concepts on anyone's part. By contrast, in a case of hermeneutical injustice the uncomprehending hearer is normally epistemically non-culpable; and there is always, definitively, a paucity of shared concepts. However, I hope to identify where the two phenomena overlap.

Most generally speaking, 'white ignorance' is a racialised form of ideological thinking. It names a certain kind of collective *interested* or *motivated cognitive bias* in what social interpretations and/or evidence for such interpretations a racially dominant group attends to and integrates into the rest of their beliefs and deliberations. More specifically the label 'white ignorance' names a motivated bias on the part of white people taken as a group that leaves them 'ignorant' (in this special sense) of the situation of their black compatriots taken as a group. We might say it names a form of collective *denial* in the white community about some uncomfortable truths.[15] It therefore typically exhibits a culpable motivated irrationality. Indeed in most cases of 'white ignorance' as that phenomenon is discussed it involves some self-serving *epistemic fault* on those inhabiting the standpoint of whites – a conscious or unconscious resistance to accepting

---

[13] See Strawson (1974).

[14] See the substantial discussion of this issue in Medina (2013); and discussions in Mason (2011), Pohlhaus (2012) and, in different terms, Dotson (2012).

[15] In Mills' list of elements it is clear that various forms of motivated irrationality, denial, or other forms of epistemic culpability characterise the phenomenon. He says, for instance: 'the dynamic role of white group interests needs to be recognized and acknowledged as a central causal factor in generating and sustaining white ignorance' (Mills 2007, p.34).

or learning about the sources of their social advantage, for instance. Such epistemic faults are generally culpable. As Rebecca Mason succinctly puts it: 'white ignorance is a kind of epistemically culpable and morally noxious *mis*cognition that facilitates the maintenance of the status quo' (Mason 2011, p. 302).

Mills first discussed the phenomenon in the framework of the United States, but more recently he has made clear that he considers the issue to have global application. Referring back to his paper 'White Ignorance' (Mills 2007) he explains:

My discussion in the essay was focused mainly on the United States, but I intended the application of the concept to be much broader. Insofar as the modern world has been created by European colonialism and imperialism, and insofar as racist assumptions/frameworks/norms were central to the theories justifying white Western conquest and domination of that world, we would expect white ignorance to be global. (Mills 2015, p. 217)

We might illustrate his point with another example drawing on British colonial history, as pointed out by Mike and Trevor Phillips in their discussion of the ignorance produced by the sheer absence of black soldiers from the many British films about the war made in the post-War period:

... it comes as a shock now to note the complete absence of black Caribbean or African participants in the plethora of British films about the Second World War. After all, the involvement of black colonials was a fact that was a part of our experience ... Our astonishment was, and still is, to do with the extent to which they had disappeared, had been expurgated from the story, as if they had never existed. (Phillips and Phillips 1998, p. 5)

Let us look closely at Mills' characterisation of white ignorance in order to see (a) whether all cases are epistemically culpable, and (b) whether any involves the paucity of concepts that is definitive of hermeneutical injustice. Mills presents two main forms of white ignorance, and they share what he calls 'racialized causality' – that is, each involves the white community failing to grasp certain facts or to hold certain truthful interpretations of their social world where a significant part of the explanation why not is *race*.

First, such racially caused ignorance might take the form of an individual's active racism blocking certain truths; or, second, it might be more structural in form. Mills says in this connection:

[T]he racialized causality I am invoking needs to be expansive enough to include both straightforward racist motivation and more impersonal social-structural causation, which may be operative even if the cognizer in question is not racist ... But in both cases, racialized causality can give rise to what I am calling white ignorance, straightforwardly for a racist cognizer, but also indirectly for a nonracist cognizer who may form mistaken beliefs (e.g., that after the abolition of slavery in the United States, blacks generally had opportunities equal to whites) because of the social suppression of the pertinent knowledge, though without prejudice himself. (Mills 2007, p. 21)

In the case of the straightforward 'racist cognizer', the epistemic culpability is clearly on display: depending on quite what form the racism takes, such prejudiced cognizers are allowing some racist motive (perhaps racial contempt, or some kind of racial self-aggrandisement) to distort their perception of the social world and their place in it. Such motivated irrationality is plainly epistemically culpable (though of course there can be mitigating circumstances that reduce the degree of appropriate blame). In cases of hermeneutical injustice, by contrast, neither speaker nor hearer need be blameworthy for the failure of intelligibility. In itself hermeneutical injustice is a purely structural phenomenon with no individual perpetrator.[16] In some cases the hearer *would* of course be blameworthy – for instance if she were self-interestedly to resist the meanings being offered.[17] But no such fault is a necessary feature of hermeneutical injustice per se. Indeed part of the intrigue of the phenomenon is that it can happen so widely without epistemic fault, which is why it calls not only for increased individual virtue but also for structural remedy through social policies and institutional arrangements that would increase equality of hermeneutical participation.

What about the question of conceptual poverty – the requisite hermeneutical gap? In the case of the straightforward racist cognizer's white ignorance there *is* no hermeneutical gap, indeed no poverty of *concepts* at all, for the racist cognizer's ignorance is not caused by any lack of conceptual-interpretive resources. Let all the hermeneutical resources stand available to him, what he lacks is the epistemic discipline to apply the extant resources in an epistemically responsible way so as to achieve cognitive contact with social reality. Given these features, the white ignorance of the straightforward racist cognizer is clearly not any kind of hermeneutical injustice. It is an independent phenomenon, played out at the level of belief and (culpable) epistemic conduct.

---

[16] Medina develops the point that individuals can however collude in hermeneutical injustice by failing to be virtuous hearers (see Medina 2012, 2013, chapter 3). The point is well taken, but I would resist his conclusion that this reveals that there are, after all, individual 'perpetrators' of hermeneutical injustices. Failures of virtue are bad in themselves, and when we fail to be appropriately open to the perspectives of others we are doing something bad and may even be wronging them as individuals. But being culpable for one's part in a broader injustice makes one a perpetrator only of that part; it does not make one a perpetrator of the broader injustice itself.

[17] See Mason (2011), Pohlhaus (2011), Dotson (2012) and Medina (2013).

Let us look now to the second sort of case that Mills gives us. This is the 'more impersonal, social-structural' case of the non-racist cognizer who nonetheless 'may form mistaken beliefs ... because of the social suppression of the pertinent knowledge, though without prejudice himself'. Perhaps such social suppression could be a matter of certain parts or aspects of history not being taught at school; or perhaps another example might be the cultural forgetting of the involvement of black Caribbean and African soldiers in the Second World War, as noted by Mike and Trevor Philipps in relation to British film. In most of these social-structural cases of white ignorance, I take it, the individual remains epistemically culpable to some significant degree inasmuch as it is likely that she ought to be able to remain critically alive to at least some of the ways in which the epistemic situation has been distorted. But equally one can imagine (I emphasise, *imagine*) scenarios in which the individual is not culpable, insofar as it is also possible that the epistemic fault driving the 'social suppression of the pertinent knowledge' could be exclusively in the collective, or in some sub-group who is manipulating collective knowledge, in a manner that no individual could reasonably be expected to detect.[18] This in-principle possibility of individually non-culpable white ignorance suggests that Mill's social-structural kind of white ignorance can in principle be non-culpable – which prompts one to ask whether it might also constitute a case of hermeneutical injustice.

As before, however, we must also look for some kind of conceptual gap caused by hermeneutical marginalisation, for it cannot be a hermeneutical injustice without at least some impoverishment in shared conceptual resources. But in itself the 'social suppression of the pertinent knowledge' does not involve any loss of interpretive concepts or conceptions. The white-ignorants[19] in question might continue to have available to them perfectly adequate conceptual resources for knowing that X, and yet fail to know that X owing to the suppression of the requisite knowledge itself – once again, a dysfunction at the level of belief and evidence rather than the level of conceptual repertoire and intelligibility. White British forgetfulness about the involvement of African and Caribbean soldiers in the Second World War, for instance, involved no deficit of intelligibility, for the shared hermeneutical repertoire was quite rich enough to have supported the lost knowledge.

---

[18] I have argued elsewhere that such a case might represent one of epistemic agent-regret (Fricker 2016).

[19] As Mills makes entirely clear, and by way of parallel with the phenomenon of false consciousness on a Marxist picture, one does not have to be white to become embroiled in white ignorance (Mills 2007, p. 22). But it helps.

We might go on, however, to envisage a third, albeit non-standard, case. One can imagine structural cases where the 'social suppression of the pertinent knowledge' *has* included suppression of concepts requisite for that knowledge. If this conceptual suppression is confined to the privileged group, a genuine *deficit in hermeneutical resources* for the white community would result, and thereby a deficit in the shared hermeneutical resource. With the hermeneutical gap so envisaged, we are closer to a case of white ignorance that is also one of hermeneutical injustice.

Given that the paucity of concepts in this case is all on the part of whites, someone might wonder whether it was the white community that was subject to the hermeneutical injustice. Not so; for in order for such a case to constitute a hermeneutical injustice the deficit of concepts in the white population would also have to be *unfair to them* in some way. It is true enough that, as Medina emphasises (Medina 2013, p. 108), such a hermeneutical deficit would clearly be bad for the white community in a purely epistemic sense, for there is important social knowledge they would be missing out on.[20] (So it was for Carmita Wood's harasser.) It may well be morally bad for them too (as it was for the harasser, who was prevented from grasping the ethical significance of his own behaviour, and was to that degree alienated from the meaning of his own actions).[21] But still, the disadvantage cannot be an injustice done *to them*, because *ex hypothesi* this very epistemic disadvantage plays more generally to their social advantage – that is the whole point: white people are represented as having an interest in not knowing certain threatening facts, and if the very concepts required for such unsettling knowledge have been suppressed, then they are all the safer from having to confront it. Rather it is the black community who suffers the hermeneutical injustice, for it is they who are asymmetrically socially disadvantaged by the whites' conceptual deficit that entails the equivalent deficit in the shared hermeneutical resource.

What we have now arrived at in pursuing the overlap between hermeneutical injustice and white ignorance is a form of hermeneutical injustice that belongs in the range of cases identified in the previous section as *midway* between maximal (Carmita Wood) and minimal (Joe) forms. Such cases are those in which one group's communicative attempts meet with failure owing to a paucity of concepts on the part of an out-group and

---

[20] Laura Beeby too has emphasised the importance of the purely epistemic disadvantage suffered by the more powerful party in such cases (Beeby 2011).

[21] Jason Stanley expresses a general version of this point in relation to legitimising myths: 'false ideologies harm the elites in ways that cut deeper than material interest. The reason that members of unjustly privileged groups are led to adopt legitimizing myths is that they cannot confront the possibility that their actions are unjust. False ideologies blind even those they seem to help, by making them "untrue to themselves"' (Stanley 2015, p. 265).

therefore in the shared hermeneutical resource. Among those cases, we can locate the racially motivated concept-suppression scenario that we have identified as a (non-standard) case of white ignorance. The motivated concept suppression among the dominant white community means that the hermeneutically marginalised black community nonetheless possesses locally operative meanings that capture their experiences but which cannot function properly in communicative attempts with social bodies that operate with the impoverished shared conceptual repertoire. However rich the black community's conceptual resources might be, these resources do not get integrated into the shared resource, because the white community has an interest in keeping them out. This, at last, is the overlap we have been looking for: a white ignorance whose explanation is a conceptual deficit (on the part of whites, and *ipso facto* a deficit in the shared hermeneutical resource) that is significantly caused by the black community's hermeneutical marginalisation. In such a case, motivated conceptual poverty on the part of a dominant racial group works to preserve their local ignorance of a significant dimension of the social world and blocks another racial group from making good that ignorance.

What about the question of epistemic culpability? In our earlier discussion of Mills' *knowledge*-suppression case I suggested that such cases might normally be epistemically culpable, though we could imagine scenarios where there was no epistemic culpability. The matter turned on how far it was reasonable, in any given case, to expect the uncomprehending hearer to be alert to the distortions in the epistemic system. The same goes for our *concept*-suppression example. Here the hermeneutical marginalisation of the black community kettles their concepts, thereby creating a conceptual lack in the shared hermeneutical resource, and so preserving white ignorance by creating a barrier to the essential conceptual means to their understanding expressions of the relevant black experiences. The question of epistemic culpability in such cases will depend, as it does in general, upon how far the uncomprehending hearer could reasonably be expected to have been alert to the fact of her conceptual impoverishment. If she could have known better, then she should have known better.[22] These issues of individual culpability and non-culpability seem worth thinking about in principle, even if we are pessimistic about how much individuals can really do.[23] In cases of hermeneutical injustice, the requisite structural remedy involves the reduction of hermeneutical marginalisation; in cases of white ignorance, a whole

---

[22] I have argued more fully for this view of the borders of culpable and non-culpable ignorance more fully in Fricker (2010).

[23] For this concern about the limitations of increased individual virtue, see Alcoff (2010), Langton (2010) and Anderson (2012).

range of structural remedies is no doubt called for.[24] Such structural changes are called for *in addition to* individual efforts – for, after all, structural changes are often in significant part the upshot of individual efforts.

4   Hermeneutical Injustice Is Not Necessarily a Face of Oppression

I hope to have clarified and defended my original characterisation of hermeneutical injustice by showing that its core notion of hermeneutical marginalisation allows for the sorts of *midway* and/or motivated cases of hermeneutical injustice that other writers have rightly emphasised.[25] If the driving thought is that hermeneutical gaps are typically *made* rather than found, then I agree. One group's marginalisation is typically motivated by the interests of another group whose purposes are served by the marginalisation. It is therefore in the nature of any marginalisation that ideology, and other kinds of privileged motivation, will be chief among its causes. Hermeneutical injustice, like testimonial injustice, is typically a face of oppression – it tends to preserve ignorance that serves the interests of dominant groups.[26]

However, I would also affirm that it is important we air possibilities of hermeneutical marginalisation that are not themselves part of a pattern of oppression. The category is broader than that, for there can be unfair forms of hermeneutical marginalisation that are to be explained in terms of more *de facto* forms of social powerlessness, or more fleeting kinds of ideological struggle; and there can sometimes be hermeneutical gaps that are more like unforeseen consequences of social flux, or of processes that do not particularly reflect the long-term interests of one group over another. Perhaps an example might be the kind of hermeneutical marginalisation against which 'teenagers' (itself a new concept at the time) in the early Sixties rebelled. They did not get much of a look in to the processes of meaning-making before that, but they found a noisy way of making new meanings among themselves, interpreting and constructing their experiences accordingly. If we imagine early-Sixties teenagers trying and failing to convey to their parents what was so great about rock'n'roll and everything it stood for, maybe we confront a case of hermeneutical injustice of the non-oppression

---

[24] See Anderson (2012) for the proposal that racial integration is essential as a structural feature of institutional epistemic justice. For her more general case for racial integration, see Anderson (2010).

[25] See Mason (2011), Pohlhaus (2011), Dotson (2012) and Medina (2012, 2013).

[26] Using the terminology I employed in *Epistemic Injustice* (Fricker 2007), I would say that testimonial and hermeneutical injustices in their 'systematic' (as opposed to 'incidental') forms are the central cases of epistemic injustice, because it is these forms that reveal the connection with other dimensions of social injustice.

kind I aim to leave room for in my characterisation. It is of course *political*, since it involves a struggle of power – the power of one generation over the next – and even of competing ideologies. But we would not normally regard it as a matter of oppression, for nobody is a teenager for very long, and this kind of struggle represents a near inevitable process that is part and parcel of on-going historical change, including ethical change. Such intergenerational struggle might therefore play a role, even a desirable role, in any human society.

For these reasons the teenage-culture case is not the kind of power struggle we would ordinarily characterise as a fight against *oppression*. It involves the hermeneutical marginalisation of the younger generation for sure; but it would be a jaundiced view of the perennial struggle between one generation and the next to insist that this marginalisation was fundamentally oppressive in nature. It is simply (and thankfully) in the nature of young people to want to make their own world, and that involves a certain overthrow of parental regime. Where that regime has hermeneutically marginalised its young, hermeneutical injustices are bound to arise from youthful attempts to express the new social ideas to the older generation.

Hermeneutical injustice can affect people's lives in many different ways. I believe it is most useful to have a theoretical framework that makes room for all sorts of cases, so that the various degrees of wrongful unintelligibility can be seen to run from maximal to minimal (from Carmita Wood's inarticulable outrage to Joe's articulate yet ultimately frustrated communicative attempts); and so that the forms of hermeneutical marginalisation can be seen to run from actively oppressive motivated ignorance (as per the case of motivated concept-suppression white ignorance) to ordinary attempts by parents to shape a new generation according to values they understand. The purpose of placing these different formations in a single theoretical structure is to reveal the range of possibilities in all their similarities and differences. Ignorance, as we observed at the outset, is not always bad; but social ignorance that results from hermeneutical marginalisation is intrinsically likely to be bad insofar as it is likely to be conserving ignorance that sustains unequal social relations. Those cases clearly *are* oppressive, and they preserve forms of ignorance that demand to be made good.[27]

---

[27] Earlier versions of some parts of this paper were first presented at a workshop on José Medina's book (Medina 2013) at the Autonomous University of Madrid. I am grateful to all the participants there for helpful comments, and in particular to Linda Alcoff, Katharine Jenkins, José Medina and Charles Mills for helpful informal discussions. I am also grateful to Rik Peels for comments on a draft. Earlier versions of some parts were published online as part of the *Social Epistemology Review and Reply Collective* (Fricker 2013a).

10   Ignorance and Racial Insensitivity

José Medina

Some insidious forms of racial oppression operate through patterns of ignorance that contribute to the stigmatization of racial minority groups. In this paper I offer an analysis of how racial ignorance produces systematic distrust and miscommunication across racial lines. I explore ways in which people could become aware of their racial ignorance and of their complicity with racial injustices. I offer an account of racial insensitivity as a kind of *numbness*, reflecting on the affective and cognitive aspects of people's inability to respond to racial injustices. I analyze insensitivity as a form of *narrow-mindedness* that involves the incapacity to see the point of view of the other and the resistance to acknowledge certain things that are hard to live with (such as one's complicity in the suffering of others). I argue that *epistemically responsible agency* demands that we live up to certain epistemic responsibilities with respect to oppressed groups: these include our responsibilities for knowing and caring for the injustices they suffer, and also our responsibilities to fight against their exclusion or marginalization as communicators and fellow citizens. On my view, epistemic responsibility is the precondition of and the basis for other social responsibilities we have; and until the epistemic responsibilities breached in racial ignorance are repaired, complicity with racial injustices cannot be uprooted. The work toward racial justice must begin with the acknowledgment of racial ignorance and the epistemic limitations it creates for social relationality.

In Section 1, I develop an account of racial insensitivity that begins with classic accounts of racial ignorance as a form of *blindness* and continues with more contemporary analyses of racial insensitivity as a form of *numbness* that includes not only perceptual and cognitive elements, but also conceptual and affective elements. In Section 2, I draw from my epistemic interactionism and contextualism to articulate a robust notion of epistemic responsibility. According to my polyphonic view, multiply situated, overlapping and intersecting perspectives and sensibilities call

I am grateful to Rik Peels, Martijn Blaauw and Ben Ferguson for their critical feedback and their suggestions for revisions on an earlier draft of this paper.

for multiply situated, overlapping and intersecting forms of responsibility. I argue that the accountability and responsivity required to address epistemic injustices can be of all sorts, but it must always start with the *acknowledgment* of one's epistemic positions and relations, and with the *acknowledgment* of the epistemic privileges and epistemic limitations one has. Finally, in Section 3, I discuss experiences of *epistemic discomfort* in educational processes that offer the possibility of ethical growth and the expansion of one's epistemic sensibilities.

1   Insensitivity: From Blindness to Numbness

> I am an invisible man ... I am invisible, understand, simply because people refuse to see me ... it is as if I have been surrounded by mirrors of hard, distorting glass. When they approach me they see only my surroundings, themselves, or figments of their imagination – indeed, everything and anything except me.
>
> Prologue to *Invisible Man*, by Ralph Ellison

A great deal of social interaction happens in the dark, with people acting "blindly" toward each other and exhibiting a stubborn resistance to recognize crucial aspects of each other's identities and lives. In classic race theory, racial ignorance has been described as analogous to a perceptual deficit, as a form of *blindness*.[1] But although the traditional account of racial ignorance as a form of blindness contains many rich and powerful insights, there are at least three reasons why "numbness" is a more apt term than "blindness" to describe the deficient epistemic sensibilities involved in racial insensitivity.

In the first place, the problem of having been desensitized to certain aspects of social relationality has a perceptual dimension, but the perceptual numbness involved is multidimensional and affects not only sight, but all our senses simultaneously – in particular, it affects our capacity to hear, to respond to voices and accents and to listen to them properly.

In the second place, the term "numbness" is more appropriate than "blindness" because, although both are clearly related to our embodied sentience, the former can be more easily extended to the non-perceptual, and indeed the epistemic deficiencies involved in racial ignorance go beyond our perceptual organs. There is an important disanalogy between the failure of a sensory organ (such as sight) and the communicative and interpretative failures involved in racial ignorance.

In the third place, the metaphor of blindness does not capture (in fact, it hides) a crucial feature that characterizes racial insensitivity in its most

---

[1] See, for example, Du Bois ([1903], [1994]).

insidious forms: its *self-effacing* nature, its self-hiding and self-denying mode of operation. Whereas the blind person is acutely aware that there are things that escape her and she leads her life adjusting to this perceptual deficit, the racially insensitive person is typically quite oblivious of there being anything at all she is missing. This is what I have called the *meta-level* aspect of racial insensitivity. Racial insensitivity becomes insidious and recalcitrant when it contains *meta-ignorance*, that is, when the racially insensitive person is ignorant of her own ignorance, unable to recognize that there is anything she is missing concerning racial experiences and meanings.

Racial insensitivity creates dysfunctional communicative dynamics. And the very attempt to unmask the lack of attention and sensitivity to racial issues often triggers communicative dysfunctions: complaints about *racial insensitivity* are often answered with complaints about *racial oversensitivity*. Especially when claims about racist attitudes and behavior are voiced by members of racial minorities, these claims are often neutralized and countered by the charge of being *oversensitive*. And thus what was meant to be an objective claim about social interaction is transformed into (or heard as) a purely subjective expression or an emotional reaction—and a misplaced one at that! The same often happens when women make the claim that an attitude or action is sexist. Let me say something brief about the gender case in order to capture some important insights in the feminist literature, to then focus on the case of race and the dysfunctional communicative dynamics in allegations of racial insensitivity and racial oversensitivity.

As Naomi Scheman (1993) argues, the anger voiced by women as a reaction to gender injustices is a rational response to facts about their situation and a communicative act that demands recognition and action. But the kind of social sensitivity that understands women's anger in that way and can enter in that non-dismissive communicative dynamic has not been easy to achieve; it has been one of the achievements of the Women's Movement, the result of the consciousness-raising practices that started in the 1970s; and of course a social achievement that is still partial and unfinished. For as long as women's emotional speech acts receive uptake only as mere expressions of emotions, they are not taken to make any epistemic or political demand on people: they are not taken to demand that people revise their beliefs or that they take appropriate action to respond to them. Because of their emotional nature and because of the limited uptake they receive as a result, women's speech acts of protestation—the communicative acts of denouncing and contesting gender oppression—are neutralized, rendered devoid of normative content, and in fact they are transformed into something else: a pure venting without any basis, a hypersensitive or hysterical reaction. This communicative dysfunction amounts to an *epistemic injustice*:[2] in these contexts women's discursive agency becomes constrained, unable to perform the speech acts of contestation, and subject to unfair communicative expectations – for it is unfair to expect from those who are oppressed to communicate about their oppression without emotions such as anger and without affective reactions that reveal how they are personally affected. The communicative dysfunction in question involves an *epistemic injustice* because it involves interpretative and testimonial disadvantages that diminish women's capacity to make sense of their experiences and to use them as compelling reasons for their claims.

The same analysis applies also to claims about racism voiced by racial minorities. These minority subjects denouncing racism are often depicted as hypersensitive. They often encounter epistemic obstacles that result in their unfair treatment as communicators and epistemic agents; that is, they encounter epistemic injustices that makes it difficult for them to communicate about their experiences of oppression and thus function as defense mechanisms that hide and protect the relations of oppression.[3]

Following the literature on the epistemology of race, in this chapter I develop an analysis of racial insensitivity in terms of *numbness* to the perspectives of racial others and their experiences. In this analysis I want to emphasize three things about racial insensitivity: (1) that racial insensitivity involves epistemic labor and that in its most insidious form this insensitivity protects itself through *cognitive and affective* mechanisms that make people socially *numbed* to racial injustices; (2) that racial insensitivity becomes insidious and recalcitrant when it operates at two levels: at the *object* level and at a *meta*-level; and (3) that racial insensitivity is a *numbness* directed both *outwards* – to the social world, to others – and *inwards* – to oneself, thus involving blind spots that result both in social ignorance and in self-ignorance. The next three sections will discuss those three epistemic features of racial insensitivity. Sections 5 and 6 will sketch a notion of epistemic responsibility in the light of this analysis. The focus of sections 5 and 6 will be the issue of *complicity* and *shared responsibilities*.

---

[2] The notion of epistemic injustice has been defined by Miranda Fricker (2007) "as a kind of injustice in which someone is *wronged specifically in her capacity as a knower*" (2007, p. 20). Within the category of epistemic injustice Fricker has distinguished between *testimonial* injustice, which involves unfair credibility assessments in testimonial exchanges, and *hermeneutical* injustice, which involves unfair limitations in one's capacity and resources for making sense of and for communicating one's perspective.

[3] For a full account of racial epistemic injustices and the protective mechanisms inscribed in racial ignorance, see Medina (2013) and Medina (forthcoming).

2   Racial Insensitivity as *Active* (Self-Protecting) Ignorance

Describing racial insensitivity as being *numbed* captures well how it can become an *active* form of epistemic withdrawal, the kind of ignorance that protects and hides itself through a whole battery of defense mechanisms, which include both cognitive and affective elements.

Racial insensitivity consists in being cognitively and affectively *numbed*. This numbness involves epistemic deficits and vices. It can involve, for example, a lack of openness to discuss racial problems, to take claims about racism seriously as claims that make demands on all of us and require a response. This lack of openness has an important affective dimension. For example, it can take the form of hearing claims about racism as personal attacks that call for defensive reactions, or as attempts to be divisive that should be met with contempt. The kind of closed-mindedness characteristic of racial insensitivity consists in epistemic dysfunctions that limit the production and passing of knowledge in epistemic activities. Racial insensitivity is the kind of epistemic dysfunction that involves not only epistemic lacunas and epistemic distortions (absence of true beliefs or presence of false beliefs), but also the inability to fill those lacunas or correct those distortions, that is, the inability to learn. In its most insidious forms, racial insensitivity involves not just a regular kind of ignorance about racial matters, but what is called in the epistemology of race *"active ignorance"*:[4] the kind of ignorance that involves a whole battery of mechanisms of avoidance and resistance to know and to learn; the kind of ignorance that is deeply invested in not knowing. This kind of recalcitrant ignorance has to be distinguished from the *basic or plain* kind of ignorance that involves nothing more than the absence of true belief or the presence of false belief.[5] Basic or plain ignorance tends to be innocuous, for, when our ignorance is nothing more than the absence of true belief and/or the presence of false belief, learning is relatively easy (we just unmask false beliefs and inculcate true ones), and education does not encounter psychological obstacles and resistances. However, in the case of *active (self-protecting)* ignorance, besides epistemic lacunas and distortions, there are also defense mechanisms that keep the ignorance in place by making it immune to criticisms and neutralizing stimulations to learn what conflicts with it. The following diagram offers a schematic illustration of the distinction between *basic* and *active* ignorance and the defense mechanisms that protect the latter:

[4] See Mills (1998), Sullivan and Tuana (2007) and Medina (2012).
[5] What I am calling *basic or plain* ignorance fits well with the New View of ignorance articulated and defended by Peels (2013).

Basic ignorance:

(1) absence of (true) belief
(2) presence of false belief

Active ignorance:

(3) cognitive resistances (e.g., prejudices, conceptual lacunas)
(4) affective resistances (e.g., apathy, interest in not knowing – "the will *not* to believe"[6])
(5) bodily resistances (e.g., feeling anxious, agitated, red in the face)
(6) defense mechanisms and strategies (deflecting challenges, shifting burden of proof, etc.)

3   Racial Insensitivity as Active *Meta*-Ignorance

The carefully cultivated disinterest in knowing (sometimes even the interest in *not* knowing) that underlies racial insensitivity is socially orchestrated and nurtured by social habits and dynamics, such as not talking about race in certain contexts or in the presence of "mixed company." But this closed-mindedness is rarely explicit and consciously cultivated. Insidious forms of insensitivity are forms of active ignorance that become invisible to the subject despite his or her active participation in it. They are deeply entrenched blind spots that remain unconscious. Racially insensitive people of this sort are not only numbed to particular racial issues, they are also *numbed to their own numbness*, that is, incapable of reacting to it or even of recognizing how they have become numbed; they are insensitive to their own insensitivity. This is what I call *meta-ignorance*, which consists in a pronounced difficulty in realizing and appreciating the limitations of one's social sensibility and horizon of understanding.

Meta-ignorance involves meta-attitudes about one's first-order propositional attitudes and cognitive repertoires, such as, for example, believing or disbelieving that one has certain beliefs/disbeliefs, epistemic abilities/disabilities, epistemic lacunas, etc. Meta-ignorance can often be encountered *associated with privilege*, that is, as resulting from having lived a privileged and sheltered life in which one does not encounter much *epistemic friction*[7] in one's interactions, a life in which one is encouraged to be inattentive to certain things, to disbelieve certain things, to trust people like oneself and distrust people who are different, and to develop an inflated sense of one's capacities and epistemic contents.

---

[6] For an account of this phenomenon, see Medina (2016).
[7] For a full account of "epistemic friction", see Medina (2012), especially chapter 1.

According to the epistemic interactionism I have developed and defended following Wittgenstein and pragmatists such as Jane Addams, John Dewey and G.H. Mead, *epistemic friction* occurs in communicative interactions when different perspectives or standpoints challenge and contest each other; and this kind of friction is required for becoming sensitive to the perspectives of those who are different from us and to the limits of one's own perspective. Those who live privileged and sheltered lives are less likely to encounter friction in their interactions; they are less likely to run into communicative and epistemic obstacles that leave their experiences, problems and even their entire lives at a disadvantage; and as a result of not ever feeling severely constrained as speakers and subjects of knowledge, privileged subjects tend to be more reluctant to acknowledge the limitations of the horizon of understanding that they inhabit; that is, they tend to be *numbed to their own numbness*, insensitive to the blind spots that they have inherited and they recirculate in their epistemic lives.

In some cases, meta-ignorance can be basic or plain and, therefore, relatively innocuous. These are cases in which the subject simply does not have meta-attitudes about their first-order epistemic attitudes, or have incorrect meta-attitudes that she or he is willing to correct. For example, we can find a case of basic meta-ignorance in a subject who is not aware of ignoring important cultural facts about a minority group within her community, but she is willing to acknowledge this epistemic deficit and to take steps to repair it when the opportunity arises. But there are also cases of *active* meta-ignorance. *Active* meta-ignorance can be characterized as *resistance to epistemic friction* – to acknowledge and engage epistemic viewpoints that can challenge and contest one's own. In fact, in active meta-ignorance we find a *double resistance* to epistemic friction: the inability to recognize alternatives (a first-order resistance to friction, a lack of openness to epistemic counterpoints), plus the inability to recognize one's inability (a second-order resistance or meta-resistance, a resistance to identify and acknowledge one's lack of openness to epistemic counterpoints). This meta-ignorance blocks possible paths for fighting and repairing epistemic injustices. If one is not even able to recognize one's own blind spots – if one is numbed to his/her own numbness – how is this subject going to be able to embark on a journey to improve his/her epistemic perspective and sensitivity? This is what I call the *problem of meta-ignorance*, which becomes more intractable in cases of *active* meta-ignorance in which the subject is not only incapable of recognizing her epistemic deficits but resistant to do so when prompted by others.

Precisely because of the obstacles and defense mechanisms that operate at the meta-level, the racially insensitive individual will need external help. In the case of the actively meta-insensitive person particular kinds of epistemic interventions will be needed, for example, those interventions that penetrate the resistances and the defense mechanisms of the subject producing cognitive discomfort, which is sometimes expressed in affective and embodied ways (e.g., taking things too personally, getting angry, getting red in the face). Sometimes these epistemic interventions may come in the form of specific challenges raised in particular interpersonal interactions: interlocutors raising challenges or provocations that make the subject rethink what she thinks she knows or doesn't know. But in other cases, the epistemic interventions may take a more generalized form. They may relate to changes in social practices and dynamics that create new social pressures and expectations, and force subjects to explain themselves when they say certain things or when they take certain things for granted. An example could be found in recent shifts in practices of telling jokes in which people are made accountable for what they find humorous and/or offensive. The generalized and concerted forms of epistemic interventions of the latter kind are particularly important given that the hard cases of active meta-ignorance – such as in racial insensitivity – concern not only particular individuals, but entire groups and cultures. The actively meta-ignorant group or culture will need the help of other groups or cultures, or of alternative viewpoints within them.[8] But, of course, the more empowered the insensitive (and actively meta-ignorant) individual, group or culture is, the more difficult it will be for others to do the proper interventions and to set in motion the process of transformation and cognitive-affective amelioration.

4   Racial Insensitivity as Involving Both Social Ignorance and Self-Ignorance

The recalcitrant blind spots of racial insensitivity are both a form of social ignorance and, at the same time, a form of *self-ignorance*. It is very important to appreciate the connection that often exists between our ignorance about others and our (typically more implicit and harder to see) ignorance about ourselves. I have argued elsewhere that when an individual is epistemically irresponsible with respect to others, it is very often the case that his social ignorance involves *self-ignorance*: ignorance about his own relationality with respect to those ignored others, and quite possibly also ignorance about certain aspects of himself that he is unable

[8] Luckily, social groups and cultures are not so homogeneous and monolithic that they contain no discordant or dissenting voices, or at least their possibility. In my *Speaking from Elsewhere* (2006) I have argued that this possibility is always there.

to recognize, which prevents him from taking responsibility for his perspective and how it relates to the perspectives of others. As Charles Mills
(1997, 1998) suggests in his account of "white ignorance," white subjects
often don't know what it means to be white; they are ignorant about the
presuppositions and consequences of their own racial identity. More
recently, in *Revealing Whiteness*, Shannon Sullivan (2006) has offered an
analysis of how privileged white subjects maintain the ignorance of their
own racialization through well-entrenched cognitive habits that hide
themselves: whiteness is often rendered invisible for white subjects and
needs to be revealed.

As the analyses of white ignorance in race theory show, privileged white
subjects tend to lack the motivation and the opportunity to develop
expressive activities and interpretative tools to make sense of their own
social experiences of racialization and to understand how their lives have
been affected by racism and its legacy. And this self-ignorance, this
inability to interpret their social experiences on racial matters, undermines their testimonial and hermeneutical sensibilities in their communicative interaction with others. The phenomenon of the active ignorance
and interpretative impoverishment of the privileged has also been analyzed by epistemologists of ignorance with respect to gender and
sexuality.[9] Feminist and queer theorists have argued that gender and
sexual experiences are particularly opaque to gender and sexual confor-
mists who, not having interrogated their own trajectories in these areas of
social life, become especially ill-equipped to understand their own gender
and sexuality, lacking interpretative tools and strategies specifically
designed to apply to their own case.[10] This is why what passes for
obviousness or transparency in relation to masculinity, femininity and
heterosexuality typically hides a lack of awareness and sensitivity to
nuanced and plural gender and sexual meanings. As epistemologists of
ignorance have shown, the epistemic gaps that emerge from structures of
oppression and identity prejudices create bodies of active ignorance for
those subjects whose privileged positions are protected by the blind-spots
and insensitivities in question – racial, sexual or gender insensitivity; and
those bodies of ignorance include their lack of knowledge and their
inabilities to learn not only about racial, sexual and gender others, but
about themselves, their position in the world and the perspective that they
share with their social group. As a long tradition of philosophers from

---

[9] See especially the pioneering work of Nancy Tuana (2004, 2006). See also Sullivan and
  Tuana (2007).
[10] On this point, see especially Scheman (1997).

Strawson (1974) to Bilgrami (1998, 2012) and beyond[11] have argued, in order to become a responsible agent, a subject needs to have some minimal self-knowledge; and this thesis can now be taken to entail that epistemic responsibility requires eradicating the kind of self-ignorance involved in racial insensitivity. This point will be part of my argumentation in the next section.

5   Racial Insensitivity and Epistemic Responsibility

Racial insensitivity is the kind of insensitivity that is indicative of moral and political patterns that go well beyond the individual; it concerns group behavior, clusters of individuals in relation to other clusters of individuals (such as families, communities, racial groups and sometimes even entire regions, nations and cultures). Racial insensitivity is misunderstood if it is conceived as a purely individualistic problem, for although we can say that particular individuals are racially insensitive, the production of insensitivity is a collective enterprise in which there are shared responsibilities: the responsibilities of parents, educators, friends, neighbors, citizens and so on. Accordingly, repairing racial insensitivity and developing new forms of sensitivity that can make people more epistemically responsible require cooperative and collective efforts directed at establishing new patterns of relationality and responsivity. The efforts at overcoming insensitivity have to be oriented toward action and they have to be sustained in particular contexts of action and interaction. They cannot be carried out in a purely spectatorial and detached way. Developing racial sensitivity is more than acquiring racial knowledge or familiarity in an impersonal way; it requires an *engaged perspective* that makes itself vulnerable to challenges and contestations from other perspectives in actual interactions with diverse others.[12]

---

[11] For a full discussion of this thesis and the philosophical literature on it, see section 4.1 of Medina (2012).

[12] One worry here may be that the task of becoming epistemically responsible can become an *infinite* and *unattainable* task given our epistemic obligations towards indefinitely many minority groups. This is a serious worry. But I think my contextualized interactionism has resources to handle it. As I have argued elsewhere, as long as we have strategies that enable us to *prioritize* in any given context which obligations we should address first in order to open ourselves to the epistemic friction of other perspectives, the task of achieving epistemic responsibility can be embarked upon and we can assess whether we are faring better or worse in that task *even if* we accept that it is a neverending task that will never be completed once and for all, that is, even if at no point can one say: "Ok, I am done with opening my mind, I have stretched my sensitivity fully and cannot possibly become more open-minded" (an expression of epistemic arrogance which seems to perform meta-blindness). For these purposes, I have proposed the *Maxim of Eminent Relevance* (Medina 2012, pp. 156–157), according to which in any given context we have to identify the *eminently relevant* others with whom we are connected and interact, and

The account of racial insensitivity as active ignorance that I have articulated above and elsewhere (Medina 2012, 2016) lends itself to an expansive notion of *epistemic responsibility* that I will explore in this section. In the first place, it is important to notice that the kind of responsibility that attaches to various forms of racial insensitivity involves a broader notion than the notion of *doxastic responsibility*. Although *doxastic* responsibility[13] is contained in my notion of *epistemic* responsibility, the responsibility that we need to take for our epistemic positions and attitudes does not only concern the *beliefs* that we hold, but also the absence of belief and the epistemic mechanisms of avoidance and resistance that protect doxastic lacunas and distortions (or patterns of false beliefs). And in the second place, my notion of epistemic responsibility is broader than standard notions of epistemic *culpability* or *blameworthiness*.[14] In some cases the issue can be whether racial insensitivity springs from culpable ignorance or blameworthy beliefs, but in other cases, even when we find doxastic attitudes or lacunas that can be said to be free from blame,[15] there still remain normative issues concerning complicity and shared responsibility for maintaining a body of ignorance in place. In other words, even when we say of a racially insensitive subject that *she or he could not have known better* and therefore she or he is *not to blame* for his or her ignorance (any more than her or his peers, mentors, etc.), we may still hold her or him partially responsible for not taking any steps to displace the ignorance in question. Although broader and more diffused, my expansive notion of epistemic responsibility (unlike standard notions of culpability and blameworthiness) is particularly adept at handling cases of widespread forms of harmful ignorance that no single individual (or identifiable cluster of individuals) is solely responsible for and culpable of. Let me illustrate what is most distinctive of my expansive notion of

---

their perspectives should be prioritized as we start expanding our epistemic sensitivities and making them progressively more open to multiple others.

[13] The debates around doxastic responsibility are not unrelated to my notion of epistemic responsibility, but they only concern one aspect of it: the permissibility, praiseworthiness or blameworthiness of the beliefs that we hold. See Booth and Peels (2010, 2014).

[14] For a full account of doxastic blameworthiness, see Nottelmann (2007).

[15] I fully agree with Peels and Booth's (2014) minimalist position in the literature on doxastic deontologism, which they call DDB. According to DDB, responsible belief is blameless belief and not praiseworthy belief – a position they call DDP and which is more epistemically demanding. For the cases they examine, being free from blame in the beliefs one holds is sufficient to qualify as epistemically responsible and praiseworthiness is not required. However, as I argue below, in cases of collective racial insensitivity, there is a form of widely shared ignorance in which individuals participate without any fault of their own (without choosing to ignore or being aware of their ignorance), and, nonetheless, they fall short of being epistemically responsible given their complacency and complicity in maintaining doxastic lacunas and systematically distorted doxastic attitudes.

epistemic responsibility by summarizing a real-life example that I have analyzed at greater length elsewhere.[16]

As reported by the local media, on Saturday, October 8, 2005, at the Vanderbilt University campus, after a fraternity party in which a pig had been roasted and eaten, an intoxicated frat boy walked across the street with the pig's head and left it at the doorsteps of the Ben Schulman Center for Jewish Life. The following morning the Jewish community on campus was outraged. The incident happened during the Jewish High Holy Days that begin with Rosh Hashanah and end with Yom Kippur, and many thought that "someone was sending Vanderbilt's Jewish community a chilling message during the holiest days of the year."[17] The student who had dropped the pig's head at the doorsteps of the Schulman Center came forward and apologized, but he emphasized that he did not know that the building in question was a Jewish Cultural Center and he also did not know that pig's parts had been used to stigmatize Jewish people and attack them. What is interesting for our purposes is his exculpatory move of appealing to ignorance in order to relieve himself of responsibility for what had been taken to be an anti-Semitic act.[18]

If we accept the pig-head dropper's account, the issue of epistemic responsibility concerning ignorance and racial insensitivity that arises in this case is a peculiar one. In the first place, if we believe that the student did not know that the building in question was a Jewish Cultural Center and that pig parts had been used to denigrate Jews, there is no harmful false belief we can blame him for, but only a doxastic lacuna. And, in the second place, the ignorance in question could reasonably be said not to be *culpable*, for the student is free from blame if he has in fact not been given opportunities to acquire the beliefs that would have made him aware that there was an anti-Semitic layer to his act. This ignorance does not seem to result from any specific irresponsible act that the subject

---

[16] See Medina (2012, pp. 135–145). The next Section is adapted from that section of my book.

[17] Quote from p. 1 of www.nashvillescene.com/Stories/News/2005/10/20/Pig_Heads_at_ Vanderbilt

[18] It is worth noting that the university administrators also appealed to ignorance in order to minimize the significance of the incident. The *Nashville Scene* reported: "'It was a bad decision, a very bad decision,' says Kristin Torrey, the school's director of Greek Life, who believes the student genuinely didn't understand the religious overtones of his action ... the University has taken the position that its student may be dumb, but he's no bigot. 'This incident happened out of stupidity and shockingly bad taste,' says Michael Schoenfeld, Vice Chancellor for Public Affairs. 'But coming out of it is an opportunity to advance understanding about how the university is diversifying, and about other traditions and cultures and religions and beliefs that may not necessarily be part of the traditional mainstream at the university'" (pp. 2–3 in www.nashvillescene.com/Stories/ News/2005/10/20/Pig_Heads_at_Vanderbilt).

had previously carried out and can be blamed for. It is not clear that the student *could have known better*. And yet, there is still an important issue of epistemic responsibility here that goes beyond the particular student who desecrated the Jewish Cultural Center. The epistemic responsibility in question here is not reducible to *blameworthy* beliefs or *culpable* ignorance.[19] Rather, it concerns the issue of taking *collective* responsibility for the doxastic lacuna that left the student in the dark as to the symbolic significance of the pig's head and the cultural significance of the building he vandalized: how can the community arrange its epistemic practices so that they make sure that students will know better and will not maintain such harmful bodies of ignorance concerning the cultural minority groups with the university community? In an important sense, we could not reasonably expect the pig-head dropper, considered in isolation, to have known any better, and he is not more responsible for his ignorance about Jewish history and anti-Semitic symbolism than his parents, his teachers, his college peers, his fraternity friends and so on. So, aren't we all collectively responsible for sustaining an epistemic climate in which certain symbols and backgrounds (e.g., those that relate to Christianity) are made familiar to everybody and expected to be known by all, whereas the familiarity with other symbols and backgrounds (e.g., those that relate to Judaism) is left to epistemic luck?

Cases of *inherited* ignorance raise a particularly challenging problem for epistemic responsibility. On the one hand, we do not want to blame individuals for a body of ignorance they have inherited from their social milieu, without their choosing to do so and without doing anything in particular to partake in the ignorance. But, on the other hand, we do not want to dissolve the issue of responsibility entirely without acknowledging the epistemic wrongs involved in it, and without issuing normative demands that can correct the situation and result in epistemic amelioration. The epistemic responsibility that attaches to cases of collective and inherited ignorance is a more diffused and expansive notion of responsibility than the standard notion of culpable ignorance, one that is not confined to the cognitive repertoire and functioning of particular individuals considered in isolation. But it is nonetheless a notion of responsibility whose scope can be clearly identified (in terms of particular clusters of subjects or communities), and whose demands can be concretized (in terms of particular activities and dynamics that can be demanded of

---

[19] As Rik Peels (2011b) puts it, a subject could be deemed *culpably* ignorant if "he performed a culpable action [or omission] in the past which resulted in that culpable ignorance" (2011b, p. 576). This standard notion of epistemic culpability is heavily individualized and, as I will argue below, unfit to address the shared and diffused form of epistemic responsibility involved in cases of collective insensitivity.

particular groups of people). In the case of widespread racial insensitivity, we have to take collective responsibility for the mechanisms of transmission and inheritance of the epistemic deficits in question, that is, for the collective actions and omissions through which the ignorance and epistemic dysfunctions are formed, propagated and passed on from generation to generation. As illustrated by the pig-head incident, it is problematic to assume that a subject can simply appeal to inherited ignorance and thus shake off *all* responsibility for his action. For, even if it exculpates the individual to some degree, it does not dissolve the issue of responsibility altogether, but brings it to another level: the level of shared and collective responsibility at which the relevant question is not simply whether or not one is responsible for the ignorance in question, but rather, in what ways and through which actions and omissions we partake in the ignorance and share responsibility for it. By calling attention to the normative significance of the alleged ignorance of the pig-head dropper, I am interested not only in highlighting how the individual student falls short of achieving full epistemic responsibility in his thinking and action, but also and more importantly in underscoring the responsibilities of the communities that shaped this individual and made his ignorance possible, and the communities that continue to influence his development and can do something to repair his ignorance – including (and especially) the Vanderbilt University community in which the incident took place (and of which I am also a member).

Although I want to underscore the collective side of epistemic responsibility in cases of widespread insensitivity and shared ignorance, I also want to call attention to the ways in which the individual and the collective levels of responsibility are inextricably intertwined, rather than simply shifting from one to the other. Indeed, as I have argued elsewhere, "one cannot hide oneself completely in the collective ignorance in which one partakes, at least not for long. The collective ignorance may not be of one's choosing, but one cannot inhabit it comfortably and without making any effort to combat it (even when opportunities to do so present themselves), and legitimately use this inherited ignorance to excuse one's actions. Even if indirectly, by omission and inaction, one becomes an active participant in one's own ignorance if one lets it sit and grow, paying no attention to its roots and its ramifications" (Medina 2012, p. 140). One's *inattention* to the ignorance one partakes in can become *complicity and active participation*. One's participation in the collective bodies of ignorance one has inherited becomes *active* when and because one acts on it and fails to act against it. As Shannon Sullivan (2006) has shown convincingly in her transactional account of white habits in the United States, racial ignorance recruits agents to act on it habitually in their daily lives and it gets transmitted across generations through a complex array of (largely unconscious) habits and dispositions that we have to take responsibility for, both individually and collectively.

The formation and transmission of epistemic sensitivities and insensitivities with respect to a racial, ethnic or cultural group requires some knowledge of that group, that is, minimal familiarity with their history, their experiences and struggles, their symbols and aspirations, and so on. When the experiences and perspectives of one particular group are highly visible within a culture at the expense of the visibility of those of other groups, this epistemic imbalance creates obstacles for developing adequate epistemic sensibilities with respect to minority and/or marginalized groups. For example, in a context in which the symbols and meaning of WASP Americans become mainstream and acquire default status, the symbols and meanings of African Americans or of Jewish Americans are less likely to be properly understood and to be given adequate uptake. Subjects easily develop an epistemic sensitivity with respect to the perspectives of those who live and speak like them, but it is harder to become equally sensitive and open-minded to viewpoints, lifestyles and forms of expressions that are unfamiliar or, worse yet, in conflict with one's perspective. Fricker (2007) and other scholars of epistemic injustice have called attention to the hermeneutical obstacles against the adequate understanding and interpretation of marginalized groups and perspectives, and to the testimonial obstacles against giving them adequate levels of trust and credibility. These scholars also emphasize that the work toward epistemic justice involves removing those obstacles and expanding our hermeneutical and testimonial sensitivities. Becoming epistemically sensitive to other people who are very different from us – becoming capable of understanding them, interpreting them, and trusting them adequately – involves more than knowing facts about them; it involves knowing *how* to listen to them in the light of those facts, knowing *how* to respond to their concerns and aspirations, and learning *how* to take into account their viewpoints. In other words, it involves the acquisition of an epistemic sensitivity that can only be developed through communicative interactions and engagements in which there is *epistemic friction* (i.e., challenge and mutual contestation), the kind of friction that can make each perspective aware of itself and of its own limitations, and open and vulnerable to other perspectives. This kind of epistemic sensitivity or openness is not developed simply by acquiring factual knowledge about diversity. It does not consist in knowledge that can remain purely detached or external to us; rather, it is a practical knowledge – a *know-how* – that deeply affects our sense of who we are in the social world and our understanding of our relationality with others. This is what my *episte-mic interactionism* emphasizes.

By epistemic interaction with heterogeneous others I do not mean simply being exposed to information about them, or even mere exposure to the presence and the voices of those who are different from us, because these exposures typically do very little to change the kinds of insensitivity and meta-insensitivity underlying social injustices. Becoming *epistemically responsible* involves experiencing epistemic friction in actual interactions with heterogeneous others; it involves learning how to *acknowledge* the limitations of our standpoint and the distance and differences between our standpoint and alternative ones. As suggested by Stanley Cavell (1969), *acknowledging* is a hybrid notion: it is an *epistemic* and *ethical* notion that involves minimally knowing or recognizing the existence of something *and* being able to avow it to oneself and to others, thus accepting the normative implications of that knowledge as it positions ourselves with respect to others. In some cases subjects may *know* something and they may not yet be ready to *acknowledge* it to themselves or to others (e.g., that one has an addiction, that one is depressed, or that one has internalized some racist prejudices). Acknowledging has the role of normatively positioning oneself with respect to the knowledge in question and taking *responsibility* for it by accepting the normative consequences that it has in one's life and in one's relations to others. There are negative forms of acknowledgment in which what one recognizes and avows is not an epistemic content, but an epistemic absence, that is, the limits of one's knowledge: one's ignorance and epistemic limitations. Recognizing and avowing an epistemic limitation – acknowledging that one does not know what something means, for example – can be a great epistemic and ethical achievement. Acknowledging that a meaning or an experience lies outside one's horizon of understanding can be crucial for learning how to position oneself with respect to that meaning or experience and for learning how to interact with those who have knowledge of that meaning or experience. Acknowledgment marks an epistemic and ethical relation that, through cognitive and affective means, we establish with others (with their experiences, problems, aspirations, values, etc.). Through the epistemic and ethical relation of acknowledgment, we can learn to respect differences we are not familiar with or cannot claim to understand, opening up the possibility of epistemic and ethical growth and the formation of new forms of sensitivity. Of course acknowledging one's epistemic limitations and the distance between one's perspective and that of others, by itself, will not repair insensitivity and the epistemic harms it can produce; but acknowledgment of this kind can be a crucial first step toward instilling epistemic virtues such as humility and open-mindedness and toward eradicating epistemic vices such as arrogance and closed-mindedness.[20] Acknowledgment is a central notion for the ethics of knowing and ignoring, for acknowledging is a crucial mechanism for establishing and accepting *epistemic responsibility*: we have to take *individual* responsibility for what we know and don't know as well as *collective* responsibility for the social production of knowledge and ignorance.[21] In any given case, it is a contextual issue whether the focus should be on individual or on collective responsibility, that is, on the specific epistemic actions/omissions that particular individuals are responsible for or on the widespread patterns of action/omission and interaction that communities maintain and individuals simply participate in.[22]

Developing a sense of epistemic responsibility in relation to the epistemic harms produced by racism (such as undeserved lack of credibility, differential access to communicative and interpretative resources, etc.), involves becoming more sensitive and responsive to racial epistemic injustices as they appear in our daily activities, that is, more sensitive and responsive to the testimonial and hermeneutical dysfunctions that surface in our epistemic practices. Trying to fight racial epistemic injustices is a very complex and difficult task; but, minimally, it should involve being *attentive* to racially motivated epistemic mistreatments, *acknowledging* dysfunctional epistemic dynamics that unfairly harm certain racial groups, and *resisting complicity* with undeserved epistemic privileges and disadvantages apportioned to members of different racial groups. Besides being action-based and action-oriented, my notion of epistemic responsibility (and of the obligation to resist contained in it) has two other key features. Our responsibility as epistemic agents and communicators is (1) *situated and polyphonic* – to be determined contextually, practice by

---

[20] In *The Epistemology of Resistance* (2012) I have developed an account of these epistemic virtues and vices as they appear under conditions of oppression and epistemic injustice. See especially Chapter 1.

[21] For a full discussion of the relation between individual and collective epistemic responsibility, see Medina (2012) and Code (1987, 2014).

[22] Although the individual and collective levels of epistemic responsibility typically go together, there are cases in which they can be decoupled and even go in separate ways. There are cases in which individuals take responsibility for racial insensitivity in their own actions and omissions, while remaining unable to recognize and acknowledge their involvement in widespread forms of racial insensitivity. For example, there are white Americans who have become racially sensitive to the perspectives of African Americans in their personal interactions, but nonetheless they still support policies and social arrangements that stifle the participation of African Americans in public life (for example, the recently proposed new requirements for voter registration and new boundaries of election districts in the United States). There are also cases in which individuals are willing to accept shared responsibility for widespread racial insensitivity and yet they remain unable to recognize how such insensitivity surfaces in their personal actions and omissions in daily life.

practice, given one's positions and relations within those practices; and (2) it is *essentially shared* – it always requires cooperation with others and collective efforts.

We all have a prima facie obligation to resist racial oppression and the epistemic injustices associated with it whatever social locations we happen to occupy and whatever racial privileges or disadvantages (if any) we happen to have. But of course what counts as our responsibility in any given context will depend on how we are positioned in the practices relevant in that situation and how we are related to others within those practices. We are all responsible to resist epistemic injustices, but we do not bear the same responsibilities. Piecemeal, practice by practice, and in all corners of our life, we need to carry out the contextualist task of figuring out what we can and should do given our position in the social world and our relationality with others across practices. I claim that there are *special responsibilities that the racially privileged have* in the fight against racial epistemic injustices. While oppressed subjects are typically epistemically better equipped to resist, their agency is constrained and they do not always have opportunities to make their resistance effective; and even when they can resist effectively, there may be extremely high costs for them in that resistance,[23] and it would be unfair to demand it from them as an obligation. On the other hand, privileged subjects, although they may have more power and agency to speak up against racial epistemic injustices and to change racial dynamics at a lesser cost for them, they often are epistemically ill-equipped to fight epistemic injustices and they have little motivation to do so (and often strong pressures *not* to make that fight their own). This suggests that different groups must cooperate and *jointly* discharge the shared obligation to remove racial ignorance and insensitivity – oppressed groups providing the requisite knowledge, insight and perspective while privileged groups providing support and yielding the required power and agency.

If becoming epistemically responsible was an individual task, then it would be utterly impossible for corrupted epistemic subjectivities to fulfill epistemic demands and achieve responsibility: actively meta-ignorant individuals by themselves are unable to detect their blind-spots and recognize their insensitivities, and therefore they are incapable of becoming epistemically responsible agents. But becoming epistemically sensitive is not only or primarily an *individual* responsibility – it is not even something that the individual can always accomplish fully by herself, in

---

[23] The result for these subjects can be being perceived as non-compliant, as unruly, and this can result in more exclusion and marginalization from the epistemic activities in question. Think for example of classroom dynamics and how a student trying to change the argumentative dynamics can be perceived by the other students and by the teachers.

isolation. Rather, it is a *shared* responsibility that can only be discharged *cooperatively and collectively*. In the first place, it can only be discharged *cooperatively* because individuals have blind-spots and insensitivities that they cannot overcome (sometime they cannot even detect) if left to their own devices; they need the critical interventions, provocations, and challenges (the *friction*) of others. And, in the second place, since insidious forms of epistemic insensitivity involve widely shared forms of ignorance and inattention, the epistemic responsibility in question can only be discharged *collectively* because it is the responsibility of groups, publics, and institutions, and of individuals *qua* members of those social groups, publics, and institutions.

Sometimes even well intentioned racially privileged subjects, willing to resist epistemic injustices, are not yet capable of doing so by themselves. In my view, this doesn't mean that their obligations disappear—they are not off the hook. Rather, what this means is that they will need the *help and guidance* (as well as the *provocations and pressures*) of others. And besides breaking their racial insensitivity with the help of others, privileged subjects will also need help to find *opportunities* to resist and develop new forms of sensitivity. Typically this means that the social world around them needs to change: the institutional settings and social practices that have supported their racial insensitivity need to undergo structural changes, so that new social conditions can block insensitive attitudes, produce costs and negative consequences for displays of insensitivity, and create incentives for the interruption of insensitivity and the formation of new forms of social sensitivity. Some of this can be done, for example, in educational contexts and educational practices that shape our epistemic sensibilities by instilling epistemic habits and by establishing dynamics of epistemic interaction with others. To this area I now turn.

6   Becoming Epistemically Responsible: Toward an Ethics and Pedagogy of Discomfort

I have argued that in order to be able to expand and meliorate our social sensibilities, we need to start by exposing ourselves and making ourselves vulnerable, by *acknowledging* our epistemic limitations and taking responsibility for epistemic injustices, opening up our perspective to processes of critical scrutiny and resistance. As I have argued elsewhere (2012), epistemically responsible social interaction requires resistance, and resistance begins *at home*, that is, in the most intimate aspects of our cognitive-affective functioning. Resistance has to begin within ourselves and in the activities in which we feel at home. This is why I contend that for our epistemic sensibilities to be truly open and responsive to differences, they must be *self-questioning*, rather than being defensive and self-protecting. Self-questioning sensibilities can only be established when subjects make themselves vulnerable to challenges and become exposed (either by choice or by social design) to processes of self-questioning.[24] Looking at ourselves with fresh eyes through processes of self-questioning affords us opportunities to interrogate what we find in the most intimate corners of our perspective, and to recognize its limitations and the possibilities of correction and improvement. In very different ways, Queer Theory, Feminist Standpoint Theory and Critical Race Theory teach us the importance of unmasking and undoing the processes of social construction of our perspective, of interrupting the flow of familiarity and obviousness, making the familiar unfamiliar and the obvious bizarre. And this critical exercise should not be thought of simply as the quaint activity of some peculiar activists and intellectuals, but rather, as a crucial part of the growth and development of critical subjects of knowledge, of subjects who learn how to resist their cognitive-affective limitations and to improve their sensibilities and capacities.

We all have a prima facie obligation to interrogate received attitudes and habits, that is, to open ourselves to processes of self-questioning. If we fail this obligation, the failure of other epistemic responsibilities will ensue and possibilities of critique and resistance will be thwarted. Cultivating this openness to being challenged about one's own perspective involves experiences of *epistemic discomfort* in which we feel disoriented, losing our epistemic bearings as it were, not being able to rely on epistemic norms and presuppositions that we have taken for granted, and therefore being open to other perspectives in new ways. Undergoing processes of self-questioning of this kind involves experiencing the kind of epistemic discomfort that makes us re-evaluate our own perspective vis-à-vis alternative ones; and these experiences constitute invaluable learning opportunities, occasions for epistemic and ethical growth, for remaking our epistemic habits and attitudes and reassessing the norms and presuppositions of our epistemic practices. The *ethics and pedagogy of discomfort* that I propose (2014) focuses on experiences of epistemic friction that make us

---

[24] These processes of self-questioning can sometimes lead to processes of *defamiliarization* and *self-estrangement* (Medina 2014, 2016). Challenging one's own perspective to the point that it becomes unfamiliar – to the point that one becomes a *stranger* to oneself – is something that may or may not happen depending on the challenges, interrogations and provocations available to oneself, and on how one processes them. All we can demand of subjects is that they remain open to these processes, and we can hold them accountable when they are not. We can also demand of communities (e.g., in relation to educational policies) that they make these processes readily available to all subjects, and that they try new techniques and strategies of interrogation and provocation if the ones in use prove to be unsuccessful.

re-evaluate the normative structure of our familiar practices and dynamics. The kind of epistemic friction that triggers processes of self-questioning is required for the formation of open-minded subjects and open communities.

Building on my view, Lorraine Code (2014) has argued recently that an "open society" and its members have epistemic responsibilities to live up to: in particular, the responsibility to make available "accurate knowledge/information" about all the problems and injustices that occur in every corner of the social fabric, so that the plight of every member of society becomes visible and no one is forced to live an invisible social existence. Code rightly adds that the responsibility in question is primarily *"pedagogical*: educators, investigative journalists, and public intellectuals (among others) have a presumptive duty to know, address, communicate, and debate these issues in their complexity; and responsible citizens have some obligation to learn how to evaluate them, negatively or positively. Yet assuming such responsibilities is, again, a fraught, often frustrating task, and questions about where to confer trust are not easily addressed" (Code 2014, pp. 672–673). Indeed lack of *trust* is one of the characteristic features of the kinds of social insensitivity that exclude and marginalize subjects; and building trust to repair those forms of insensitivity and the injustices they keep in place is a difficult *pedagogical* challenge. Should students trust educators? Should educators trust the educational system within which they work? As Code emphasizes, "pedagogical responsibilities are multiply challenging": to begin with, teachers, journalists and public intellectuals who should educate the public and promote less exclusionary forms of social sensibilities have themselves been socialized breathing the prejudices, biases and insensitivities in question and should not be presumed to be free from them (Code 2014, p. 673).

The multiple challenges and social constraints of our pedagogical responsibilities makes it clear that the expansion of social sensibilities "could not be a purely individual effort" (Code 2014, p. 675), but it is a challenge for the whole of society that requires the concerted efforts of all communities and their members. It is a challenge that involves *community building* and the *making and remaking of social networks*.[25] It is crucial to foster solidarity with those who are marginalized in our epistemic practices and suffer epistemic injustices, being disproportionately and unfairly disbelieved and misunderstood because of lack of trust, lack of credibility and lack of access to epistemic and interpretative resources. It is crucial that subjects resist their complicity with unfair and

---

[25] See especially section 5.3 of Medina (2012, pp. 225–249).

dysfunctional epistemic dynamics, and that they interrupt such dynamics and make those who participate in them *uncomfortable* by questioning habitual and familiar assumptions that skew communication and bias assessments of intelligibility and credibility. In this sense, I have argued (Medina forthcoming) that the micro-aggressions through which the epistemic status and agency of racial minorities are routinely undermined in epistemic activities should be countered with *micro-practices of resistance* in which participants in epistemic practices (whatever their racial identity) express epistemic solidarity with those unfairly treated.

Examples of micro-practices of resistance against epistemic micro-aggressions are the following: calling out and making explicit a differential treatment – even if that means stopping the interaction and/or making the participants uncomfortable; responding to a stare, gesture or insinuation that calls into question someone's competence with a stare, gesture or insinuation that calls into question the aggressor's authority or ability to call into question other people's competence; and so on. Micro-resistance does not need to come from the person suffering from the epistemic micro-aggression, but it can be produced effectively (sometimes even more effectively) by others involved in the interaction even though they were not targeted (including bystanders and even eavesdroppers). For example, imagine passengers on a bus in a major US city overhearing someone lecturing to some kids about blacks or Hispanics being oversensitive when being questioned by the police; instead of extricating oneself from the uncomfortable situation, everybody present (and not just the kids involved) can and should feel responsible to intervene and not let it stand, that is, not let the micro-aggression go unquestioned and the micro-aggressor get away with it. Sometimes racial micro-aggressions take the form of micro-invalidations such as "you feel that way just because you are black," "you are making it a racial issue," "you are overreacting and making something out of nothing." These micro-aggressions vitiate communicative dynamics by biasing hearer's receptivity to some racial perspectives and invalidating the credibility or trust deserved by testimonial contributions from those perspectives. Unfair micro-invalidations can be countered by anyone present at the interaction with a who-are-you-to-invalidate response, or with a way of deflecting or shifting the unfair argumentative burden being posed. Micro-invalidations can also be countered through resistant micro-validations, or alternative ways of validating and supporting subjects who, in the given context, are likely to face challenges and obstacles in their status of participants with full or equal epistemic agency. These micro-practices of resistance that produce friction are at the core of my ethics and pedagogy of discomfort, which recommends epistemic interventions and subversions that produce epistemic discomfort in dysfunctional dynamics in order to motivate agents to change their epistemic attitudes and habits and to experiment with alternative dynamics.[26]

Epistemic responsibility is intertwined with ethical and pedagogical responsibilities. Under conditions of epistemic injustice, when there are dysfunctional epistemic dynamics, our ethical and pedagogical responsibilities call for critical interventions that turn experiences of epistemic discomfort into learning opportunities for individuals and communities to become more sensitive to patterns of unfair epistemic treatment and more active in producing epistemic solidarity and facilitating fair epistemic cooperation. The ethics and pedagogy of discomfort that I propose targets our complacency and complicity with epistemic injustices and demands that we confront and live up to our epistemic responsibilities through sustained pedagogical practices that disrupt epistemic habits and attitudes that protect unfair privileges and disadvantages. "Sometimes people need to be made *uncomfortable* so that they wake up from their numbness, sometimes their familiar spaces and comfortable activities need to be interrupted so that they become aware of their complicity and their motivational obstacles to pay attention to an injustice and to join the fight against it. Part of what needs to happen to counter the protective mechanisms of privilege is to call attention to the unfair consequences of keeping areas of epistemic neglect unchecked and thus to make painfully visible the *price of epistemic comfort* under conditions of oppression, so that people cannot avoid the realization that the epistemic comfort of some comes at the cost of the epistemic discomfort of others" (Medina 2014, p. 66), and that leaving the epistemic appraisals of some uncontested means that the epistemic appraisals of others are always in question. All of us (but those who occupy positions of privilege especially) need to get out of our comfort zones and familiar spaces and to open ourselves to the epistemic friction that can make perspectives vulnerable and accountable to each other. Nothing short of this complicated and concerted effort at epistemic resistance will be effective in eradicating patterns of racial ignorance, uprooting racial insensitivity and repairing the harms it produces.

7   Epilogue

I want to conclude my discussion of ignorance and racial insensitivity with a caveat and a closing reflection on ongoing research and future work in

---

[26] This section has been adapted from my essay "Epistemic Injustice and Epistemologies of Ignorance" (Medina 2016), where the reader can find a fuller discussion of microaggressions and micro-resistance.

this area. First, the caveat. This paper has focused on racial ignorance and insensitivity in privileged groups (such as white people in the United States), but although privilege can be associated with particular dynamics of racial ignorance and insensitivity, there is also racial ignorance and insensitivity within and across oppressed groups, and not only against privileged groups (e.g., anti-white biases among peoples of color in the United States), but also against other oppressed groups and even against members of their own group (e.g., the phenomenon of *racial self-hatred*). A full account of racial insensitivity should include an analysis of how the defense mechanisms of racial ignorance operate in differently situated subjects and groups.

In closing, I want to acknowledge recently developed areas of empirical research that have sparked theoretical discussions of racial ignorance and have turned the epistemology of race into an area of vibrant interdisciplinary research. In particular, I want to highlight the significance and fruitfulness of two areas of interdisciplinary research: *implicit bias* (Brownstein and Saul 2016) and *micro-aggressions* (Sue 2010). On the one hand, the paradigm of implicit bias and the empirical evidence gathered within it illustrate well my conception of racial ignorance as a form of self-hiding and unconscious insensitivity that is hard to displace because it consists in well-entrenched habits of mind. On the other hand, micro-aggressions are the perfect arena for the detailed analysis of how racial insensitivity operates in situated interpersonal dynamics. I am confident that these and other venues of empirical research will bear many empirical and theoretical fruits for the discussion of racial ignorance. At the same time, I also want to point out that there are *cognitivist* and *individualist* biases in these areas of research that obscure (or at least minimize) the *affective* and *collective* aspects of racial ignorance. While a lot of research has been done on the cognitive mechanisms underlying racial biases, the emotions and affective resistances that protect racial ignorance have received little attention. And while a lot has been written recently about the psychological mechanisms within the individual that keep racial biases in place, there has been little discussion of racial insensitivity as a collective pattern of shared ignorance, and about the structural and institutional elements that are responsible for the propagation and perpetuation of racial ignorance at the collective level. I hope that the insights and suggestions contained in this essay contribute to expand the research on racial ignorance along those lines.

References

Adler, J. 1996. 'Transmitting Knowledge'. *Noûs* 30 (1): 99–111.

Alcoff, L. 2010. 'Epistemic Identities'. *Episteme: A Journal of Social Epistemology*, 7 (2): 128–137. Symposium on *Epistemic Injustice: Power and the Ethics of Knowing.*

Alston, W. 1996. 'Belief, Acceptance, and Religious Faith'. In *Faith, Freedom, and Rationality: Philosophy of Religion Today*, Jordan, J. & Howard-Snyder D. (eds). London: Rowman & Littlefield, pp. 3–27.

Anderson, E. 2010. *The Imperative of Integration.* Princeton University Press.

2012. 'Epistemic Justice as a Virtue of Social Institutions'. *Social Epistemology* 26 (2): 163–173.

Aquinas, T. 1989. *Summa Theologiae: A Concise Translation.* Translated by McDermott, T. Allen. Texas: Christian Classics.

Aristotle 2003. *The Nicomachean Ethics.* Translated by Rackham, H. Cambridge, MA: Harvard University Press.

Armstrong, D.M. 1978. *Universals and Scientific Realism.* Cambridge, UK: Cambridge University Press.

Artemov, S. & Fitting, M. 2012. 'Justification Logic'. In *The Stanford Encyclopedia of Philosophy* (Fall 2012 Edition), Zalta, E.N. (ed.). http://plato.stanford.edu /entries/logic-justification/

Augustine 2009. *Confessions.* Translated by Chadwick, H. Oxford: Oxford World Classics.

Audi, R. 2011. *Epistemology: A Contemporary Introduction to the Theory of Knowledge.* New York: Routledge.

Austin, J.L. 1979. 'Other Minds'. In *Philosophical Papers*, Austin, J.L. (ed.). New York: Oxford University Press, pp. 67–116.

Baehr, J. 2011. *The Inquiring Mind: On Intellectual Virtues and Virtue Epistemology.* Oxford: Oxford University Press.

Baltag, A. & Smets, S. 2008. 'Qualitative Theory of Dynamic Interactive Belief Revision'. *LOFT07, Texts in Logic and Games* 3: 13–60.

Beardsley, E.L. 1979. 'Blaming'. *Philosophia* 8 (4): 573–583.

Beeby, L. 2011. 'A Critique of Hermeneutical Injustice'. *Proceedings of the Aristotelian Society* 111: 479–486.

Bengson, J. & Moffett, M. 2007. 'Know-How and Concept-Possession'. *Philosophical Studies* 136 (1): 31–57.

Bierwisch, M. 1989. 'The Semantics of Gradation'. In *Dimensional Adjectives*, Bierwisch, M. & Lang, E. (eds.). Berlin: Springer-Verlag, pp. 71–261.

Bilgrami, A. 1998. 'Self-Knowledge and Resentment'. *In Knowing Our Own Minds*, Wright, C., Smith, B. & Macdonald, C. (eds.). Oxford University Press, pp. 207–241.

2012. *Self-Knowledge and Resentment*. Cambridge, MA: Harvard University Press.

Bishop, J. 2010. 'Faith'. In *The Stanford Encyclopedia of Philosophy* (Fall 2010 Edition), Zalta, E.N. (ed.).

Blaauw, M. 2008. 'SSI: in memoriam'. *Philosophical Quarterly* 58 (231): 318–325.

2013. 'The Epistemic Account of Privacy'. *Episteme* 10 (2): 167–177.

Blome-Tillmann, M. 2007. 'Contextualism and the Epistemological Enterprise'. *Proceedings of the Aristotelian Society, New Series* 107 (1/3): 387–394.

2009a. 'Contextualism, Safety, and Epistemic Relevance'. *Philosophical Studies* 143 (3): 383–394.

2009b. 'Knowledge and Presuppositions'. *Mind* 118 (470): 241–294.

2013. 'Contextualism and the Knowledge Norms'. *Pacific Philosophical Quarterly* 94 (1): 89–100.

2014. *Knowledge and Presuppositions*. Oxford University Press.

2015. 'Skepticism and Contextualism'. In *Skepticism: From Antiquity to the Present*, Reed, B. & Manchuca, D. (eds.). Bloomsbury.

Booth, A. & Peels, R. 2010. 'Why Responsible Belief Is Blameless Belief'. *Journal of Philosophy* 107 (5): 257–265.

Brandt, R.B. 1969. 'A Utilitarian Theory of Excuses'. *Philosophical Review* 78 (3): 337–361.

Brogaard, B. 'Staying Indoors: How Phenomenal Dogmatism Solves the Skeptical Problem Without Going Externalist'. In *Internalism*, Bergmann, M. (ed.). Oxford University Press.

2005. 'I Know. Therefore, I Understand', unpublished manuscript.

2007. 'Attitude Reports: Do You Mind the Gap?' *Philosophy Compass* 3 (1): 93–118.

2008. 'Knowledge-The and Propositional Attitude Ascriptions'. *Grazer Philosophische Studien* 77 (1): 147–190.

2009. 'What Mary Did Yesterday: Reflections on Knowledge-wh'. *Philosophy Phenomenological Research* 78 (2): 439–467.

2010. 'Perspectival Truth and Color Primitivism'. In New Waves in Truth, C. Wright and N. Pedersen (eds.), 249–266. New York: Palgrave Macmillan.

2011. 'Knowledge-How: A Unified Account'. In *Knowing How: Essays on Knowledge, Mind, and Action*, Bengson, J. & Moffett M. (eds.). Oxford University Press, pp. 136–160.

Bromberger, S. 1992. *On What We Know We Don't Know: Explanation, Theory, Linguistics, and How Questions Shape Them*. University of Chicago Press and Stanford: CSLI.

Brooks, A. 2007. *Who Really Cares: The Surprising Truth About Compassionate Conservatism*. New York: Basic Books.

Brown, J. 2008. 'The Knowledge Norm for Practical Reasoning and Subject Sensitive Invariantism'. *Noûs* 43 (2): 167–189.

Brownmiller, S. 1990. *In Our Time: Memoir of a Revolution*. New York: The Dial Press.

Brownstein, M. & Saul, J. (eds.) (2016). *Implicit Bias and Philosophy, Volume I: Metaphysics and Epistemology*. Oxford University Press.

Brueckner, A. 1994. 'The Structure of the Sceptical Argument'. *Philosophy and Phenomenological Research* 54 (4): 827–835.

Carnap, R. 1947. *Meaning and Necessity*. Chicago University Press.

2002. *Thoughts and Utterances – The Pragmatics of Explicit Communication*. Oxford: Blackwell.

Carter, J.A. & Pritchard, D.H. (forthcoming). 'Intellectual Humility, Knowledge-How, and Disagreement'. In *The Virtue Turn*, Slote, M., Sosa, E. & Mi, C. (eds.). London: Routledge.

Carston, R. 2002. *Thoughts and Utterances: The Pragmatics of Explicit Communication* (Oxford: Blackwell)

Cavell, S. 1969. 'Knowing and Acknowledging'. In *Must We Mean What We Say?*. New York: Cambridge University Press, pp. 238–266.

Chalmers, D.J. & Bourget. D. 2014. 'What Do Philosophers Believe?' *Philosophical Studies* 170 (3): 465–500.

Chan, W. 1963. *The Way of Lao Tzu*. New York: Macmillan Publishing Company.

Clegg, J.S. 1979. 'Faith'. *American Philosophical Quarterly* 16 (3): 225–232.

Coady, C.A.J. 1992. *Testimony: A Philosophical Study*. Oxford: Clarendon Press.

Code, L. 1987. *Epistemic Responsibility*. Hanover, N.H.: University Press of New England.

2014. 'Culpable Ignorance?' *Hypatia* 29 (3): 670–676.

Cohen, L. J. 1992. *An Essay on Belief and Acceptance*. Oxford: Clarendon Press.

Cohen, S. 1987. 'Knowledge, Context, and Social Standards'. *Synthese* 73 (1): 3–26.

1988. 'How to Be a Fallibilist'. *Philosophical Perspectives* 2: 91–123.

1997. 'Contextualist Solutions to Epistemological Problems: Scepticism, Gettier, and the Lottery'. *Australasian Journal of Philosophy* 76 (2): 289–306.

1999. 'Contextualism, Scepticism, and the Structure of Reasons'. *Philosophical Perspectives* 13: 57–89.

2004. 'Contextualism and Unhappy-Face Solutions: Reply to Schiffer'. *Philosophical Studies* 119 (1–2): 185–197.

Collins, R. 1999. 'A Scientific Argument for the Existence of God'. In *Reason for the Hope Within*, Murray, M. (ed.). Grand Rapids: Eerdmans, pp. 47–75.

Comesaña, J. 2005. 'Unsafe Knowledge'. *Synthese* 146 (3): 395–404.

Craig, W.L. 1991. 'Talbott's Universalism'. *Religious Studies* 27 (3): 297–308.

Cresswell, M.J. 1977. 'The Semantics of Degree'. In *Montague Grammar*, Partee, B. (ed.). New York: Academic Press, pp. 261–299.

DePaul, M. 2001. 'Value Monism in Epistemology'. In *Knowledge, Truth, and Duty: Essays on Epistemic Justification, Virtue, and Responsibility*, Steup, M. (ed.). Oxford University Press, pp. 170–186.

DeRose, K. 1992. 'Contextualism and Knowledge Attributions'. *Philosophy and Phenomenological Research* 52 (4): 913–929.

1995. 'Solving the Skeptical Problem'. *The Philosophical Review* 104 (1): 1–52.

2011. 'Contextualism, contrastivism, and X-Phi surveys'. *Philosophical Studies* 156 (1): 81–110.

Descartes, R. 1647. *Meditations on First Philosophy*. English edition of *Meditationes de Prima Philosophia*, Cottingham, J. (ed., transl.) 1996. Cambridge University Press.

De Ridder, J. 2013. 'Epistemic Dependence and Collective Scientific Knowledge'. *Synthese* 191(1): 37–53.

Donagan, A. 1977. *The Theory of Morality*, Chicago: University of Chicago Press.

Dotson, K. 2012. 'A Cautionary Tale: On Limiting Epistemic Oppression'. *Frontiers* 33 (1): 24–47.

Dretske, F. 1970. 'Epistemic Operators'. *Journal of Philosophy* 67 (24): 1007–1023.

Driver, J. 1989. 'The Virtues of Ignorance'. *The Journal of Philosophy* 86 (7): 373–384.

Du Bois, W.E.B. [1903] 1994. *The Souls of Black Folks*. New York: Dover.

Ellison, R. 1995. *Invisible Man*. New York: Vintage Books.

Enqvist, S. 2009. 'Interrogative Belief Revision in Modal Logic'. *Journal of Philosophical Logic* 38 (5): 527–548.

2011. *Interrogative Belief Revision*, Doctoral Dissertation. Department of Philosophy, Lund University.

Fagin, R. & Halpern, J.Y. 1988. 'Belief, Awareness and Limited Reasoning'. *Artificial Intelligence* 34 (1): 39–76.

Fagin, R., Halpern, J.Y., Moses, Y. & Vardi, M.Y. 1995. *Reasoning about Knowledge*. Cambridge, MA: MIT Press.

Fantl, J. & McGrath, M. 2002. 'Evidence, Pragmatics and Justification'. *The Philosophical Review* 111 (1): 67–94.

2007. 'On Pragmatic Encroachment in Epistemology'. *Philosophy and Phenomenological Research* 75 (3): 558–589.

2009. *Knowledge in an Uncertain World*. Oxford University Press.

2010. 'Pragmatic Encroachment'. *Routledge Companion to Epistemology*, Bernecker, S. & Pritchard, D.H. (eds.). London: Routledge, pp. 558–568.

Farkas, K. 2016. 'Know-wh Does Not Reduce to Know-that'. *American Philosophical Quarterly* 53 (2): 109–122.

Faust, J. 2000a. 'Proof Beyond a Reasonable Doubt: An Annotated Bibliography'. *The APA Newsletters* 99 (2): 229–235.

2000b. 'Reasonable Doubt Jury Instructions'. *The APA Newsletters* 99 (2): 226–229.

Feltz, A. & Cokely, E.T. 2012. 'The Virtues of Ignorance'. *Review of Philosophy and Psychology* 3 (3): 335–350.

Fields, L. 1994. 'Moral Beliefs and Blameworthiness'. *Philosophy* 69 (4): 397–415.

Firestein, S. 2012. *Ignorance: How It Drives Science*. Oxford: Oxford University Press.

Fischer, J.M. & Ravizza, M. 1998. *Responsibility and Control: A Theory of Moral Responsibility*. Cambridge University Press.

Flanagan, O. 1990. 'Virtue and Ignorance'. *The Journal of Philosophy* 87 (8): 420–428.

Flew, A. 1976. *The Presumption of Atheism and Other Philosophical Essays on God, Freedom, and Immortality*. Amherst, New York: Prometheus Press.

Franke, W. 2015. 'Learned Ignorance: The Apophatic Tradition of Cultivating the Virtue of Unknowing'. In *Routledge International Handbook of Ignorance Studies*, Gross, M. & McGoey, L. (eds.). London/New York: Routledge, pp. 26–35.

Fricker, E. 1987. 'The Epistemology of Testimony'. *Proceedings of the Aristotelian Society*, supplementary volume 61: 57–83.

Fricker, M. 2007. *Epistemic Injustice: Power and the Ethics of Knowing*. Oxford University Press.

   2010. 'The Relativism of Blame and Williams's Relativism of Distance'. *Proceedings of the Aristotelian Society Supp.* LXXXIV: 151–177.

   2013a. 'Epistemic Justice as a Condition of Political Freedom'. *Synthese* 190 (7): 1317–1332.

   2013b. 'How Is Hermeneutical Injustice Related to 'White Ignorance'? Reply to José Medina's 'Hermeneutical Injustice and Polyphonic Contextualism: Social Silences and Shared Hermeneutical Responsibilities'. *Social Epistemology Review and Reply Collective* 2 (8): 49–53.

   2016. 'Fault and No-Fault Responsibility for Implicit Prejudice – A Space for Epistemic 'Agent-Regret'. In *The Epistemic Life of Groups: Essays in the Epistemology of Collectives*, Brady, M. & Fricker, M. (eds.). Oxford University Press.

Fumerton, R. 1995. *Metaepistemology and Skepticism*. Maryland: Rowman & Littlefield.

Geach, P. 1956. 'Good and Evil'. *Analysis* 17 (2): 32–42.

Gendler, T.S. 2014. 'The Third Horse: On Unendorsed Association and Human Behaviour'. *Proceedings of the Aristotelian Society Supplementary* Volume XXXVIII: 185–218.

Ginet, C. 1975. *Knowledge, Perception, and Memory*. Boston: D. Reidel.

Goldman, A. 2002b. 'The Unity of the Epistemic Virtues'. In *Pathways to Knowledge: Private and Public*. Goldman, A. (ed.). Oxford University Press, pp. 51–72.

Goldman, A.I. 1970. *A Theory of Human Action*. Princeton University Press.

   1986. *Epistemology and Cognition*. Cambridge, MA: Harvard University Press.

   1999. *Knowledge in a Social World*. Oxford: Clarendon Press.

   2002a. 'Social Routes to Belief and Knowledge'. In *Pathways to Knowledge: Private and Public*. Goldman, A.I. (ed.). Oxford University Press, pp. 164–181.

   2002c. 'What Is Social Epistemology? A Smorgasbord of Projects'. In *Pathways to Knowledge: Private and Public*. Goldman, A.I. (ed.). Oxford University Press, pp. 182–204.

Goldman, A. & Olsson, E.J. 2009. 'Reliabilism and the Value of Knowledge'. In *Epistemic Value*. Haddock, A., Millar, A. & Pritchard, D.H. (eds.). Oxford University Press, pp. 19–41.

Greco, J. 2009. 'The Value Problem'. In *Epistemic Value*. Haddock, A., Millar, A. & Pritchard, D.H. (eds.). Oxford University Press, pp. 313–321.

Greenough, P. & Pritchard, D. (eds.) (2009). *Williamson and His Critics*. Oxford University Press.

Groenendijk, J. & Stokhof, M. 1982. 'Semantic Analysis of Wh-complements'. *Linguistics and Philosophy* 5 (2): 175–233.

Gross, M., and L. McGoey. 2015. 'Introduction'. In *Routledge International Handbook of Ignorance Studies*, Gross, M. & McGoey, L. (eds.). London/New York: Routledge, pp. 1–14.

Grove, A. 1988. 'Two Modellings for Theory Change'. *Journal of Philosophical Logic* 17 (2): 157–170.

Guerrero, A.A. 2007. 'Don't Know, Don't Kill: Moral Ignorance, Culpability, and Caution'. *Philosophical Studies* 136 (1): 59–97.

Haack, S. 2001. 'The Ethics of Belief" Reconsidered'. In *Knowledge, Truth, and Duty: Essays on Epistemic Justification, Responsibility, and Virtue*, Steup, M. (ed.). Oxford University Press, pp. 21–33.

Haas, J, and K. Maria Vogt. 2015. 'Ignorance and Investigation'. In *Routledge International Handbook of Ignorance Studies*, Gross, M. & McGoey, L. (eds.). London/New York: Routledge, pp. 17–25.

Hallie, P. 1979. *Lest Innocent Blood be Shed*. New York: HarperCollins.

Harman, E. 2011. 'Does Moral Ignorance Exculpate?' *Ratio* 24 (4): 443–468.

Hasker, W. 1985. 'Foreknowledge and Necessity'. *Faith and Philosophy* 2 (2): 121–157.

2004. *Providence, Evil, and the Openness of God*. New York: Routledge Press.

Hawley, K. 2003. 'Success and Knowledge-How'. *American Philosophical Quarterly* 40 (1): 19–31.

Hawthorne, J. 2004. *Knowledge and Lotteries*. Oxford University Press.

Hawthorne, J. & Stanley, J. 2008. 'Knowledge and Action'. *Journal of Philosophy* 105 (10): 571–590.

Heatherington, S. 2011. *How to Know: A Practicalist Conception of Knowledge*. Oxford: Wiley-Blackwell.

Heim, I. 1985. 'Notes on Comparatives and Related Matters', unpublished manuscript, University of Texas: Austin.

Hendricks, V. 2006. *Mainstream and Formal Epistemology*. Cambridge University Press.

Hetherington, S. 2001. *Good Knowledge, Bad Knowledge*. Oxford University Press.

Hick, J. 1989. *An Interpretation of Religion*. New Haven, CT: Yale University Press.

Hill, C. & Schechter, J. 2007. 'Hawthorne's Lottery Puzzle and the Nature of Belief'. *Philosophical Issues* 17 (1): 102–122.

Hintikka, J. 1962. *Knowledge and Belief*. Ithaca, NY: Cornell University Press.

Holroyd, J. 2012. 'Responsibility for Implicit Bias'. *Social Philosophy* 43 (3): 274–306.

Hookway, C. 2010. 'Epistemic Injustice and Reflections on Fricker'. *Episteme: A Journal of Social Epistemology* 7 (2), Symposium on *Epistemic Injustice: Power and the Ethics of Knowing*, pp. 151–163.

Houlgate, L.D. 1968. 'Knowledge and Responsibility'. *American Philosophical Quarterly* 5 (2): 109–116.

Howard-Snyder, D. 2017. '*The Skeptical Christian*'. In Oxford Studies in the Philosophy of Religion, Vol VIII, ed. Jonathan L. Kvanvig (Oxford: Oxford University Press).

Hume, D. 1739–40. *A Treatise of Human Nature*. Oxford: Clarendon Press.

Hyman, J. 2006. 'Knowledge and Evidence'. *Mind* 115 (460): 891–916.

Ichikawa, J. 2011a. 'Quantifiers and Epistemic Contextualism'. *Philosophical Studies* 115 (3): 383–398.

2011b. 'Quantifiers, Knowledge, and Counterfactuals'. *Philosophy and Phenomenological Research* 82 (2): 287–313.

Jacobs, J. 2015. 'The Ineffable, Inconceivable, and Incomprehensible God: Fundamentality and Apophatic Theology'. In *Oxford Studies in Philosophy of Religion*, ed. J.L. Kvanvig, Vol. 6. Oxford: Oxford University Press, pp. 158–176.

James, W. 1912. *The Will to Believe and Other Essays in Popular Philosophy*. London: Longmans, Green, and Company.

1997. 'Why Do We Value Knowledge?' *American Philosophical Quarterly* 34 (4): 423–440.

Jones, W.E. 1997. 'Why Do We Value Knowledge?', *American Philosophical Quarterly* 34(4): 423–439.

Jordan, J. 2006. *Pascal's Wager: Pragmatic Arguments and Belief in God*. New York: Oxford University Press.

Kallestrup, J. & Pritchard, D.H. (forthcoming). 'Intellectual Humility'. In *Pride*, Carter, J.A. & Gordon, E. (eds.). Lanham, MD: Rowman & Littlefield.

Kaplan, D. 1989. 'Demonstratives'. In *Themes from Kaplan*, Almog, J. Perry, J. & Wettstein, H. (eds.). Oxford University Press, pp. 481–563.

Kennedy, C. 1999. *Projecting the Adjective: The Syntax and Semantics of Gradability and Comparison*. New York: Garland.

2007. 'Vagueness and Grammar: The Semantics of Relative and Absolute Gradable Adjectives'. *Linguistics and Philosophy* 30: 1–45.

Klein, E. 1980. 'A Semantics for Positive and Comparative Adjectives'. *Linguistics and Philosophy* 4 (1): 1–45.

Kolodiejchuk, B. 2009. *Mother Theresa: Come Be My Light*. New York: Image/ Random House Press.

Kornblith, H. 1983. 'Justified Belief and Epistemically Responsible Action'. *Philosophical Review* 92 (1): 33–48.

Künne, W. 2006. 'Properties in Abundance'. In *Universals, Concepts and Qualities. New Essays on the Meaning of Predicates*, Strawson, P.F. & Chakrabarti, A. (eds.). Aldershot: Ashgate, pp. 249–300.

Kvanvig, J.L. 2003. *The Value of Knowledge and the Pursuit of Understanding*. Cambridge University Press.

2013. 'Affective Theism and People of Faith'. *Midwest Studies in Philosophy* 37 (1): 109–128.

Kvanvig, J.L. (ed.) 1996. *Warrant in Contemporary Epistemology*. New York: Rowman & Littlefield Publishers.

Lackey, J. 2005. 'Testimony and the Infant/Child Objection'. *Philosophical Studies* 126 (2): 163–190.

2007. 'Norms of Assertion'. *Noûs* 41 (4): 594–626.

2008. *Learning from Words*. Oxford University Press.

Langton, R. 2010. Review of *Epistemic Injustice: Power and the Ethics of Knowing*. *Hypatia* 25 (2): 459–464.

Le Morvan, P. 2002. 'Is Mere True Belief Knowledge?' *Erkenntnis* 56 (2): 151–168.

2005. 'Goldman on Knowledge as True Belief'. *Erkenntnis* 62 (2): 145–155.

2010. 'Knowledge, Ignorance, and True Belief'. *Theoria* 77 (1): 309–318.

2011. 'On Ignorance: A Reply to Peels'. *Philosophia* 39 (2): 335–344.

2012. 'On Ignorance: A Vindication of the Standard View'. *Philosophia* 40 (2): 379–393.

2013. 'Why the Standard Conception of Ignorance Prevails'. *Philosophia* 41 (1): 239–256.

2015. 'On the Ignorance, Knowledge, and Nature of Propositions'. *Synthese* 192 (11):3647–3662.

Lehrer, K. 1965. 'Knowledge, Truth and Evidence'. *Analysis* 25 (5): 168–175.

2000. *Theory of Knowledge*. Boulder/Oxford: Westview Press.

Leibniz, G.W. 1989. *Philosophical Essays*. Translated by Ariew, R. & Garber, D. Indianapolis: Hackett.

Leslie, S.J. (forthcoming). 'The Original Sin of Cognition: Fear, Prejudice and Generalization'. *Journal of Philosophy*.

Levinson, S. 2000. *Presumptive Meanings*. Cambridge, MA: The MIT Press.

Lewis, D. 1973. *Counterfactuals*. Cambridge, MA: Harvard University Press.

1996. 'Elusive Knowledge'. *Australasian Journal of Philosophy* 74 (4): 549–567.

Locke, J. 1690. *An Essay Concerning Human Understanding*. Chicago: Britannica.

1975. *An Essay Concerning Human Understanding*. Translated by Nidditch, P.H. Oxford University Press.

Ludlow, P. 2005. 'Contextualism and the New Linguistic Turn in Epistemology'. In *Contextualism in Philosophy: Knowledge, Meaning and Truth*, Preyer, G. & Peter, G. (eds.). Oxford University Press.

MacFarlane, J. 2005. 'Knowledge Laundering: Testimony and Sensitive Invariantism'. *Analysis* 65 (286): 132–38.

Madison, B.J.C. 2012. Review of How to Know. Notre Dame Philosophical Reviews. (ndpr.nd.edu/news/28899-how-to-know-a-practicalist-conception-of-knowledge/. Last accessed 29/12/2014.)

Maimonides, M. Translated by Friedlander, M. 1956. *Guide for the Perplexed*. Dover Publications.

Mason, R. 2011. 'Two Kinds of Unknowing'. *Hypatia* 26 (2): 294–307.

Mathiesen, K. 2006. 'The Epistemic Features of Group Belief'. *Episteme* 2 (3): 161–175.

McBrayer, J. 2010. 'Skeptical Theism'. *Philosophy Compass* 4 (1): 1–13.

2014. 'The Wager Renewed: Believing in God is Good for You'. *Science, Religion & Culture* 1 (3): 130–140.

McEwan, I. 1998. *Enduring Love*. London: Vintage.

Medina, J. 2006. *Speaking from Elsewhere: A New Contextualist Perspective on Meaning, Identity, and Discursive Agency*. Albany: SUNY Press.

2012. 'Hermeneutical Injustice and Polyphonic Contextualism: Social Silences and Shared Hermeneutical Responsibilities'. *Social Epistemology* 26 (2): 201–220.

2013. *Epistemologies of Resistance: Gender and Racial Oppression, Epistemic Injustice, and Resistant Imaginations*. Oxford University Press.

2014. 'Towards An Ethics and Pedagogy of Discomfort: Insensitivity, Perplexity, and Education as Inclusion'. *Civitas Educationis* 3 (1): 51–67.

(2016). 'The Will *Not* to Believe: Pragmatism, Oppression, and Standpoint Theory'. In *Feminist Interpretations of William James*, Sullivan, S & Tarver, E. (eds.). University Park: Penn State University Press, pp. 256–289.

(forthcoming). 'Epistemic Injustice and Epistemologies of Ignorance'. In *The Routledge Companion to the Philosophy of Race*, Alcoff, L., Anderson, L. & Taylor, P.(eds.). London and New York: Routledge.

Menzel, C. 2015. 'Possible Worlds'. In *The Stanford Encyclopedia of Philosophy*, Zalta, E.N. (ed.).

Mills, C. 1997. *The Racial Contract*. Ithaca: Cornell University Press.

1998. *Blackness Visible: Essays on Philosophy and Race*. Ithaca: Cornell University Press.

2007. 'White Ignorance'. In *Race and Epistemologies of Ignorance*, Sullivan, S. & Tuana, N. (eds.). New York: SUNY Press, pp. 11–38.

2015. 'Global White Ignorance'. In *Routledge International Handbook of Ignorance Studies*, Gross, M. & McGoey, L. (eds.). London/New York: Routledge, pp. 217–227.

Mion, G. 2012. 'God, Ignorance and Existence'. *International Journal for Philosophy of Religion* 72 (2): 85–88.

Moser, P.K., ed. 2005. *The Oxford Handbook of Epistemology*, Oxford: Oxford University Press.

Mulligan, K. & Correia, F. 2013. 'Facts'. In *The Stanford Encyclopedia of Philosophy*, Zalta, E.N. (ed.).

Nagel, J. 2014. 'Intuition, Reflection, and the Command of Knowledge'. *Proceedings of the Aristotelian Society Supplementary* Volume XXXVIII: 219–241.

Newman, L. 2005. 'Descartes' Rationalist Epistemology'. In *A Companion to Rationalism*, Nelson, A. (ed.). Oxford: Blackwell, pp. 179–205.

Noë, A. 2005. 'Against Intellectualism'. *Analysis* 65 (4): 278–290.

Nottelmann, N. 2007. *Blameworthy Belief*. New York: Springer.

Nozick, R. 1981. *Philosophical Explanations*. Cambridge, MA: Harvard University Press.

Olsson, E. & Westlund, D. 2006. 'On the role of the research agenda in epistemic change'. *Erkentnis* 65 (2): 165–183.

Peels, R. 2010. 'What Is Ignorance?' *Philosophia* 38 (1): 57–67.

2011a. 'Ignorance Is Lack of True Belief: A Rejoinder to Le Morvan'. *Philosophia* 39 (2): 344–355.

2011b. 'Tracing Culpable Ignorance'. *Logos and Episteme* 2 (4): 575–582.

2012. 'The New View on Ignorance Undefeated'. *Philosophia* 40 (4): 741–750.

2014. 'What Kind of Ignorance Excuses? Two Neglected Issues'. *Philosophical Quarterly* 64 (256): 478–496.

Peels, R., ed. 2016. *Perspectives on Ignorance from Moral and Social Philosophy*, London: Routledge.

Peels, R. & Booth, A. 2014. 'Why Responsible Belief If Permissible Belief'. *Analytic Philosophy* 54 (4): 75–88.

Peirce, C.S. 1958. *Collected Papers*. Boston: Harvard University Press.

Pelikan, J. 1993. *Christianity and Classical Culture: The Metamorphosis of Natural Theology in the Christian Encounter with Hellenism*. New Haven: Yale University Press.

Phillips, M. & Phillips, T. 1998. *Windrush: The Irresistible Rise of Multi-Racial Britain*. London. Harper Collins.

Plantinga, A. 1993a. *Warrant: The Current Debate*. Oxford University Press.

1993b. *Warrant and Proper Function*. Oxford University Press.

2000. *Warranted Christian Belief*. New York: Oxford University Press.

Plato 1997. *Complete Works*. Edited by Cooper, J.M. Cambridge and Indianapolis: Hackett.

Pohlhaus, G. 2012. 'Relational Knowing and Epistemic Injustice: Toward a Theory of Willful Hermeneutical Ignorance'. *Hypatia* 27 (3): 715–735.

Pojman, L. 1991. 'Faith, Hope, and Doubt'. In *Contemporary Classics in Philosophy of Religion*, Loades, A. & Rue, L. (eds.). New York: Open Court, pp. 183–207.

Pritchard, D.H. 2007. 'Recent Work on Epistemic Value'. *American Philosophical Quarterly* 44 (2): 85–110.

2009. 'Knowledge, Understanding and Epistemic Value'. In *Epistemology*, O' Hear, A. (ed.). Cambridge University Press, pp. 19–43.

2011. 'What is the Swamping Problem?' In *Reasons for Belief*, Reisner, A. & Steglich-Petersen, A. (eds.). Cambridge University Press, pp. 244–259.

2012. 'Anti-Luck Virtue Epistemology'. *Journal of Philosophy* 109 (3): 247–279.

2014. 'Truth as the Fundamental Epistemic Good'. In *The Ethics of Belief: Individual and Social*, Matheson, J. & Vitz, R. (eds.). Oxford University Press, pp. 112–129.

2015. 'Engel on Pragmatic Encroachment and Epistemic Value'. *Synthese* [Online First, DOI: 10.1007/s11229-015-0755-8].

(forthcoming*a*). 'Intellectual Virtue, Extended Cognition, and the Epistemology of Education'. In *Intellectual Virtues and Education: Essays In Applied Virtue Epistemology*, Baehr, J. (ed.), London: Routledge.

(forthcoming*b*). 'Veritism and Epistemic Value'. In *Alvin Goldman and His Critics*, Kornblith, H. & McLaughlin, B. (eds.). Oxford: Blackwell.

Pritchard, D.H., Millar, A., & Haddock, A. 2010. *The Nature and Value of Knowledge: Three Investigations*. Oxford University Press.

Pritchard, D.H. & Turri, J. 2011. 'Knowledge, the Value Of'. In *The Stanford Encyclopedia of Philosophy*, Zalta, E.N. (ed.).

Proctor, RN., and L. Schiebinger, eds. 2008. *Agnotology: The Making and Unmaking of Ignorance*, Stanford: Stanford University Press.

Ramsey, F.P. 1926. 'Truth and Probability'. In *Philosophy of Probability: Contemporary Readings*, Eagle, A. (ed.). London: Routledge, pp. 52–94.

Rasmussen, D.B. 1974. 'Austin and Wittgenstein on Doubt and Knowledge'. *Reason Papers* 1: 51–60.

Ravetz, J. 1993. 'The Sin of Science: Ignorance of Ignorance'. *Science Communication* 15 (2): 157–165.

Rawls, J. 1971. *A Theory of Justice*, Cambridge, MA: Harvard University Press.

Reed, B. 2010. 'A Defence of Stable Invariantism'. *Noûs* 44 (2): 224–244.

Rescher, N. 2009. *Ignorance: On the Wider Implications of Deficient Knowledge*. University of Pittsburgh Press.

Riggs, W. 2008. 'The Value Turn in Epistemology'. In *New Waves in Epistemology*, Hendricks, V. & Pritchard, D.H. (eds.). London: Palgrave Macmillan, pp. 300–323.

Rivera-López, E. 2006. 'Can There Be Full Excuses for Morally Wrong Actions?' *Philosophy and Phenomenological Research* 73 (1): 124–142.

Roberts, R.C. & Wood, J.W. 2007. Intellectual Virtues: An Essay in *Regulative Epistemology*. Oxford University Press.

Rosen, G. 2003. 'Culpability and Ignorance'. *Proceedings of the Aristotelian Society* 103 (1): 61–84.

2008. 'Kleinbart the Oblivious and Other Tales of Ignorance and Responsibility'. *The Journal of Philosophy* 105 (10): 591–610.

Ross, W.D. 1939. *Foundations of Ethics*. Oxford: Clarendon Press.

Rumfitt, I. 2003. 'Savoir Faire'. *Journal of Philosophy* 100 (3): 158–166.

Russell, B. 1984. *Theory of knowledge*. London: Allen and Unwin.

Ryle, G. 1945. 'Knowing How and Knowing That'. *Proceedings of the Aristotelian Society* 46: 1–16.

1946. 'Knowing How and Knowing That'. In *Collected Papers*, vol. 2: *Collected Essays* (1929–1968), Ryle G. (ed.). New York: Barnes and Noble, Inc, pp. 222–235.

1949. *The Concept of Mind*. London: Hutchinson.

1973. *The Concept of Mind*. Aylesbury: Hazell Watson & Viney.

Sartwell, C. 1991. 'Knowledge Is Merely True Belief'. *American Philosophical Quarterly* 28 (2): 157–165.

1992. 'Why Knowledge Is Merely True Belief'. *The Journal of Philosophy* 89 (4): 167–180.

Saul, J. 2013. 'Implicit Bias, Stereotype Threat, and Women in Philosophy'. In *Women in Philosophy: What Needs to Change*, Hutchison, K. & Jenkins, F. (eds.). Oxford University Press.

Schaffer, J. 2006. 'The Irrelevance of the Subject: Against Subject-Sensitive Invariantism'. *Philosophical Studies* 127: 87–107.

2007. 'Knowing the Answer'. *Philosophy and Phenomenological Reseach* 75 (2): 383–403.

Schaffer, J. & Szabó, Z.G. (2014). 'Epistemic Comparativism: A Contextualist Semantics for Knowledge Ascriptions'. *Philosophical Studies* 168 (2): 491–543.

Schellenberg, J.L. 1993. *Divine Hiddenness and Human Reason*. Ithaca, NY: Cornell University Press.

Scheman, N. 1993. *Engenderings: Constructions of Knowledge, Authority, and Privilege*. New York: Routledge.

Scheman, N.1997. 'Queering the Center by Centering the Queer: Reflections on Transsexuals and Secular Jews', in D.T. Meyers (ed.), *Feminist Rethink the Self*, pp. 124–162. New York: Westview.

Schiffer, S. 1996. 'Contextualist Solutions to Scepticism'. *Proceedings of the Aristotelian Society* 96: 317–333.

Smith, H.M. 1983. 'Culpable Ignorance'. *Philosophical Review* 92 (4): 543–571.

Snowdon, P. 2004. 'Knowing How and Knowing That: A Distinction Reconsidered'. *Proceedings of the Aristotelian Society* 104 (1): 1–29.

Somin, I. 2015. 'Rational Ignorance'. In *Routledge International Handbook of Ignorance Studies*, Gross, M. & McGoey, L. (eds.). London/New York: Routledge, pp. 274–281.

Sosa, E. 1999. 'How to Defeat Opposition to Moore'. *Noûs*, Supplement Philosophical Perspectives 13: 141–153.

2001. 'For the Love of Truth?' In *Virtue Epistemology: Essays on Epistemic Virtue and Responsibility*, Fairweather, A. & Zagzebski, L. (eds.). Oxford University Press, pp. 49–62.

2002. 'The Place of Truth in Epistemology'. In *Intellectual Virtue: Perspectives from Ethics and Epistemology*, DePaul, M. & Zagzebski, L. (eds.). Oxford: Clarendon Press, pp. 111–134.

2010. 'How Competence Matters in Epistemology'. *Philosophical Perspectives* 24 (1): 465–475.

2011. *Kowing Full Well*. Princeton University Press.

2015. *Judgment and Agency*. Oxford University Press.

Stanley, J. 2005. *Knowledge and Practical Interests*. Oxford University Press.

2011. *Know How*. Oxford University Press.

2015. *How Propaganda Works*. Princeton University Press.

Strawson, P.F. 1974. *Freedom and Resentment and Other Essays*. London: Methuen.

Stanley, J. & Williamson, T. 2001. 'Knowing How'. *Journal of Philosophy* 98 (8): 411–444.

Steup, M. 2005. 'Epistemology', *Stanford Encyclopedia of Philosophy*, http://plato.stanford.edu/entries/epistemology/, first published December 14th 2005.

Stroumsa, G. 2005. *Hidden Wisdom: Esoteric Traditions and the Roots of Christian Mysticism*. Leiden: Brill Academic Press.

Sue, D.W. 2010. *Microaggressions in Everyday Life: Race, Gender, and Sexual Orientation*. New York: Wiley.

Sullivan, S. 2006. *Revealing Whiteness: The Unconscious Habits of Racial Privilege*. Bloomington: Indiana University Press.

Sullivan, S. & Tuana, N. (eds.) 2007. *Race and Epistemologies of Ignorance*. Albany: SUNY Press.

Swinburne, R. 2004. *The Existence of God*. Oxford: Clarendon Press.

Swoyer, C. & Orilia, F. 2014. 'Properties'. In *The Stanford Encyclopedia of Philosophy*, Zalta, E.N. (ed.).

Talbott, T. 1990. 'Providence, Freedom, and Human Destiny'. *Religious Studies* 26: 227–245.

Thagard, P. 2004. 'What Is Doubt and When Is It Reasonable?' *Canadian Journal of Philosophy* 34: 391–406.

Townley, C. 2011. *A Defense of Ignorance: Its Value for Knowers and Roles in Feminist and Social Epistemologies*. Lanham: Rowman & Littlefield.

Treanor, N. 2013. 'The Measure of Knowledge'. *Noûs* 47 (3): 577–601.

2014. 'Trivial Truths and the Aim of Inquiry'. *Philosophy and Phenomenological Research* 89 (3): 552–559.

Tuana, N. 2004. 'Coming to Understand: Orgasm and the Epistemology of Ignorance'. *Hypatia: A Journal of Feminist Philosophy* 19 (1): 194–232.

Tuana, N. 2006. 'The Speculum of Ignorance: The Women's Health Movement and Epistemologies of Ignorance'. *Hypatia: A Journal of Feminist Philosophy* 21 (3): 1–19.

Unger, P. 1975. *Ignorance: A Case for Scepticism*. Oxford: Clarendon.

Van Benthem, J.F.A.K. 2007. 'Dynamic Logic for Belief Revision'. *Journal of Applied Non-Classical Logics* 17 (2): 129–155.

Van der Hoek, W. & Lomuscio, A. 2004. 'A Logic for Ignorance'. *Electronic Notes in Theoretical Computer Science* 85 (2): 117–133.

Van Fraassen, B. 1980. *The Scientific Image*. Oxford University Press.

Van Inwagen, P. 2006. *The Problem of Evil*. Oxford University Press.

Van Woudenberg, R. 2009. 'Ignorance and Force: Two Excusing Conditions for False Beliefs'. *American Philosophical Quarterly* 46 (4): 373–386.

Vlastos, G. 1985. 'Socrates' Disavowal of Knowledge'. *The Philosophical Quarterly* 35 (138): 1–31.

Von Stechow, A. 1984. 'Comparing Semantic Theories of Comparison'. *Journal of Semantics* 3 (1–2): 1–77.

Warren, R.P. 1946. *All the King's Men*. New York: Harcourt Brace & Company.

Weatherson, B. 2011. 'Defending Interest-Relative Invariantism'. *Logos and Episteme* 2 (4): 591–609.

Welbourne, M. 1979. 'The Transmission of Knowledge'. *Philosophical Quarterly* 29 (114): 1–9.

Wilholt, T. (forthcoming). 'On Knowing What One Does Not Know: Ignorance and the Aims of Research'. In *Agnotology: Ways of Producing, Preserving, and Dealing with Ignorance*, Kourany, J. & Carrier, M. (eds.).

Williamson, T. 1994. *Vagueness*. London: Routledge.

 2000. *Knowledge and Its Limits*. Oxford University Press.

 2005. 'Contextualism, Subject-Sensitive Invariantism, and Knowledge of Knowledge.' *Philosophical Quarterly Special Edition on Contextualism* 55 (219): 213–235.

Wittgenstein, L. 1969. *On Certainty*. Anscombe, G.E.M. & von Wright, G.H. (eds.). New York: Harper & Row.

 2009. *Philosophical Investigations*. Revised fourth edition by P.M.S. Hacker and Joachim Schulte. Chichester: Wiley-Blackwell.

Wright, C. 1975. 'On the Coherence of Vague Predicates'. *Synthese* 30 (4): 325–65.

Zagzebski, L. 2003. 'The Search for the Source of the Epistemic Good'. In *Moral and Epistemic Virtues*, Brady, M.S. & Pritchard, D.H. (eds.). Oxford: Blackwell, pp. 13–27.

Zimmerman, M.J. 1988. *An Essay on Moral Responsibility*. Totowa, NJ: Rowman and Littlefield.

 1997. 'Moral Responsibility and Ignorance'. *Ethics* 107 (3): 410–426.

 2008. *Living with Uncertainty: The Moral Significance of Ignorance*. Cambridge University Press.

Index

For EU product safety concerns, contact us at Calle de José Abascal, 56–1°,
28003 Madrid, Spain or eugpsr@cambridge.org.

www.ingramcontent.com/pod-product-compliance
Ingram Content Group UK Ltd.
Pitfield, Milton Keynes, MK11 3LW, UK
UKHW020438120925
462827UK00008B/403